The Job
of the
Practicing Planner

The Job of the Practicing Planner

ALBERT SOLNIT
with
CHARLES REED,
PEGGY GLASSFORD,
and
DUNCAN ERLEY

Planners Press
American Planning Association
Washington, D.C.   Chicago, Illinois

Copyright 1988 by the American Planning Association
1313 E. 60th St., Chicago, IL 60637
ISBN 0-918286-52-2
Library of Congress Catalog Card Number 87-72375

Contents

Foreword

In late 1986 Al Solnit was in the process of completing two books: a new edition of *The Job of the Planning Commissioner*, and a manuscript as yet not completed for this book, *The Job of the Practicing Planner*.

As Al would periodically do, he was taking several months off for overseas travel. He once spent almost a year on a boat sailing around the South Pacific. This time he was going to spend about three months in Europe and the Middle East.

Meanwhile, we here at the Planners Press were to review the manuscript and correspond with him about the draft, look for illustrations, suggest revisions, and in general work with Al toward a completed manuscript and eventually a book.

In the first week of January 1987 we were stunned when we were informed by his family that he had unexpectedly passed away while traveling. We were, of course, saddened and reflected on his life of professional contributions as a practitioner, consultant, author, workshop leader, and teacher. His book, *The Job of the Planning Commissioner*, had gone through several editions and made him very well known in the field. The workshops he conducted for APA at its national conferences, at APA chapters, and a large number of state and local organizations, brought his wit and practicality to thousands of planning commissioners and planners throughout the nation. He also spoke to the development community through his book, *Project Approval*, which was designed to help developers and builders through the local and government regulatory system.

As we turned to the as yet uncompleted manuscript, we found that a number of chapters on important topics were still in rough form and, as Al knew, needed additional work before publication.

We thought about how to complete the manuscript so that it would be a coherent whole. Given the amount of work that he had put in on the manuscript up to that point in time, and given that no book like it was available elsewhere, we felt that it was inconceivable to not move ahead. We found several pieces of work by others that we felt would complete the manuscript. We were able to adapt materials that now appear as Chapters 5, 6, 7, and 8.

We are deeply indebted to the following for permission to adapt the materials for this book. For Chapters 5 and 6, we thank Charles Reed for materials that originally appeared in his newsletter, *The Zoning Report*.[1] For Chapter 7, our thanks go to APA's Planning Advisory Service and to Peggy Glassford.[2] For Chapter 8 we again thank the Planning Advisory Service and Duncan Erley.[3] All of these chapters represent the kind of practical, how-to-do-it approach that Al took when writing for or speaking to the practicing planner.

Frank S. So

NOTES

1. Chapters 5 and 6 appeared originally in a slightly different form in *The Zoning Report*. Chapter 5 appeared in the issues of March 9 and March 23, 1984. Chapter 6 originally appeared in the issues of November 11 and November 25, 1985. Planning practitioners would find *The Zoning Report* an excellent source of practical information on a regular basis. Subscription information is available by writing *The Zoning Report*, 1404 North State Rd. 7, Suite 269, P.O. Box 6529, Margate, FL 33063.
2. Chapter 7 originally appeared in a different form as *Appearance Codes for Small Communities*, Planning Advisory Service Report No. 379, by Peggy Glassford (Chicago: American Planning Association, 1983).
3. This material orignally was published as *Writing Better Zoning Reports*, Planning Advisory Service Report No. 321, by Duncan Erley (Chicago: American Planning Association, 1976).

Introduction

God told Moses that he had good news and bad news.

"The good news first," said Moses.

"I'm planning to part the Red Sea to allow you and your people to walk right through and escape from Egypt," said God, adding, "and when the Egyptian soldiers pursue, I'll send the water back on top of them."

"Wonderful," Moses responded, "but what's the bad news?"

"You write the environmental impact statement."

This book is for the people who are the practitioners on the regulatory side of the planning profession. Much of the material in this book has been developed during short university extension courses I gave to such practitioners. Among those taking the courses in "Fundamentals of Effective Current Planning," less than 5 percent had received any instruction in the course's main topics during their years of professional education at universities. Many observed that most of the professional literature is commentary on the theoretical side of the profession by writers who have never worked inside a planning agency. Exhaustive searches in university libraries, periodical files, and bookshops indicate that except for the specialized reports issued from time to time by the Planning Advisory Service of the American Planning Association, there is virtually no professional literature on this aspect of planning practice. This book is designed to help fill that gap.

While this book is in large part derived from my 20 years of experience in local planning agencies plus feedback on the performance of planners during dozens of courses for planning commissioners, developers, architects, engineers, administrators, and others who deal with them on a day-to-day basis, this book does not dwell on the techniques of practice alone. Wherever possible, common practices and standards will be tied to their theoretical sources.

Above all, this book should demystify the work of development review for those who are about to enter it and improve the performance of those already at work and attempting to learn on the job.

John W. Dyckman observed that students:

> To the extent they have internalized the conception of planning taught in the schools in which they are prepared, they are likely to fall victim to feelings of malaise or the "what is planning all about blues". . .The newly minted graduate planner stuffed with social science and armed with the image of planning as "societal guidance" is likely to experience stunning culture shock in the environment of bureaucratic life. [1]

While the environment of bureaucratic life was treated extensively in my previous book, *What Do I Do Next? A Manual for People Entering Government* (with Warren Jones, American Planning Association, 1981), this book tries to achieve a balance between the development of technical skills and the bureaucratic and organizational skills needed to make the planner effective in the climate of local government. As Dyckman pointed out,

> Substantive rationality or what planning is about takes second place to procedural efficiency in this environment. Any planner preparing environmental impact studies knows that these will be judged more for how they are done than for what they imply. And while universities may be bureacratic in their practices, different skills are required for advancement in a government bureaucracy. . . .[2]

Dennis O'Harrow said:

> An awful lot of planners and an awful lot of planning

vii

commissioners spend an awful lot of time working with and worrying about zoning problems. . . .

How well are the schools preparing our youth for the great adventure? We have also in the course of our annual survey recently assembled the curricula of the universities that are educating our young to be planners, fitting them for their careers in the real world. *We did not find* a single course that used zoning in its title, although we did not have curricula from all planning schools and there still may be one school that is not ashamed to clearly label a course in zoning. . . .We have met young graduates with master's degrees in city planning who have never even seen a zoning ordinance.[3]

Based on my own experience with a fair sample of the people who work in the zoning and current planning sections of local agencies, things haven't changed very much in almost 20 years in the universities. However, the job market has changed and those MCP graduates who used to be able to find asylum in consulting firms, think tanks, and research programs are now finding that a slot in the current planning or zoning division of a local agency is the only game in town for those who seek employment. So in addition to culture shock many are experiencing the fear of the unknown as they process their first subdivision application.

For these reasons, this book will present its topics without presumption of prior knowledge or training on the part of the reader.

Albert Solnit

NOTES

1. John W. Dyckman, "Three Crises of American Planning," in *Planning Theory in the 1980s*, Robert W. Burchell and George Sternlieb, eds. (Piscataway, N.J.: Rutgers University Center for Urban Policy Research, 1981), p. 284.

2. Dyckman, p. 238.

3. Dennis O'Harrow, "Zoning May Not Be Planning, But . . .," in *Dennis O'Harrow: Plan Talk and Plain Talk* (Chicago: American Planning Association), 1981, p. 277.

1

The Tools of
Local Regulation of
Private Development

Albert Solnit

Pogo explains how the country ticks: "There's the public, business, and the ever-luvin' gummint. The public elects the gummint and works in business. The gummint controls business, so that business won't control the public and the public controls the gummint so that it can't control business too much or the public wouldn't elect the gummint which would hurt the controls to save the public."

Tad: "What's all these enemies of each other got to do with the country?"

Pogo: "They's not enemies, they's all the same thing. They's the country." WALT KELLEY

Many learned discussions and scholarly articles written by academics and lawyers advance the impression that land use regulation is really a diabolical scheme to extend the powers of a faceless bureaucracy whose basic motivation is to strip away the rights of property owners, forever shackle the initiative of free enterprise, and curtail the rightful returns of business initiative. In point of fact, the United States has a vast history of disasters caused by unfettered business initiative ranging from the sweatshops and the slums of the East to the more recent land frauds in the West perpetrated by a lack of subdivision controls. Many of the regulations that are on the books today were not the initiatives of bureaucrats seeking to extend their powers over the private sector, but rather were the result of a public outcry that government should do something to protect people from further calamities. Despite all the rhetoric about over-regulation, there still are new disasters, such as Times Beach, Missouri, or the Love Canal District in New York, where lack of regulation allowed the endangerment of the public health, welfare, and safety.

TRADITIONAL PURPOSES OF LAND USE REGULATION

Traditionally, the purposes of land use regulation have been fairly simple. They include the following.

1. To maintain property values. This purpose is based on the theory that building and land values are preserved and enhanced by orderly, as opposed to haphazard, development. An emerging concern in this area has been the enhancement and preservation of the tax base.

2. To stabilize neighborhoods and preserve their quality. The quality of neighborhoods is not determined only by the standard at which one person maintains a house, but by the desirability of all the homes surrounding a home. Traditionally, the leading indicator of neighborhood quality has been density. The folklore of real estate has it that neighborhoods with low density are generally of higher quality. This produces one of the most common battles in zoning and planning. Developers have a great incentive to locate higher density development in high-quality, low-density neighborhoods because of the obviously greater return to the same building in the more desirable location. On the other hand, the owners of the low-density housing fight vigorously to prevent the entry of such developments, contending that there is a strong tendency for high-quality, low-density neighborhoods to decline once the homogeneity of such neighborhoods is breached.

Another consideration that enters into this conflict is that economies of scale in public services and in capital improvements are present in the higher density areas, while many low-density neighborhoods really do not pay their way. In strictly fiscal terms, mixed densities are often more economically attractive to the municipal treasury. In addition, the argument is often advanced that housing mixtures are more socially desirable because they provide a wider range of affordable housing for all the residents of a community. However, one of the unspoken understandings between city officials and the owners of high-quality housing is that the city officials are expected to act as stewards of the collective investment the owners have in good neighborhoods, and woe to any public official who seems to betray that responsibility.

3. To provide uniform regulations throughout each district. For many years, the idea was that similar properties similarly situated should be treated similarly, and one of the worst deeds in the world of zoning was discriminating against or allowing a special advantage to one piece of land. This was called spot zoning—the blackest of planning sins—and is something the courts have struck down again and again.

But with the trend toward negotiable controls in the 1960s, rigid zoning controls began to give way to more flexible controls that allowed the exercise of the widest administrative discretion. In other words, a zone change under common special permit procedures or planned unit development requirements does not have to rely on the standards, lists of permissible uses, and other matters of right in a zoning ordinance. The local government's approval is very often based on the best deal it can get.

These changes meant that the practicing planner had to evolve from a plan checker to a skilled negotiator. The skill of negotiating for better development in the public interest is something that is critical to the planning agency that wants to do an effective job. This matter is so important that it will be treated later in a separate section.

4. To move traffic rapidly in safety. Probably no other purpose of land use regulations is used more frequently to argue against nonresidential development in residential areas than traffic safety. Complaints most commonly used are dangers to children and increased noise. In these types of regulations, street widths are often keyed to the intensity of activity allowed in each district. Off-street parking requirements also are justified on the basis of maintaining street capacity and public safety. As cities become more congested and parking from high-traffic generators spills into other areas, the American "right" to park anywhere on the street increasingly is being challenged by such things as residents-only permit systems (e.g., San Francisco). Reduction of traffic often is used to justify density controls and it is common for street dedications and large projects' off-site dedications to be made a condition of variances or zone changes related to lessening congestion in the streets.

5. To control aesthetics and architectural harmony. In architectural control, the courts have upheld the denial of permits for structures that are so at odds with existing structures or the nature of the district that they cause a depreciation of property values. Nevertheless, this is usually a very hazy area, and unless every structure in a district has to go through design review it is virtually impossible to regulate against bad taste in design. Many home owners to not understand that bad architecture cannot be prohibited everywhere. The city really needs to set its priorities in the general planning process and then subject to design review those new structures that might block views or desecrate historic areas or simply ruin the unity of Main Street.

Many cities and counties have enacted such architectural controls in an effort to assure that development will be compatible and harmonious with the use and enjoyment of nearby properties. The controls deal with such things as the harmony of external design, colors, materials, and architectural features that must relate to other structures and the natural environment.

There seems to be little doubt that these regulations are legally permissible. As far back as 1960, a test case involved the city of Laguna Beach, California, which had adopted an ordinance requiring all future buildings to conform to a particular type of architecture. The California Court of Appeals upheld the validity of this action, and said that it would help to assure orderly development in the vicinity.

But the movement almost from the outset was in the direction of eventually recognizing aesthetics alone as being a sufficient reason for an ordinance. With a relatively minimal shift in emphasis, the California Court of Appeals in *Van Silkin* v. *Brown* in 1971 was able to use the word "aesthetics" broadly enough to include maintaining property values, protecting tax revenues, providing neighborhood social and economic stability, attracting business and industry, and encouraging conditions that make a pleasant community for living and working. With a definition as broad as that, there can be little question but that "aesthetics" is regarded by the courts as a proper subject of regulation.

NEW VISTAS FOR LAND USE REGULATION

Many land use controls, either indirectly or in effect, regulate competition. Attorneys continue to debate the business of compensation and unfair takings as a result of the regulation of competition, but generally it is held that preserving the stability and profitability of existing business districts is as valid a use of the police power as stabilizing the property values (read: resale prices) of high-quality neighborhoods. There has been some talk in the legal fraternity about challenging under anti-trust statutes the prohibition of the entry of ruinous competition to existing businesses. What will come of this remains to be seen.

In recent years, any act of government that the law interprets as protection of "public health, safety, morals, and welfare" can be applied to private property. Thus, some of the newer concerns, such as the protection against negative impacts on environmental resources and the control of pollution, have become part of land use regulation. Even more recently, the enhancement of the future economy of an area and the protection of the economic stability of the governmental entity are concerns that are being upheld as valid exercises of regulations. The point here is that the law constantly adjusts and redefines powers of an owner to use his land. Very often a new situation arises that is completely outside the scope of existing regulation.

One good example occurred in Portland, Oregon, which had fairly rigorous regulations to control nude and topless dancing in taverns. However, problems arose when a new kind of business emerged, namely, "soda pop" nude and topless dancing establishments in which liquor was not served. The mixture of sex and liquor was tightly controlled by the city, but since liquor was not involved in this circumstance, neither the activity nor the age of the patrons who could order topless table dancing or private nude shows could be controlled.

These businesses could locate next to schools and churches and in established neighborhoods. Outraged citizens picketed and shook their fists at the television cameras. The city leaders clearly needed new regulations to handle the new situation. Therefore, the rationale for regulating the soda pop topless bars was that they would be a detriment to the morals of youth, and the regulation writers could consider regulations that (*a*) moved such establishments away from schools and churches and residential areas, or (*b*) allowed them to oper-ate alongside other business establishments, but with a prohibition on what the entertainers could do and who could go see such entertainers.

Situations like this occur frequently; the point is that many regulations are written as a reaction to public outcry rather than as tools to advance comprehensive plan recommendations. Rarely are regulations put on the books by staff action alone. They are there because the public and the elected representatives decided that the regulations would be for the good.

For instance, the era of the sexual revolution had a major impact on the regulatory operations of urban planning agencies. Once sex becomes a recognized business, the problem is where should it go. After considerable litigation and moralizing, it has generally been agreed that planners can focus on the effects but not the content of such businesses. But different cities handle this holding differently. Consider the following.

The Skid Row Effect. The city of Detroit decided that the effects of adult bookstores and X-rated move theaters were different from the effects of conventional bookstores and standard theaters. This then made it possible to rationalize that adult theaters and adult bookstores, like other uses in the zoning code, would be segregated in terms of the relationship between these uses and the other uses that adjoin them. The planners in Detroit noted that concentrations of certain uses, including the pornographic ones, resulted in deteriorating property values, higher crime rates, traffic congestion, and depressed neighborhood conditions. They used these assumptions in preparing an antiskid row ordinance that contained definitions of the various pornographic businesses, but no judgment was made of the content of the product sold. The objective, then, was to disperse the uses and keep them separate from each other, so that the skid row effect would not occur.

This idea was challenged by the operators of X-rated movie theaters and found its way to the U.S. Supreme Court. The Court found that the ordinance was not a restraint on free speech, did not offend the First Amendment, and thus it was possible for Detroit to disperse such businesses.

The "Combat Zone" Effect. In Boston, however, it was necessary to go in an opposite regulatory direction. There, the city already had a concentrated development of pornographic businesses (peep shows, bookstores, adult theaters, and strip joints) in an area known as the "combat zone." Boston decided to turn the concentration into an advantage. The city set up an adult entertainment district—a special overlay district—that would be the only place in the city where such uses would be permitted. To fight against the skid row effect now recognized by the Supreme Court, Boston upgraded the district with parks, new street lighting, sign removal, improved street paving, and renovated storefronts. Communities such as New Orleans and New York also have adapted a zoning approach to the control of sex businesses.

These examples seem to point to the fact that society continues to change and planners must be prepared to deal with such change. To the degree possible, planners must look to the future with a practical eye, but control of current development relies on the effectiveness of the planning to date, and on the tools the planner has at his or her disposal.

TOOLS OF THE PLANNER

The practicing planner's equipment for the control of development consists of three main types of tools.

"Regs"

The first tools are the ordinances or the "regs," as they are known to practitioners. Regs include such things as the zoning ordinance, the building regulations, the subdivision platting requirements, and the general plan. The general plan is seldom understood in terms of its being an ordinance. Nevertheless, land use attorneys have known for years that where actions of a local government can be supported by the language of a general plan, those actions are very rarely struck down in the courts as arbitrary and capricious. This is because the language of general plans is full of assurances to the judiciary that everything proposed has been carefully considered, given due process, and received a majority vote of the governing body certifying its proposals as fully in the public interest.

Standards

Standards are the second tools of the planner and deal with public facilities and the related issues of "how big" and "how much." Standards ensure the needs of local residents will be adequately met. Table 1.1 shows some of the 1961 assumptions behind standards for schools, playgrounds, and other child-oriented facilities.

These standards may have been very commendable in 1961, but they represent conditions and preferences of those times. For example, note the assumptions about average family size, where school-age children live in dwelling units containing 4.4 persons per dwelling unit with 2.23 children, 1.48 of which attend a school. This assumption took place during the height of the baby boom and before the widespread use of the birth control pill, and yet today—nearly three decades later

Table 1.1
BASIC STANDARDS FOR NEW URBAN DEVELOPMENT
(1961)

ASSUMPTIONS

Average Family Size:
(a) For purposes of schools planning: 4.4 persons per dwelling unit.
(b) For purposes of land use and public services and facilities planning: 3.8 persons per dwelling unit.

Age Distribution of Population:

Age Group	Distribution in New Residential Subdivisions* (For Schools Planning)		Distribution in Established Residential Community		Distribution in a Metropolitan Region*	
	No. Per Dwelling Unit	Percent of Total Pop.	No. Per Dwelling Unit	Percent of Total Pop.	No. Per Dwelling Unit	Percent of Total Pop.
Preschool	0.75	17.0	0.47	12.3	0.38	11.2
Kindergarten	0.15	3.4	0.09	2.4	0.07	2.1
Elementary School	0.85	19.3	0.52	13.7	0.41	12.0
Junior High School	0.25	5.7	0.20	5.3	0.17	5.0
Senior High School	0.23	5.2	0.19	5.0	0.16	4.7
Working Age	2.07	47.1	2.09	55.0	1.91	56.2
Retired (over 65)	0.10	2.3	0.24	6.3	0.30	8.8
	4.40		3.80		3.40	

* Estimates based on information supplied by Rocky Mountain School Study Council.
**Estimates based on U.S. Census Bureau information

Source: Reproduced from Urban Land newsletter, May 1961, Vol. 20, No. 5, published by the Urban Land Institute.

—in many plans and population projections the same assumptions are still in place. This is but one reason why practicing planners must critically examine the standards that are being employed in their towns. They may be working not only with hopelessly inaccurate projections of public facility needs, but also with tastes for public services and facilities that are outdated, inappropriate, and fail to recognize the current scarcity of maintenance funds, the need to lower housing costs, and the basic changes in the composition of population.

For example, if you live and work in a city that no longer has 2.23 children per household, does it make sense to maintain the same level of child-oriented playgrounds and playfields? Or, are certain requirements still in the community's best interest? For instance, in one city, regulations called for all local streets, particularly on hillsides, to be 36 feet wide. In one neighborhood laid out before such standards became popular with the engineering fraternity, annexation to the city occurred on the condition that the 20-foot streets never be brought up to engineering standards. It works fine when people are careful about parking and driving around the tree-shaded curves. The residents also take great comfort from the fact that sidewalk, curb, and gutter assessments will not be levied en masse against them by a zealous city, which leaves money available to do the serious repair work that the city can no longer afford.

Developers and planners in the Las Vegas

area recently met to learn what feasible means there were of changing standards so that housing would be more affordable. The result was Capital Approach '80, a multi-family development. The total cost savings of this project amounted to $5,492 per unit. Had Capital Approach '80 been built to Las Vegas standards, only 33 units would have been possible instead of the 38 that were built. (See Table 1.2 for distribution of cost savings.)

This project tried to show that cost savings of up to $10,000 per home could be achieved by discarding unnecessary codes and regulations, but it did not attempt to prove marketability, customer acceptance, or adaptability to other locations. It did, however, provide a very valuable methodology for reducing housing costs by reviewing standards. The method is reproduced here as a checklist in Exhibit 1.1.

Conditions, Exactions, and Dedications

The third set of tools in the practicing planner's shop—conditions, exactions, and dedications—is the most negotiable. As zoning and land use regulation have become more flexible, the effective practicing planner must know how to employ the art of putting conditions on a development so that it serves the public interest as fairly and fully as possible.

One caveat about recommending conditions on a development is that a bad development cannot be "fixed up" by placing conditions on it. Effective planners know that when something is in the wrong location and is a threat to the surrounding environment, requiring higher fencing or shrubbery or shielding the lights or dickering over architectural details will not solve the problem. Many public hearings

Table 1.2
CAPITAL APPROACH '80
TOTAL COSTS BY MAJOR COST CATEGORY
(AS-BUILT vs. CONVENTIONAL LAS VEGAS CODES AND STANDARD PRACTICES)

Cost Category	Average Cost Per Unit		
	As-Built	**Conventional**	**Savings**
Fees & engineering	$ 1,123.74	$ 1,123.74	-0-
Raw land	4,089.82	4,709.49	$ 619.67
Land development	8,298.61	11,202.09	2,903.48
Direct construction	22,904.76	24,140.60	1,235.84
Indirect construction	1,943.77	2,093.83	150.06
Overhead & financing	3,289.91	3,545.22	255.31
Sales & marketing	4,486.53	4,814.03	327.50
Totals	$46,137.14*	$51,629.00**	$5,491.86
Percent savings			10.60

* Average cost for 38 units was $46,237.14.
** Average cost for 33 units was $51,629.00.

Exhibit 1.1
CHECKLIST FOR
REDUCING HOUSING DEVELOPMENT COSTS

A. Feasibility Checklist
1. Is the project politically feasible?
   a. Compatibility with local plans and zoning
   b. Compatibility with citizen desires and expectations
   c. Perceived effect on property values
   d. Perceived cost to the community
   e. Purpose and packaging of the proposed project

2. Is land available in proximity to required infrastructure?
   a. Availability of sufficient buildable land
   b. Proximity to adequate water and sewer facilities
   c. Availability of suitable transportation services and facilities

3. Is the site environmentally suitable?
   a. Compatibility with public regulations and protections regarding flooding, wetlands, slopes, habitats for rare and endangered species, etc.

4. Is the project financially feasible?
   a. Availability of construction and permanent financing
   b. Marketability of the final product

5. Has the local government created an atmosphere receptive to affordable housing?
   a. Zoning ordinance
   b. Building code
   c. Permit and approval process
   d. Land acquisition assistance
   e. Availability of capital improvements and public services
   f. Financial assistance
   g. Neighborhood revitalization program

B. Methods of Reducing Production Costs
1. Land
   a. Increase density
   b. Land banking
   c. Write downs
   d. Innovative zoning techniques
      1. T.D.R., PUD, cluster, zero lot line
      2. flexibility techniques
      3. density bonuses
      4. accessory apartment ordinance
      5. zoning override by higher level of government
   e. Incorporate housing in mixed-use developments
   f. Zone for less density in center city areas to bring cost down and provide housing that the market will support
   g. Aggregate center city vacant lots for less costly development
   h. Plan new development in cities in conjunction with rehabilitation and adaptive reuse
   i. Restraints on resale price
   j. Upzone to make small in-fill parcels buildable

2. Professional fees and services; developer's overhead
   a. Increase density to spread cost over wider base
   b. Reduce processing delays and requirements
      1. one-step processing, permit expeditor, lead agency
      2. negotiated development strategy
      3. update zoning ordinances and building codes
      4. clear regulations for permit processing
      5. coordinate lay board review process
      6. preliminary application to reduce developer's costs
      7. train staff and lay board members
      8. reduced fees
   c. Reduce front-end cost by delivering feasible project to developer through public agency or non-profit organization

3. Capital improvements
   a. Increase density to spread cost over wider base
   b. Use of local tax-exempt financing in lieu of payment under purchaser's mortgage
   c. Contributions from county capital budget

d. State and federal grants-in-aid
   1. Environmental Protection Agency
   2. Community Development Block Grants
   3. Farmers Home Administration
   4. Heritage Recreation and Conservation Service
e. Reduce requirements
   1. sidewalks and street lights
   2. road width, cul-de-sac lengths
   3. drainage
   4. grade and paving quality
f. Cluster development
g. Build in proximity to current infrastructure; coordinate capital budget planning with development objectives
h. Build at densities that can support self-contained utility systems
i. Incorporate housing in mixed-use developments

4. Labor
   a. Reduce per unit size
   b. Special residential rates from unions
   c. Nonunion labor
   d. Use factory-built systems
   e. More efficient work rules
   f. Cost-reducing training programs

5. Materials
   a. Use of systems housing
   b. Adopt building code with performance standards that allow acceptable, cost-effective technology
   c. Reduction in required square footage
   d. Minimize common space
   e. Build at optimal density to utilize materials most efficiently
   f. Design to meet present needs—leave room for expansion
   g. Use even modules so that standard-sized materials can be used

6. Construction financing
   a. Reduce delay in processing and approvals
   b. Tax-exempt construction financing
   c. Insurance program for construction lending
   d. Interest subsidy program for construction lending
   e. Leverage deposit of public funds
   f. Draw down funds only as needed to reduce interest charges

7. Profit
   a. Increase tax advantage of housing to provide alternative benefit
   b. Less profit per unit at higher densities

C. Methods of Reducing Carrying Costs
   1. Debt service
      a. Reduce amount to be financed
         1. see production cost reduction checklist above
         2. higher down payment with down payment assistance
         3. principal reduction grant or loan
      b. Extend term of loan
         1. FHA insurance
         2. state agency insurance
         3. private insurance
         4. bank agreement
         5. revise standards of secondary mortgage market
         6. create special secondary market
         7. mortgage-backed securities
      c. Reduce interest
         1. interest reduction subsidies (various techniques)
         2. Section 235
         3. tax-exempt mortgages—local, state, or federal
         4. mortgage-backed security programs
      d. Innovative mortgage instruments
         1. graduated payments
         2. participation loans
         3. growing equity mortgages
         4. pledged accounts

   2. Real property taxes
      a. Tax abatement
      b. Tax relief legislation (refunds, credits, and exemptions)

   3. Utilities
      a. Individual meters (rental housing)
      b. Energy efficient design (may increase production costs)
         1. shared walls
         2. revised codes to provide energy-conserving site and building design
         3. proper siting of structure
         4. multi-glazed windows
         5. high efficiency furnaces

6. ventilation system energy recovery
   devices
   c. Energy efficient life-styles
   d. Tax credits for energy conservation
      measures
   e. Public sector energy grants and loans

4. Hazard insurance
   a. Counseling
   b. Insurance pools
   c. Risk reduction
   d. Location of hydrants and fire stations

5. Maintenance, repair
   a. Durable construction
   b. Home owner warranty program
   c. Home maintenance organization
   d. Publicly assisted maintenance programs

6. Rental housing
   a. Management and administration
      1. nonprofit management
      2. tenant participation in management
      3. cost-efficient management techniques
   b. Return on owner's equity
      1. nonprofit ownership
      2. public ownership
      3. tax incentives in lieu of profit

Source: Center for Community Development & Preservation, Inc., *Affordable Housing: Public and Private Partnerships for Constructing Middle and Moderate Income Housing*, White Plains, New York, 1980, pp. viii-xii.

bog down in the details of how to make conditions that will make a project minimally acceptable when the actual problem is that it is in the wrong place with the wrong use. A denial would probably be kinder than trying to mute the effects with buffering.

Planning commissioners and other locals who have an ingrained sense of place often instinctively know this. For example, one small Virginia town in the Washington, D.C., area was invaded by 11 experts from the Middle West who proposed a massive high-rise development in this rather small, residential town. Expert after expert testified as to the marketability, the desirability, the additional tax base, and so on for hour after hour with flip charts, graphs, elaborate maps, aerial photographs, and all the other public relations tools such a group would be expected to bring to the fray. It took the planning commission of this rather uncosmopolitan area exactly one minute and thirty seconds to deny the project. The attorney wanted to sue, thinking the commission was wrong to deny such an important advance in the art of construction. Some time later, an ad hoc planning commission of real planning commissioners was set up at an American Planning Association conference, and the same evidence was again presented. It took that group just thirty seconds to deny it, to the astonishment of the attorney.

What were the real-life planners doing? They were applying the principle laid down by Mr. Justice Sullivan in the definitive *Village of Euclid* v. *Ambler Realty Co.*, the case that set the legal foundation for zoning. "Each community has the right and responsibility to determine its own character...."

POLICY CONSIDERATIONS

The advance planning staff dreams of escaping the task of dealing with policy considerations, but the role of the practicing planner is to learn how to live in the real world of compromise. Every planning decision has a political context, and in that sense the distribution of cost falls unequally on people. This is where politics comes in. Planning is not politics and it cannot escape politics, although the reality is rarely as dire as is seen by some. Academicians in particular are known to view planners as workers who supply numbers while the politicians decide how—and for whom—those numbers can best be used.

In recent years, however, people have begun

to view planning in a more humanitarian light. Propositions of this view are that planning is not separate from planners and its recipients; that planning is not value-free; that planning cannot take place without a value base, indeed, that values are at the heart of planning. Consider what straight technological planning for the human future has left us today—our environmental crises alone have taught us that our oceans and earth are not bottomless dumps and that abuse leads to the Love Canals, Times Beaches, and Lake Eries of our time.

The main goal in planning no longer is to control events. Today the goal is to participate in outcomes. We now understand that we do not know what we need to know to make the world what we want it to be. We should feel our way into many futures, with special attention to the worthiness of what we do now, especially with respect to what we want to avoid. We will not have error-free reactions, and so we need to include error-detecting systems in our response. Hard data is no longer enough. Value changes must be tracked, errors embraced, and broad public participation invited.

Planning for the future means going from a control to a learning mode. However, questions remain. Can our institutions really implement plans? They must evolve, so as to be able to meet the needs of the future. Our institutions must learn to be more like the human body, where decision making is properly assigned. For example, not all the body's functioning decisions are made by the centralized brain. Some decisions are made by the spleen. The essence of the organic humanist planner's philosophy was summed up by H.G. Wells, who said, "Civilization is a race between disaster and eduction."

The role of planners with regard to their clients, therefore, is to add weight to the educational side of the race and point out the position of disaster.

2

Understanding the U.S. System of Land Use Controls

Albert Solnit

Blackacre on the edge of town is not private property. It is a thing—land and nothing more. It becomes property by virtue of law: law and property were born together. JOHN E. CRIBETT[1]

Everything depends.
Nothing is always.
Everything is sometimes. LANGSAM'S LAW

Before describing how one can guide a project through the local system of land use controls, it is important to have some understanding of the relationship between property and the public interest in the United States. This relationship is constantly evolving; it continues to change in response to shifts in politics, technology, social structure, and economics.

BEGINNINGS

After World War II, the suburbs were born with the release of a pent-up housing need that had been suppressed by depression and war. The suburbs were fathered by the freeway building program, federal sewer and water grants, Veteran's Administration and Federal Housing Authority mortgages that required little or no cash down, and by rising incomes, savings, and employment. The suburbs then were built by large firms: 4 percent of the development companies built 45 percent of the homes between 1945 and 1960. In contrast, in 1938 less than 20 percent of the home builders built more than four units per year.[2] Mass housing production and larger sites meant that site improvements such as roads, drains, and utilities could be installed by the builder/developer before selling the homes, rather than through the much more difficult system of voluntary (and forced) government special assessment districts, which are created to equitably divide the costs among the property owners. This fact was not lost on government officials and soon the system of subdivision standards and exactions, which is now almost universal, came

13

into being.

Today, a different combination of land use factors is emerging. The federal deficit crisis, the completion of 95 percent of the interstate highway system (the remaining 5 percent is estimated to cost as much as the 95 percent in place), the phasing out of federal revenue sharing and grant programs, and the probable demise of easily affordable starter houses for first-time home buyers are combining to produce changes in the rules of the game. The cheap land at the urban fringe is still there, but using it is more difficult. The public road-building programs and sewer and water grants are disappearing, and the fiscal structure of local governments is more and more hard pressed to maintain the physical plant and levels of service residents currently enjoy. The development industry is running out of affordably developable empty land.

Some developers have turned to urban areas. There, improvements are in place—the conversion of existing rental buildings to condominiums or the demolition of low-density structures and the erection of high-density development is all that needs to be done. This has resulted in a new rash of conflict and controls.

Consider the developers and their attorneys who often appear at public meetings, making statements along the lines of, "This is supposed to be a free country. In a free country like America nobody can tell you that you don't have a God-given right to do whatever you please with your own property." This fallacy has a noble history. Blackstone said it in the eighteenth century: "Regard for the law of private property is so great that it will not authorize the least violation of it even for the general good." He was followed by William Pitt, who opined "the poorest man in his cottage could defy the King—storms may enter—rains may enter—but the King cannot enter." This has

come down to us as, "A man's home is his castle." But Blackstone and Pitt were wrong even for their time.

The extent of the powers of an owner to dispose of and use his land has never been unlimited by public interests, nor have these powers remained static. Since earliest times, use of property was constrained by nuisance laws that controlled uses that were harmful, dangerous, or offensive to community values.[3] Such laws, which can be found as far back as 1692 in Massachusetts, confined obnoxious uses (e.g., uses that produce smells, noise, threaten fire, etc.) to certain special districts within settled areas. What is considered harmful changes over time. Thus in 1909 sunlight was considered essential for the enjoyment of property rights and the U.S. Supreme Court in *Welch* v. *Swasey* approved a Boston law regulating the height of buildings.[4]

ZONING'S BIRTH, EVOLUTION

As cities became bigger and more complex, local governments were unable to deal with the number of potential nuisance conflicts. There were as yet no requirements for public approval before detrimental uses might be established next to existing properties. Zoning, a giant leap in the extension of the police power, was approved in 1926 by the U.S. Supreme Court in *Ambler Realty* v. *the Village of Euclid*.

The Police Power

Police power as discussed here does not involve flashing red lights and sirens. Rather, it has to do with the power of cities and counties to make and enforce zoning regulations for the general welfare. This means that unless a state or federal law provides otherwise, a local municipality may follow its own course in adopting and enforcing land use controls. The courts, in interpreting what a city or county may or may not do, have generally been quite liberal in allowing zoning regulations to stand and, over time, the message to property owners and developers seems to have become quite clear: The best place to fight and win your battle is before the local agencies, *not* in the courts.

Protectionism

The National Commissions on Urban Problems (1968) summed up the purposes of zoning:

> The purpose of zoning becomes, in effect, to keep anyone from doing something on his lot that would make the neighborhood a less enjoyable place to live or make a buyer less willing to buy. . . . Regulations still do their best job when they deal with the type of situation for which many of them were first intended; when the objective is to protect established character and when that established character is uniformly residential. It is in the nice neighborhoods, where the regulatory job is easiest, that regulations do their best job.[5]

However, even in the nicest neighborhoods, many citizens do not feel regulation goes far enough. In some places, a regulatory process may become impossibly complex and restrictive. The rationale for such protectionism is partially explained as follows:

> If the government in a neighborhood does not perform properly the tasks that only government can accomplish, the people who live in that area will scramble to leave—and the "housing problem" in that area becomes insoluble, however hard the legislators push on the subsidy pedal, however firmly the "code requirements" are enforced.[6]

The Density Issue

Perhaps only school busing causes more local emotion than a proposal to raise density. Robert Nelson offers an explanation that goes beyond economics.

> In areas less intensively developed than those in in-

ner cities, the most important single indicator of housing quality is density. Because neighborhoods with low density generally have a high environmental quality, developers of high-density housing will have a strong incentive to locate it in low-density neighborhoods. Moreover, high-density housing economizes greatly on land costs, so that prices of land in even the most desirable neighborhoods are usually affordable. As a result, if neighborhood entry were not controlled, there would be a strong tendency for high-quality, low-density neighborhoods to decline. . . . The means of dealing with this critical problem is, of course, land use regulation. Zoning ordinances establish minimum lot size, floor space, road frontage, setback distance, side and rear yard size, and other similar minimum quality standards for each neighborhood, while building codes and subdivision regulations establish other types of quality standards for the structures themselves.[7]

Zoning and Collective Property Rights

Zoning represented a major infringement on personal property rights by collective authority, but it did not—though it often has been seen to—constitute a threat to the concept of private property. Properly understood, zoning was a new and well-disguised extension on the collective level of private property concepts.[8] The important point is that when an individual developer's property rights are in conflict with the collective rights of the neighbors, the public officials acting as the protective trustees will usually award victory to the neighbors.[9]

Scope of Zoning

Today, zoning controls have been generally upheld with respect to the following areas of collective protection of private property in neighborhoods.

1. Maintaining property values.

2. Stabilizing neighborhoods and preserving their character.

3. Providing for uniform regulations throughout each district. Because planned unit developments do not conform to this purpose, they are often controversial and bitterly opposed.

4. Moving traffic rapidly and safely. As noted earlier, this purpose is used quite frequently to argue against higher density or nonresidential uses in residential areas.

5. Controlling aesthetics. As noted earlier, the courts have upheld a denial of permits for structures at variance with existing structures that would cause a depression of property values. However, aesthetic controls also spark the question of the imposition of one group's taste on an individual's use of his poperty.

"Negotiable" Controls

By the 1960s rigid zoning controls began to give way to more "flexible" development controls. They took many forms. Among the most common were the floating zone and the "wait and see" zone. Richard Babcock described the floating process as, "given the 'right' proposal put forward by the right developer, this textual reference would descend from the firmament and settle on the lucky owner's land—but only after extensive and careful bargaining between the applicant and the municipal legislature."[10]

In the "wait and see" form, undeveloped lands might be zoned only for exclusive agricultural or large-lot residential uses. However, the city or county actually is only waiting for the invisible hand of the market to stretch out in the form of a developer who will propose a zone change under contract or special permit conditions that allow the exercise of the widest administrative discretion. In other words, since the zone change does not have to rely on standards, list of permissible uses, and other matters of right in a zoning ordinance, the city approval is often based on the best deal it can get. These "wait and see" zones may extend to much of the buildable land in a jurisdiction, even though the comprehensive plan shows more extensive use.

Other Flexible Regulations

Special permits is another category of techniques that allows individualized review and controls certain uses under terms specifically spelled out in the zoning ordinance. Planned unit developments (PUDs) and overlay zones are often administered through the special permit system. These generally deal with the types of uses that have special problems to the community, such as massage parlors, pornographic bookshops, treatment centers for drug and alcohol abuse patients, and so on. They present a challenge to the practicing planner, inasmuch as the dangers to the surroundings are often more perceived than real.

Site plan review is another of the more common flexible techniques used by many communities. Long employed as part of the planned unit development procedure, the general idea behind site plan review is that the local community receives an assurance that the detailed plans presented by the developer will be followed.

In using such flexible development review techniques, the practicing planner has much more to do than simply determining whether a proposed development is in compliance with existing ordinances and codes. He or she must have the skills required to negotiate not only on behalf of the municipality with the developer, but for several other interest groups, such as the general public, the residents, property owners near the proposed development, and other landowners and speculators who will be affected by the approval of the development under review. The practicing planner does have discretion in these situations, but the process also takes considerable time and much more professional and technical skill in evaluating site plans, negotiating for better development, handling public relations, and managing the project as it makes its way through the approval maze.

The major results of the planner's work in administering flexible review techniques are conditions on the approval of a project. The ability to write conditions of approval that will both be fair and will also stick is one of the most difficult skills a practicing planner must acquire.

DISTINCTIONS BETWEEN PLANNING AND ZONING

Zoning is only part of the process called "planning." Zoning separates a municipality into districts and regulates, on various bases, building and structures, but planning has a much broader focus—it concentrates on development in relation to the community's current and future social and economic well being. For someone attempting to work with the system, a practical distinction is that planning measures, such as adopted plans, goals, and so forth, are official policy for the future, whereas zoning lists the permissible uses for specific properties right now. For a long time, the official plans and the zoning covering the same areas could be in conflict. This meant that the name of the game for development was rezoning. Today, the story is changing.

An increasing number of states now require that zoning conform to a "well considered plan" or a "comprehensive plan." This reflects a belief that zoning cannot truly be effective unless the long term is considered, and that the comprehensive plan is the means by which the rational allocation of land can be achieved. It should be a prerequisite for zoning.

Comprehensive planning was institutionalized by federal grants (Section 701 of the Housing Act of 1954) and other federal requirements that made having a comprehensive plan a criterion for winning urban renewal, transportation, and other capital grants. But federal grants for comprehensive planning have disappeared in recent years, so that even those plans that were relevant a few years ago are probably now approaching obsolescence. Very few communitites have the funds (or the will) to hire the platoons of planners and squads of consultants that used to produce those thick reports, those massive research efforts, and those wonderful audiovisual materials for public hearings. Nevertheless, the planning process must be kept current. Likewise, the planning-zoning relationship must be assessed as it exists in the present.

THE REAL WORLDS OF ZONING AND PLANNING

In recent years, there has been a trend toward using land use controls to carry out social policy ranging from the distribution of pornographic movie houses to redistribution of wealth. Martin Mayer pointed out that "politicians must also understand that land policy and social policy are very different questions, often likely to be in conflict.... The brilliantly accomplished social policy of encouraging home ownership by the lower middle class in the years after World War II was abusive land policy and recognized as such from the beginning."[11]

The practicing planner needs to understand how the land use system really works and why. In many communities there is a secret agenda that the decision makers follow in deciding how planning and zoning policies will be implemented. A developer from outside the community is often setting himself up for a disappointing joust with the status quo if his project cannot be designed in accord with the consensus on "the way things should be." In many communities, for example, unstated operating principles similar to the following examples rule development decisions, regardless of what has been said in a comprehensive plan.

• Existing desirable neighborhoods shall not suffer changes.

• For undeveloped areas, housing similar to or higher in price than existing housing is all that is wanted under growth-control policy. Clean industries, research and professional offices, and high-sales-tax-yield commercial uses are sought to give the city a fiscal boost. Every city wants to become the home of a "high tech" company that hires only $50,000-per-year Ph.Ds with no children and whose products are dispatched into the world by bicycle couriers or pneumatic tubes.

• Entry is to be denied to housing that would bring in lower income people, big families, transients, or other people with undesirable traits. Housing that would be lower in cost, too different in style, or increase density are also to be excluded.

• Existing businesses are to be protected from competition, particularly where the village or town has a charming downtown center. However, if the new development is determined to be potentially profitable enough to increase tax revenues, then principles of unfettered free enterprise will be in effect.

Norman Williams, Jr., listed five basic forces affecting how land use controls really work. They are:

1. The pressure from developers to obtain as large a profit as possible from development of land, normally increasing the intensity of land use.

2. The pressure from neighboring residents to achieve and protect quality in the physical environment, in part by decreasing the intensity of land use.

3. The clear tendency since World War II for new development (and also the middle class population) to concentrate in the outer parts of metropolitan areas. . . .

4. The gradually dawning realization that opportunities available in suburban areas—in terms of new jobs, better public services, and a more pleasant environment are barred to those lower income groups who need them most, and that conscious public policy (in the form of land use controls) has played a major role in this connection. . . .

5. The increasing resistance in the suburbs to any new development, partly for fiscal reasons and partly for less creditable ones.[12]

Given such pressures, it seems amazing that the system has performed as well as it has. Most of the literature has been critical of the American system of land use controls, but the system has generally, and in combination with good times and technological advances, given Americans a better built environment in each succeeding decade. The look-alike houses of the suburbs of the 1950s and 1960s have not disintegrated into the slums that the cities had predicted. Where the environment was protected, housing has appreciated in price several times over original purchase prices and the rates of inflation. Even the older central cities have not suffered the death forecasted for them.

Americans are not people who will suffer a system that does not deliver. Much of the criticism of the land use system concerns how it handled problems that have or soon will have passed into history (overcrowded schools, impacts of freeways, and even sprawl). The system has been remarkably adaptive because every state, city, and county is a laboratory where solutions can be developed, tested, and then exported to other communities to adapt to their own needs and values. This may not have the concentrated focus and power of an edict from a Ministry, but it is the only feasible public system in balance with the workings of a free enterprise system.

NOTES

1. John E. Cribbett, "Private Property and the Public Interest Conflict," in *Proceedings of the Institute on Law and Planning* (Urbana: University of Illinois, 1968), p. 273.

2. Miles Colean, *American Housing* (New York: Twentieth Century Fund, 1947).

3. Many of today's building requirements, such as density limits, minimum side and rear yards, and width of streets, are probably corrective police power measures against the abuses following the Civil War. In *The Good Old Days: They Were Terrible* (New York: Random House, 1974, p. 27), Otto Bettman offers the following description of middle-class apartments: "Families were shelved in layers...(in) three or four tiny rooms providing no insulation from the neighbors' cooking smells or babies squalling. Garbage removal and sanitary facilities were comparably wretched, and overcrowding made the buildings more difficult to manage than the tenement houses of the slum districts....(These apartments) were not the only fire traps, but they accounted for the heaviest loss of life in the great conflagrations of the period."

4. It is interesting to note that another ramification of this kind of regulation has arisen with the energy crisis—namely, regulation of buildings, trees, and other objects that would impair solar access for neighboring structures and properties whose owners are using or may wish to use solar energy devices.

5. National Commission on Urban Problems, *Building the American City* (New York: Praeger, 1969), p. 7.

6. Martin Mayer, *The Builders* (New York: W.W. Norton & Co., 1978), p. 419.

7. Robert H. Nelson, *Zoning and Property Rights* (Cambridge, Mass.: M.I.T. Press, 1977), p. 16 ff.

8. Nelson, pp. 17-18.

9. The U.S. Supreme Court blessed this principle in a 1971 decision (*James* v. *Valtierra*) that upheld a provision of the state constitution saying that no low-rent housing project could be developed, constructed, or acquired by a public body unless the project were first approved by a majority voting in the community where such a project were proposed.

10. Richard F. Babcock, *The Zoning Game* (Madison: University of Wisconsin Press, 1969), p. 89.

11. Mayer, *The Builders,* p. 79.

12. Norman Williams, Jr., "Land Use and Growth," *Future Land Use,* Robert W. Burchell and David Listokin, eds. (Piscataway, N.J.: Rutgers University Center for Urban Policy Research, 1975), p. 153.

3

Skills Needed to Be an Effective Practicing Planner

Albert Solnit

Wanted: Candidates to work in local agencies as planners, administrators, and community development or social service specialists.

Must be willing to:

• Sit through many meetings, some of which are poorly organized and managed,

• Adjust to a bureaucracy and bureaucrats and "company men,"

• Accept and work within a climate of increasing public distrust,

• Provide services on limited and dwindling funds, with limited staff and budget,

• Be available and answerable at all times to politicians and community residents on every local problem, real or imagined,

• Work with officials, some of whom want inexpensive instant solutions on the one hand (when there are none), or, on the other hand, resent being confronted (by you) with issues and problems they can't or won't solve (and wish would just go away),

• Work long hours at times, especially if you are in a responsible position,

• Implement federal and state policies and regulations, sometimes whether you like them or not,

• Understand and cope with the diminishment of local government's role.

Source: University of California Extension Course; Notes, by Warren Jones

Today's practicing planners are multifaceted individuals who have been academically prepared and have or are just cutting their teeth in real-world agencies and departments. Those who are drawn to the profession have basic interests in the field; those who survive have skills they can develop and hone to make them effective planners.

PERSPECTIVES ON PLANNERS

The attributes of a good practicing planner can be viewed from several perspectives, the most important being those of the employer, the applicant, and the citizen. From the employer's point of view, a good planner should be able to:

1. Know what is a good development from the public point of view,

2. Know what the development means in terms of the general plan,

3. Know the potential politics of a proposal,

4. Know how to apply the laws, standards, and policies in a positive way,

5. Know to analyze zone changes, subdivisions, and complex projects by applying the ordinances, codes, checklists, design principles, and local objectives.

In essence, the employer expects a good planner to have a sense of what the community is all about. A good practicing planner also is able to control his or her personal preferences for certain types of design or site plan solutions, and controls any tendency to build an extra-legal power base. The good planner does not add to the stereotype of the petty bureaucrat who grasps and uses his or her piece of discretionary power to hold up, redesign, or otherwise control and obstruct the development process when it is not necessarily in the public interest.

Other attributes of good practicing planners include:

• The ability to write well and present reports that organize data clearly and bring together ours, theirs, and anyone else's data for a balanced and comprehensive presentation.

• The ability to make recommendations that are supported by the facts and developed with enough attention to precedents and existing policies that they influence decision making. Such recommendations have to build a bridge

to the viewpoint of the decision makers.

• A knowledge of the legal basis for planning plus what the courts currently are saying. Planners should be able to help the hearing bodies issue findings of fact which include conclusions of law and fact, the reasoning by which the hearing body reached its conclusions, and the basic fact on which the decision is made.

• The ability to function in an office: Knowledge of procedures, how they work, how to change them, and even how to circumvent them. A planner needs to know how to get support staff to work with his or her deadlines and also how to write clear work orders to ancillary personnel, such as draftsmen and typists.

• The ability and desire to stay current and stave off obsolescence. University educations can be broadened by reading materials in the office, taking extension courses, and going to conferences.

• The ability to identify the interests of many different clients. There are many publics, many special interest groups, and other agencies in addition to the private applicants to whom the planner must effectively respond.

• The ability to learn to judge effectiveness. Planners who will advance to management will learn how to determine the adequacy of the planning agency, the staff-commission relationship, and the staff-council relationship, as well as the adequacy of agency products such as ordinances, the general plan, and special studies. Setting performance standards is one way to do this.

• Character traits such as enough intelligence to handle the complexities of the planning process, a mind open to new ideas, a tolerance for change, and vision for future prospects of the community. This requires imagination and flexibility.

• The ability to bounce back after losing an

item or two on the agenda. The planner needs to be able to come back and give 100 percent to the next item on the agenda.

The applicant wants the practicing planner to be a "good bureaucrat." Good bureaucrats know how to clearly explain procedures, rules, and requirements so that applicants do not lose time, money, and their place in line for approval. The good planner can explain what the options are on any development proposal. He or she should know what kind of job the planning department can (or will be allowed to) do on an application. Above all, the good planner does not treat the applicant as the enemy. The applicant should be treated fairly, informed of what is required every step of the way, and points of conflict should be pointed out as early as possible.

The citizen wants the planner to understand and be sympathetic to—though not necessarily in agreement with—the point of view of citizens. The planner should know how people really feel about where they live. This requires a degree of empathy beyond being able to recite the goal statements in a general plan.

Consider, for example, residents who have strong feelings about losing the quiet sanctity of an established residential zone or the small-town flavor of a business district because something in the name of progress might be too large in scale. The good planner uses these attitudes and aspirations as part of the analysis of the proposed project, and figures out how to mitigate the impacts at all levels.

GETTING HIRED

The rules for entering local government employment are often crazy. There are layers of employment laws and procedures that must be followed. Personnel offices rarely make valid evaluations of job applicants because they are geared to find the best "applicant." And once

hired, the new planner may find the job does not quite fit textbook descriptions.

Most entry-level job holders seem adequately served by the universities that provide planning theory and substantive knowledge. They are taught useful research, analytic, evaluative, and policy development methods. However, many indicate that they are not satisfied with university curriculums that exclude the skills the practicing planner needs to obtain and keep a job. These practical abilities include management skills, administration techniques, grantsmanship skills, environmental and economic impact assessment methods, and oral and visual presentation skills. The following lists represents what should be the minimum requirements for placement and advancement in a planning division.

1. Planners should be able to organize time and work effectively doing a fixed amount of work in a fixed amount of time with a fixed amount of money. This means the ability to create and stick to work programs, project management procedures, and understand budgeting, including its justification for unfriendly legislators. Successful consultants have this skill. They can relate time to money and always have the meter running when at work.

2. A desire to serve the community objectively while retaining a broad-based view of the public interest.

3. An interest in planning activities and impacts beyond the planner's jurisdiction.

4. Awareness of the planner's agency's strengths, weaknesses, and biases, and the measures to take for mitigating them. The people working with the planner should be known as human beings, not as paper generators.

5. The capacity to distinguish between fact and opinion. This is critical for evaluating testimony in public hearings.

6. The ability to speak clearly and react quickly in public. This means that a good planner must be able to assemble information in both written and oral testimony and then go on to make recommendations that are meaningful to the people he or she advises.

7. The ability to take the initiative in policy issues. Good planners should be able to do more for their communities than react to the applications they receive over the counter.

SKILLS FOR SURVIVAL

There are essential skills for survival on the job.[1] First and foremost is the word. Whether in memos, reports, technical studies, or oral presentations, the important thing is that whatever message is attempted, it must be understood. Voltaire said: "We have the natural right to make use of our pens, as of our tongues, at our peril, risk, and hazard."

Consider how communication is critical in every aspect of the planner's job.

Working with the Public

Students rarely learn in school how to deal with the public. A planner's first job often will involve explaining the rules of the game to a citizen who wants to do something that the government regulates. For many ordinary people, that is their one big face-to-face contact with government and the planner may make a lasting impression that will add to the widely held belief that government workers are unresponsive and hard to deal with unless an attorney is in tow. Appendix 3.A shows a positive way to help the public. But the opposite is shown in the encounter between Flotilla Marsh, recently widowed home owner, and Pincus Flornoy II, variance, exception, and special permit analyst.

Flotilla: [huffing and puffing after a long search for the right bureau] Hello there, is this where I get a zoning variation?

Pincus: Well, that depends, what do you want to do?

Flotilla: I'm all alone since Hanibal, my husband, died, and I'd like to convert my front bedroom and porch into a plant emporium and juice bar.

Pincus: Do you know your zoning?

Flotilla: What's that got to do with what I want to do?

Pincus: Well, we don't just hand out variances to anyone who asks. It depends on a lot of variables, including your existing zoning designation.

Flotilla: [visibly shaking] Well, could you look it up, please? I live at 314 Stone Street.

Pincus: Of course not, you'll need your assessor's parcel number and proof of ownership, such as a current tax bill. Then I can locate your place in our map books. The assessor is in our downtown annex, so you'd better hurry if you want to get there before that office closes.

Flotilla: I've already come clear across town on the bus to see you. Couldn't you help me while I'm here? Could you, for instance, call the assessor for me?

Pincus: I'm sorry, we don't offer that service in this section. We only process applications from bona fide property owners and it's your responsibility to establish that as a prerequisite to making application under the requisite sections of the zoning ordinance.

Flotilla: [grips her shopping bag and leaves, muttering imprecations about snotty bureaucrats].

Technically, Pincus was playing by the rules. In terms of human relations, his treatment of Flotilla Marsh was a disaster. Here are three things he did that he should not have done.

1. *He was uncooperative.* He also did not give good directions. His job is to give people all the information he can. It would not have been out of line from the standpoint of decency to have checked out the zoning himself after phoning in for the parcel number, or to let Mrs. Marsh use his phone to do it. Instead he gave her a runaround. Most people have been mishandled by people in government whose approach to the public has been to make things as difficult as possible. The right thing to do is to make things as simple as possible for the public, even if the planner is not at all responsible for the system in which he or she must work. The people planners deal with should be considered as clients, and the fees they pay as the psychic rewards that are earned by helping people cope with a complex process that the planner understands better than they do.

2. *He engaged in evasions and put-downs.* The public generally does not know the rules and jargon of the planner's job and such lack of knowledge does not justify treating people with disrespect. Public employees often must be educators if communication is to ultimately take place. Pincus was willing to teach Flotilla about the procedures she needed to follow to get started with him, but she couldn't learn about what she really wanted to do without being brushed off. Many new employees consider this behavior as being objective; actually, it is the essence of stonewalling and unresponsiveness.

3. *He maintained his social distance.* Pincus avoided person-to-person contact with Flotilla by speaking stilted jargon instead of plain English. Even if she wasn't put off by his uncooperative attitude, resentment certainly would develop after having "official" words like variables, existing zoning designation, bona fide, and requisite tossed at her. Beginning planners who think it is smart to pepper their conversations with the public with such two-bit words will probably find people responding to them with frustration and disdain.

Reaching the Public

Planners often must venture out in public to communicate what their work is about to the people they need to persuade, inform, and positively impress. Unfortunately, they instead often antagonize, confuse, and negatively impress their audiences. Planners must avoid the seven deadly sins of presentation that follow.

1. *Confusing and unclear topics.* Topics often are confusing and unclear because they have been dragged out of fat, unreadable reports that have not been properly focused or summarized.

2. *Over-technical explanations.* Avoid presentations so full of technical triple-ply language that only those who have Ph.D.s in the field can follow it.

3. *Unreal topics and questions.* Why address subjects that have no real relevance? For example, one regional agency used to travel around to local meetings with a 30-minute slide show showing abstract maps and posing the question, "What Regional Form Do We Prefer?"

4. *Tech fix.* This is the kind of presentation that can result when a lot of number crunching has gone on. Too often there is a temptation to insinuate a level of precision that is not there, especially when projections and mathematical modeling results are presented to lay people by the technicians who are stakeholders in the number-crunching business.[2]

5. *Unseen assumptions.* Solutions are offered that hide important considerations. For example, a capital improvement program might be presented as easily affordable, but an unseen assumption might be that there will be no inflation in building costs.

6. *No here-there.* Very often a recommendation for something in the future includes no consideration of the current realities. For example, a neighborhood renewal scheme for a low-income neighborhood will be offered up as if its implementation would not cause displacement and relocation problems at the very outset. Such presentations do not ask the basic question of what do we have to pay, change, and give up to get from here to there. Means are dismissed by ends.

7. *No point of view.* A problem is minutely described, checked over, and defined, but the presentation lets things hang right there. No point of view on what needs to be done to alleviate this problem is expressed.

Avoiding the seven deadly presentation sins is not enough. Planners also must consider other factors when making presentations. These factors include the following.

1. A planner must know what his or her subject is about and what he or she is doing in it.

2. A planner must know what he or she wants to get from presenting and must identify the audience and what the optimum response would be. Is the goal:
- To simply impart information?
- To offer advice?
- To get approval of some proposal?

3. The planner should allow openings for discussion and feedback from listeners, and be prepared to handle it. Leaving more time for discussion than presentation is often wise.

4. The timing of the presentation should be right; it should come at the proper stage of the decision process. For example, should a planner make a presentation showing the need for more funding for transit for the elderly a short time after the city council has finally adopted next year's budget—and hope for results?

5. The highlights should be identified and focused on during the presentation.

6. Printed materials should not be distributed just before the planner will speak. Otherwise, much of the audience will be reading instead of listening to the presentation.

7. A planner needs to learn how to really listen to what people are saying, in terms of both their words and their feelings. For example, people who are resisting assisted housing in their neighborhood may talk about how such housing will damage their property values, when they really mean that they are afraid of having people who take such welfare as neighbors.

8. A planner should not be defensive or evasive when hard questions are asked. Even presidents sometimes can say, "I don't know, but I can find out." Remember, fast talking will be recognized as just that.

Written Communication

As public confidence in government has dropped, many critics have claimed that government officials are often their own worst enemies when they try to communicate in writing. Any planner worth keeping on past probation should be able to write:
- Short memos, directives, and letters;
- Brief, clear reports of medium length; and
- Well-organized long reports.

The biggest problem is that too many people who have to communicate ideas in writing cannot do it clearly. Following are some of the most common of several types of deficiencies in the use of English by governmental writers.

Jargon and psuedo-scientific prattle. In academia, one is often rewarded for obscure, murky shop talk. After all, the authorities, whose texts you have to buy, often write like that. For example:

> Thus we conclude, as we began, that both of the two common and superficially different modes of defining a region express useful, if not indispensable, truths. The less metaphorical mode is content to delimit a region as that contiguous one having the necessary geographic unities; the people with sufficiently homogeneous desires, attitudes, and wants; the sufficient bases in natural and man-made resources and technology; and the appropriate voluntary institutions and governmental organization to achieve, within the limits and opportunities of the structure of external political prose, the utmost efficiency in the fullest attainment of the major human values of the people of the area. To this comprehensive summation of the rivals or organismic mode of expression, drawing on the analogy of individual living organisms, adds an emphatic insistence that such an equilibrium of hu-

man wants is not to be achieved unless people, values, institutions, and resources are structured into functional components, as interrelated and indispensable to each other and to the healthy functioning of the whole, and as pulselike in the regularity of their interaction, as are the component parts of man and the animals.[3]

If prose like this, a 78-word sentence followed by an 81-word sentence, were put in a document for public discussion, the only response to be expected would be, "What did he say?" or just "What?". Yet, report after report is filled with the kind of pompous complexity that turns readers off.

That the prattle of academia reaches out into public writing is exemplified in this unpublished gem from an overpaid economic consultant in the San Francisco area, who wanted to sound like an irrefutable expert at any cost.

> The appropriate concepts of cost and gain depend on the level of optimization and the alternative policies that are admissible. The appropriate level of optimization and the alternatives that should be compared depends on a general acceptance of suitable criterion.

While the sentence length is not up to academic standards, the denseness of language was at the Ph.D. level. Here is how it might be rewritten in clear-speak:

> The notion of an optimum cost-benefit ratio really depends on how one defines a benefit. The level of benefits from each of various alternatives depends on the standards accepted for comparison.

Legalese or Complexosis. This is language that is so stilted, stuffy, and complex that it fogs instead of clarifies. An example is Section 6416 of the State of California's Housing Element Guidelines, presumably written for the guidance of local government people.

> In accordance with the provisions of Article 4, a housing program consisting of a comprehensive problem-solving strategy adopted by the local governing body which both establishes local housing goals, policies, and priorities aimed at alleviating unmet needs and remedying the housing problem, and sets forth the course of action which the locality is undertaking and intends to undertake to effectuate these goals, policies, and priorities. Making adequate provision for the housing needs of all economic segments in the community to plan affirmatively, through its housing element program for a balanced housing supply suited to the needs of the community as defined in Section 6418 of these regulations.

There are three basic faults in language infected with complexosis. First, each sentence contains more than one thought. Second, there are cross references to things like Article 4 and Section 6418 that murk up the meaning of the section. Third, there are newly minted word combinations strung together to produce important sounding meaninglessness, such as "a comprehensive problem-solving strategy." How does a locality meet this requirement?

Many government documents are written in a sort of legalese—the language of law, which retired Yale University professor Fred Rodell described as "almost deliberately designed to confuse and muddle the ideas it purports to convey." He wrote in 1939 in *Woe Unto You, Lawyers!*:

> No segment of the English language in use today is so muddy, so confusing, so hard to pin down to its supposed meaning as the language of the law. It ranges only from the ambiguous to the completely uncomprehensible....
>
> Yet why should people not be privileged to understand completely and precisely any written laws that directly concern them, any business documents they have to sign, any code of rules and restrictions which apply to them and which they perpetually live?[4]

Bureaucratic Flapdoodle. A twelfth century French bishop wrote to his priests: "Be neither ornate nor flowery in your speech...or the educated will think you a boor and you will fail to impress the peasants."

The idea is for planners to avoid pomposity and to try to write as they would speak. John O'Hayre reports that bureaucratic flap-doodle—defined as oily talk, having a false look of genuineness—really rankled President Franklin D. Roosevelt. He once received the following memo on what federal workers were supposed to do in case of an air raid:

> Such preparations as shall be made as will completely obscure all Federal buildings and non-Federal buildings occupied by the Federal government during an air raid for any period of time from visibility by reason of internal or external illumination. Such obscuration may be obtained either by blackout construction or obtained by termination of illumination.

FDR simplified the monstrosity:

> Tell them that in buildings where they have to keep the work going to put something over the windows; and in buildings where they can let the work stop for a while, turn out the lights.[5]

Not only memos are afflicted with filigree language. Annual reports often sound as pompous as the funeral oration for a Roman emperor. Here is one from a New England town planning department:

> This agency's activities during the preceding year were primarily oriented to continuing their primary functions of informing local groups and individuals to acquaint them of their needs, problems, and alternate problem solutions, in order that they can effect decisions in planning and implementing a total program that will best meet the needs of the people now and in the future.

An uncurling of this piece of pomposity might read: "We spent most of our time last year working with local people, going over their problems and trying to help them figure out solutions. In this way, we hoped to help them set up and carry out a program that will

solve today's problems and satisfy tomorrow's needs."

Buzz Words and Abstract Writing. It is important to use concrete words with specific meanings. Buzz words many have many meanings but mean nothing specific. They can confuse readers and impart little real meaning. Party platforms, patriotic speeches, and real estate sales brochures are common examples of this kind of mindless burbling. Technocrats often fall into this technique and fuzz up whatever meaning there might have been in what started as an attempt to inform the laity. For example, an environmental impact report tried to explain economic impacts as follows:

> The economic effects, although extremely important, are often so subtle and so confounded with other environmental effects, we neither realize nor appreciate the true economic effects and the resulting advantages of properly recognizing their linkage with environmental conditions.

The problem here is that the word effects has been used three different ways in a single sentence. Some words are so commonly and badly used that they often become part of a semantic charade.

Virtual Illiteracy. Given the growing deterioration of basic writing skills among college students, it is not surprising that much of what is written in government agencies is not only sloppy, but virtually illiterate. One county department head used to use a day per week rewriting his subordinates' reports. He complained that many of his staff, who were college graduates, expected the secretaries, who were high school graduates, to catch and correct their mistakes in grammar, spelling, and punctuation and, in many cases, to be their personal editors. Sometimes a semi-illiterate rises to the top and then there is no one to set things right. Here is an example from a county planning director's paper on rural development.

> At the outset of any discussion relative to concluding peripheral city or town land use, one must acknowledge the controversy that is generally generated by such a discussion, especially when City (all cities) and County legislators are involved. The tangents, all mind boggling, are numerous and relate to many frames of reference of the past, present, and future wherein quite frequently during any forum the context of any statement may be read a half dozen ways. In generating a functional formula that has some flexible application around the County for *total* County *application* (a very important thought) County Staff must deal with the following thoughts, acts, or proposals:
>
> (Biggest thought) There are diverse attitudes in all eight cities. In the past (and somewhat in the present) all cities that are experiencing growth have annexed following older development plans for the sole purpose of accommodating development. There has been little concern as to effects on contiguous unincorporated lands, such as speculations, taxation, incompatibility with agriculture, etc. Overnight with new state laws (LAFCo mandates) the County is called upon to reverse past trends on a wholesale basis. In most instances the cities in a plural form say, "We must bite the bullet and resolve the question of peripheral city land use, when really that we is you the county. All cities and the county should solicit the State to pass legislation enabling cities to annex everything within their sphere of influence and zone it for greenbelt with a corresponding order to the assessor to reduce taxation.

It is unfortunate that this reflects how the director actually spoke. Still, it might have been rewritten as follows.

> Land use on the city borders is controversial, especially when City councilmen and county supervisors are involved. In attempting to devise a solution that would be applicable everywhere in the county, county staff must contend with the following conditions:
> a. The cities do not all think the same about this subject.
> b. Cities that are expanding have annexed and accommodated development with little provision for the effects on the surrounding unincorporated areas.
> c. Now new state laws, such as the Local Agency Formation Commission Act mandates, require the county to reverse these effects. However, in most instances, the cities want the county to solve the problem of controlling development at the fringe by itself, until they can annex such lands. Therefore, all jurisdictions should try to get state legislation passed enabling cities to annex all lands within their spheres of influence, hold it as greenbelt, and correspondingly order the assessor to reduce the assessments on such lands.

MAKING THE GRADE

Newly hired planners quickly learn it takes more than an academic background and desire to be an effective planner. Employers, applicants, and citizens each must be served by the planner, and each has different expectations of how the planner should perform. Basic skills are critical to the planner's survival, with the most crucial of these being the ability to communicate effectively both orally and in writing. The ability and desire to continue to sharpen the skills and contribute to being an effective practicing planner also is critical.

NOTES

1. Warren W. Jones and Albert Solnit, *What Do I Do Next?* (Chicago: American Planning Association, 1981), pp. 31 ff.

2. Very often such technocrats will continue to offer tentative decisions that are precise but wrong because more variables must be considered on the next run of the model.

3. Yale University Directive Committee on Regional Planning, *The Case for Regional Planning* (New Haven: Yale University Press, 1947).

4. Stuart Auerbach, "War on Legalese Gaining Adherents in Los Angeles." *Los Angeles Times,* January 29, 1978, p. 2.

5. John O'Hayre, *Gobbledygook Has Got to Go* (Washington, D.C.: U.S. Government Printing Office, 1966), p. 39

Appendix 3.A
How to Draw a Plot Plan
City of Seattle Department of Construction and Land Use

Introduction

Many City of Seattle land use authorization applications or construction permit applications require that plot plans accompany the application. For the homeowner who is not used to preparing a plot plan this can be a formidable task. This handout has been prepared to assist homeowners in preparing plot plans. It lists the information that must appear on the plot plan, it shows what a good plot plan looks like, and it takes people step by step through the process of drawing a plot plan. Helpful hints and guidelines are also provided to aid an applicant in the preparation of the plan.

What is a Plot Plan?

A "plot plan" is an accurate drawing or map of your property that shows the size and configuration of your property and the size and precise location of most man-made features (buildings, driveways, walkways) on the property.

Plot plans show both what currently exists on your property and what physical changes you wish to make which will change the physical appearance of the land man-made features.

When do you need to draw a Plot Plan?

Plot plans are required to accompany most applications that you will make to the City in order to get approval to change how your property will be used or that are needed in order to construct something on your property. For example, plot plans are required when you apply for:

—A Building Permit to build an addition, construct a new structure, alter the roof line or do other exterior remodeling.

—A Variance to the Zoning Code requirements. (Not all Variances need complete plot plans. Check with the Zoning Counter to determine if a complete plot plan is needed.)

—A change of use authorization.

—A driveway permit where there is an existing sidewalk and curb.

A plot plan is also very helpful to have when you are asking the City questions about what you can and cannot do on your property. It will help City personnel to see the specific and unique conditions of your site. They can then provide you with specific rather than general information. The information you get will be much more reliable because it will be based on an understanding of your particular situation. This is particularly important when what you are doing involves Zoning Code and Building Code requirements.

What does a Plot Plan show?

A plot plan must contain the following information:

1. Name and address of the owner of the property.

2. Address of the property (if different from the owner's address).

3. The location and dimensions of all parking areas and driveways (existing and proposed).

4. Identification of adjacent streets (by name), alleys or other adjacent public property.

5. Legal description of the property.

6. Any easements that cross the property or other pertinent legal features.

7. A north arrow.

8. Identification of the drawing's scale (example: ⅛″ - 1′).

9. The property lines and property dimensions.

10. Location, size and shape of any structures presently on the site and proposed for construction.

11. Dimensions showing: front, side and rear yard setbacks, size of structures, paving, porches and decks.

12. Roof overhangs, and other architectural features such as bay windows and chimneys.

13. Identification of exactly what work is to be done, including the changes that are proposed to the physical features of the site or existing structures.

14. Creeks, drainage ditches and surface water lines (shorelines).

15. Ground elevations and contour lines for sloping sites or where earth grading is proposed. (This may not be required – check with the Zoning Counter or Permit Counter).

How do I show information on a Plot Plan?
Figure 1 shows a three-dimensional view of a piece of property. Such an illustration is not required to accompany a plot plan but is shown here to demonstrate how three-dimensional features are drawn on a plot plan. Figure 2 labels each of the features of the plot plan that are required to be shown on it. Specific guidelines to drawing the plot plan are given below.

How to prepare a Plot Plan
Step 1: Determine property boundaries and legal descriptions. There are several ways to determine what are your property boundaries and the legal description of your property. A legal description usually contains your property's lot number, the number of the block, and the name of the subdivision in which your lot is located.

Method #1 – Refer to the surveyor's map that often accompanies your real estate deed or the title to your property. The surveyor's plan shows the dimensions and configuration of your property, its relationship to abutting streets, where any easements exist on your property and other similar legal restrictions on the property.

Method #2 – Obtain copies of the King County Assessor's Office real estate property tax assessment records for your property. This information will include the legal description and a plot map that shows the dimensions and configurations of your property. (It does not show the location of buildings, driveways, etc.) You will have to visit the Department of Assessment Real Estate Office to obtain information on your property. Information is not available over the telephone. The office is on the 7th floor, King County Administration Building, between 4th and 5th and Jefferson and James. A copy of the Assessor's records can be made for 50¢ each.

Method #3 – If a Building Permit has been taken out on your residential property in the last four (4) years, the Seattle Building Department will have a microfilm

Figure 1
A typical property. (Note: This drawing is for illustration purposes only. It is not required by the City. The shaded portion shows the addition.)

Figure 2
A properly prepared plot plan for the property shown in Figure 1. (Figure 3 explains the markings and symbols.)

Identify streets by name.

Stippling (dotting) helps to
identify walks and pavements.

Showing setbacks is important.

Identify easements.

Show all roof overhangs
with dotted lines.

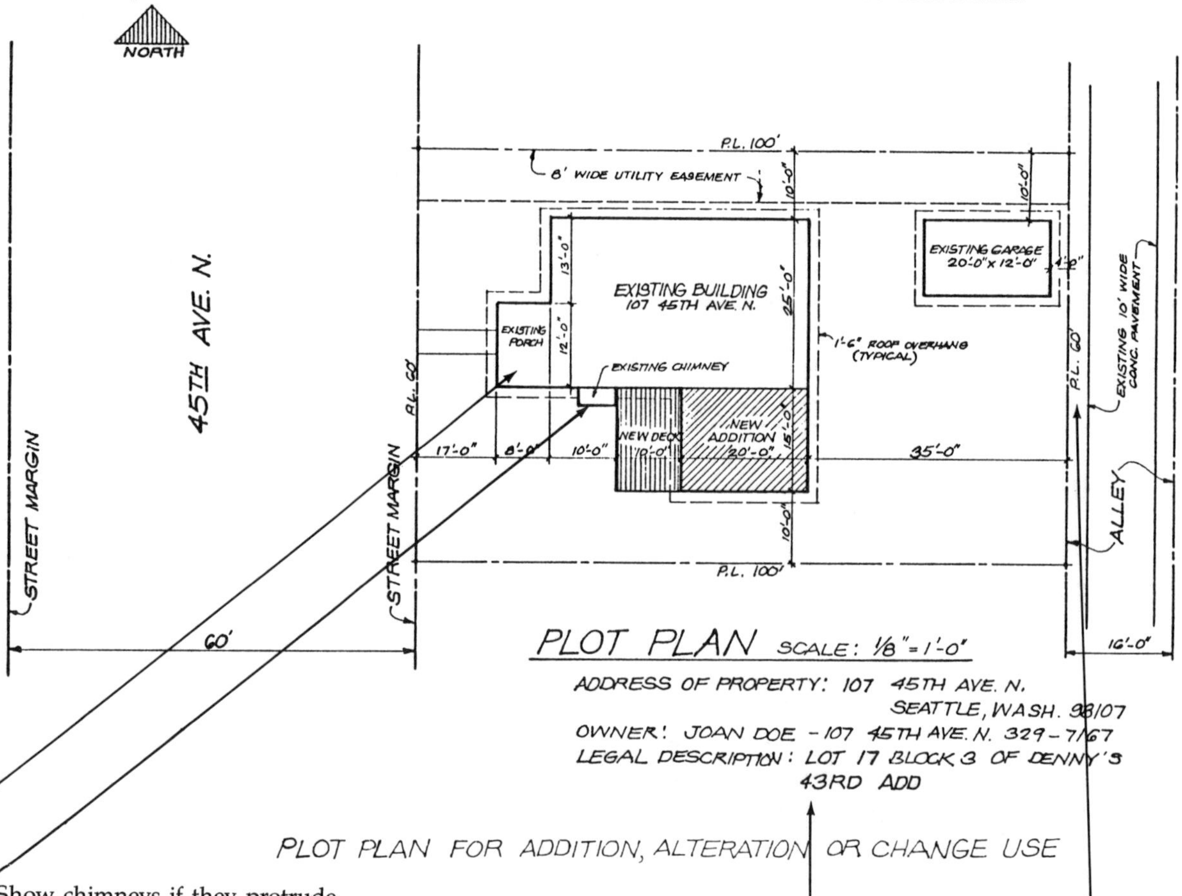

Show chimneys if they protrude.

Identify all porches and decks.

Note how property lines
dimensions are shown.

It is good to put all such
information in one, easily
found location.

PLOT PLAN SCALE: ⅛"=1'-0"

ADDRESS OF PROPERTY: 107 45TH AVE. N.
SEATTLE, WASH. 98107
OWNER: JOAN DOE – 107 45TH AVE. N. 329-7167
LEGAL DESCRIPTION: LOT 17 BLOCK 3 OF DENNY'S
43RD ADD

PLOT PLAN FOR ADDITION, ALTERATION OR CHANGE USE

copy of the building plans on file. To review the plans ask the receptionist at the Building Department (5th floor, Municipal Building) to direct you to the Building Department's microfilm center. Copies of the plan can be made for $2.00 per copy.

Step 2: Determine the location of all structures and other physical features to be shown on the plot plan. You will now have to measure the size (not including height) of all the buildings on your property as well as other important manmade structures (carport, garden shed, driveways, decks, and the like).

You will also have to determine the distance between these items and the property lines and the main buildings. In order to make these measurements you will have to locate your property lines on the ground. This is not always easy to do. For some helpful hints on how to locate your property line see the Homeowners Assistance Series handout titled "How To Locate Your Property Line" (available in May 1980).

Measuring is best done by two people, using a measuring tape long enough to avoid dividing each measured length into several segments. (A 25-foot or 50-foot tape is generally sufficient.) When measuring yards and pavements, be sure to hold up the tape level and measure perpendicularly to the property line or feature being measured. It is easiest to record all measurements on a sketch plan at the time you are doing the measuring and then later transfer all the information onto the final scale drawing.

Step 3: Draw the plan. After all of the information has been obtained, drawing the plan should be relatively easy. The first thing to do is to decide the size of the paper needed and the scale of the drawing. "Scale" is a word used in the architectural and engineering professions to mean a variety of things. In our case "drawing scale" or "scale of the drawing" denotes how many inches on the plan equals is a given length on the actual property. Thus if the scale of the drawing is $\frac{1}{8}'' = 1'0''$, a $50' \times 100'$ lot will appear as a $6\frac{1}{4}'' \times 12\frac{1}{2}''$ rectangle in the plot plan. The preparation of a scale drawing is aided by using a tool called an "architect's scale" or an "engineer's scale." These tools basically resemble rulers except that instead of being divided into inches, a given length can be measured directly by reading the markings on the scale.

A standard ruler can also be used. Usually rulers have markings which divide inches into 8 or 16 equal parts. One inch would thus equal either 8 feet or 16 feet.

An architect's scale can be used for drawing plans to $\frac{1}{8}'' = 1'\text{-}0''$, $\frac{1}{4}'' \times 1'\text{-}0''$, $\frac{3}{16}'' = 1'\text{-}0''$, **and** $\frac{3}{32}'' = 1'\text{-}0''$. An engineer's scale measures in $1'' = 50'$ and $1'' = 60'$. Inexpensive architect's and engineer's scales can be purchased at drafting supply stores, and some bookstores and stationery stores, usually for about $2.00 to $5.00. Other low-priced helpful tools are a drafting triangle (to draw right angles) and a protractor (to measure any non-right angles).

The selection of an appropriate scale for the plot plan usually depends upon the size of your property and how much information is needed to be shown on the plot plan. $\frac{1}{8}'' = 1'0''$, $\frac{1}{4}'' = 1'0''$, $1'' = 10'$ and $1'' = 20'$ are the most commonly used scales.

Select a scale that will permit you to draw the plot plan so that the information is not crowded together and so that it is large enough to be easily read by someone who is not familiar with your property. Note: If you are just interested in finding out some information about a permit and you are not applying for a permit at that time, your plot plan does not have to be complete and it may not need to be drawn to scale. It is usually only when you are filing an application that the plot plan has to be complete and accurately drawn. However, the more precise your preliminary information, the less likely that an important piece of information will be overlooked.

The plot plan must be drawn on, or attached to a sheet of paper that is at least $18'' \times 18''$, but not larger than $41'' \times 54''$. The size limits permit the plans to be microfilmed and easily stored.

Plans should be drawn on relatively heavy drafting paper such as "Crystaline", "1000H", or Mylar. Drafting supply stores can help you select suitable paper. Graph paper, poster board and card board cannot be used, since they are difficult to microfilm and store. If you prefer to draw each copy separately you may do so, or you can make good quality photocopies.

The next task is to draw the plan. It is usually easiest to begin drawing in the property lines. Next, add the existing features and then show what new additions or changes are to be made. Notes and dimensions are generally drawn last so they can be placed to avoid conflict with the lot and building elements. Printing and numbers should be at least $\frac{1}{8}''$ high so that they can be read easily once they are microfilmed. Where possible, use the symbols and abbreviations that are shown in the list below.

Varying the line weight (thickness of pencil line) will help the drawing to be more readable. Property lines and buildings are usually drawn in heavy lines while dimension lines and pavement lines are usually lighter. Refer to the example and plan shown earlier.

Indicate the new work by notes and cross hatching. The dimension line "strings" through the property should add up to the overall property dimensions. See Figure 3.

Figure 3. Symbols commonly used on Plot Plans

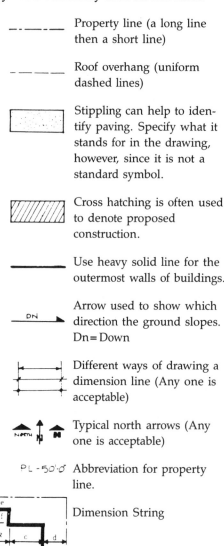

Property line (a long line then a short line)

Roof overhang (uniform dashed lines)

Stippling can help to identify paving. Specify what it stands for in the drawing, however, since it is not a standard symbol.

Cross hatching is often used to denote proposed construction.

Use heavy solid line for the outermost walls of buildings.

DN → Arrow used to show which direction the ground slopes. Dn = Down

Different ways of drawing a dimension line (Any one is acceptable)

Typical north arrows (Any one is acceptable)

PL -50'-0" Abbreviation for property line.

Dimension String

a + b + c + d = 100'

e + f + g + h = 50'

If you are proposing to build on a sloping site you may have to show contour lines which indicate how much change in ground elevation occurs across your property. For building sites that do not slope uniformly and gradually, a surveyor may be necessary to plot the contour lines. Check with the Permit Counter or Zoning Counter before drawing contour lines to see if they are needed and determine how much information you should provide concerning the slope of your property, making sure that your plot plan is complete and accurate.

Step 4: Check the drawings and make copies. You can save yourself a good deal of time in the application process by making sure that your plot plan is complete and accurate. The following check list is useful in checking your plan.

Copies of the plot plan can either be made by having the original drawing "blueprinted" at a blueprint shop or it can be photocopied at a copy center. Blueprint copies can be made with either blue lines or black lines. Determine how many copies you will need to submit along with your application. It is advisable to keep your original drawing so that you have a record of what you submitted and so that you can make additional copies if the need arises.

Checklist

Does the plan show:

Yes	No	
_____	_____	Property address
_____	_____	Legal Description
_____	_____	Owner's address and phone number
_____	_____	North arrow
_____	_____	Drawing scale
_____	_____	Property lines and dimensions
_____	_____	Existing and proposed building location(s) and their dimensions
_____	_____	Front, back and side yard setback dimensions
_____	_____	Driveways, walks

———— ———— For sloping sites:
contour lines and ground elevations at the corners of the lot and new construction

———— ———— Roof overhangs

———— ———— Porches, stairs, chimneys, decks and other architectural features

———— ———— Location and description of proposed construction if it will change the form of an existing structure or is a new building

———— ———— Names of adjacent streets

———— ———— Easements

———— ———— Dimensions showing size and location of buildings and size of property.

Definitions of Terms

• **Contour Line**–A line on the plot plan that connects the points on a piece of land that have the same ground elevation. Contour lines are shown on a plot plan when the property is not flat.

• **Dimension**–A measure in feet and inches of how long something is, such as the length of a wall, or how far something is from something else, such as the distance between a building and a property line.

• **Easement**–A legal right to use a piece of property owned by someone else. Quite often an easement states that a property owner cannot build on a portion of his or her property to allow access for utility lines or vehicular traffic.

• **Ground Elevation**–A number that states how high a specific point on the ground or on a structure is above sea level or some other recognized reference point.

• **Legal Description**–The written description of the property which legally defines the property's boundaries. It is usually written in surveyor's language stating the length and direction of a property line from a given reference point or referring to the lot and block number of a sub-division plot on file at the City. Legal descriptions are found on real property tax statements and the deed to your property; or they can be provided to you by the King County Assessor's Office.

• **Property Line**–A line on a plot plan that accurately shows the legal dimensions of your property. It shows how long each edge of the property is and shows the configuration of the property as if you were viewing the property from a point above it.

• **Scale**–An indication of a proportion which shows the size relationship between the actual size of something and the size of it as represented on a drawing. If something is acutally 8 feet long and it appears on a drawing as being 1 inch long the scale of the drawing would be 1 inch equals 8 feet or ⅛ of an inch equals 1 foot (⅛″ = 1′0″).

• **Setback**–The distance from a building or other structure to the property line.

4

Working with the Developer and the Project

Albert Solnit

It is apparent that the police power is not a circumscribed prerogative, but is elastic, and in keeping with the growth of knowledge and the belief in the popular mind of the need for its application, capable of expansion to meet existing conditions of modern life, and therefore keep pace with social, economic, moral, and intellectual evolution of the human race. In brief, there is nothing known to the law that keeps more in step with human progress than does the exercise of this power. CALIFORNIA SUPREME COURT IN *MILLER* v. *THE BOARD OF PUBLIC WORKS,* 195 Cal. 477, 485 (1925).

The scope of land use and development regulation many change with the times, as the above quote indicates. In the early days, the purpose of zoning and subdivision regulation was to keep nuisances segregated, to see that adequate public facilities were provided for new development, and to keep high property values from being diluted by uses that would diminish their resale value.

Since then, a large array of new concerns has arrived on the scene. They include such things as environmental, fiscal, social, and even moral concerns that were not present when the early regulation writers were at work. This has led to considerably more complexity in land use regulation; some say too much complexity. Table 4.1 illustrates one community's complex review process.

THE PLANNER-DEVELOPER RELATIONSHIP

Until about 50 years ago, urban development in the United States was unplanned and unregulated. Then, as now, the developer responded to market opportunities in his search for profit; this is a integral part of the American capitalist system. What has changed is that today the developer is subject to count-

Table 4.1
One Community's Complex Review Process

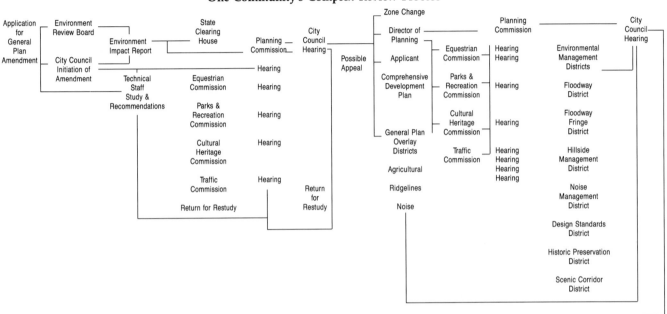

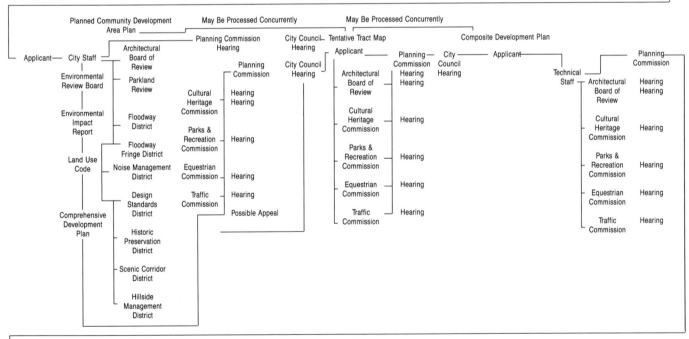

less levels of planning and environmental controls and regulations. A result is a relationship between planner and developer that can be less than idyllic.

The planner and the developer must meet often during the review and approval processes for the developer's project. In this case, the developer wants something from the planner — approval.

But the developer often is met by a planner who distrusts developers. The planner's concern with the less privileged in society has reinforced this distrust. Moreover, few planners who work in public agencies fully understand the economics of development. Their professional training rarely includes the real costs of money, of time and delays in processing, of delays in reaching the market, or even of what public services and improvements really cost the developer, the local governments, and the home buyer. Yet such data is basic to the developer.

The planner's training and tools are designed and directed toward the control of the private sector. The mechanisms of zoning, subdivision regulations, and environmental regulations are accepted tools for the controlling and directing of private development. Still, this does not mean the developer inherently is the enemy. The developer usually accepts the limits to development activities in a begrudging sort of way. Some developers do don the role of the enemy and fight all the way, with a court case always on the horizon. Others see the process as one to work with as quietly as possible without rocking the boat. Some developers even see the process as one with creative tensions, directly or indirectly encouraging them to do better in response to some publicly created roadblock.

The problem for the planner is how to tell the good guys from the bad guys. This is not always an easy job, and is part of the reason that planners tend to put all developers in the same category. A few tests that planners can apply to help separate the good from the bad follow.

1. *Past reputation.* The planner can look at portfolios of past projects and products. He or she should go see projects the developer has built and talk to other planners who have dealt with the developer on other projects. What was their experience?

2. *Financial backing.* It may be difficult, if not impossible, but the planner should try to establish who is financially backing the developer. This can be an important clue as to the developer's ability to carry out new and difficult approaches, and most important, the developer's ability to stick to his promises.

3. *Personnel supporting the developer.* What are the qualifications of in-house people, the reputation of consultants working with the developer? Are they really contributing or just being used?

4. *The developer's own words of commitment.* What is the developer saying to the outside world about the project? Is the developer entirely close-mouthed or cautious in public?

5. *Public appearance.* Does the developer appear personally at public meetings and review sessions? Developers who are really committed to their projects attend as many meetings as possible, and do not let their staffs or consultants carry the ball.

6. *Cooperation.* Does the developer understand the planner's values as they relate to the project (understanding, but not necessarily agreeing)?[1]

MEETING THE DEVELOPER'S NEEDS

Assuming that the planner is ready to meet with the developer, he or she should be prepared to deal with what the developer usually wants to know. Time frames, required forms and data, guidelines and standards for such projects, costs of application and processing, staff ability, and an assessment of the political/power environment are information items of primary interest to developers. Appendixes 4.A, 4.B, and 4.C provide examples of information that is of help to developers and, as a consequence, can help planners.

The Time Frame

How long does it take to get approval at the agency? To quote Robert Tennenbaum:

> To a developer, time is money. Money is very hard to get in the first place, and harder to keep after one gets it. Furthermore, there is no guarantee that the money will make more money. It costs money to borrow money with which to option land, buy land, hold land, plan land, engineer land, process land, develop land, and market land. It takes a while to sell land before all previous costs are reimbursed and profit or positive cash flow is impossible. All the while, inflation and rising costs and recessions get in the way to complicate everything. It follows then that the longer the review and approval processes, the more technical studies and restudies, the more revisions and dotting the i's, the most costly standards, the more it will cost the developer and the more the developer will pass through these costs to the consumer of the project's products.[2]

Paul C. Zucker, former planning director of San Diego County, has said that:

> The cost of development is 90 percent political and 10 percent bureaucratic, but we bureaucrats have to learn to handle our 10 percent better. We must reduce the time and cost of development review if we're going to be allowed to continue to keep the gains made in the recent decades in favor of planning. The process therefore is very important. We need to get organized. Very few, I estimate perhaps only 5 percent of planning agencies, have good management practices. Good management practices would include technical guidelines, codes, and ordinances that can be understood

by the applicant. Set times for production. This includes protected time for professionals to do their thinking.[3]

According to Melville C. Branch,

> the time taken to obtain various municipal approvals for a proposed project is probably the "original sin." For the past 25 years or more, private enterprise has protested that the time taken to process a request to develop or redevelop real property has been progressively lengthened as new legislation imposes additional conditions or inefficiency lengthens bureaucratic review. Many city officials agree that what once took less than a year in larger cities has been drawn out to an average closer to two years and in some cases to three years or more. Many private developers cannot afford to wait this long for the necessary local governmental approvals...Often, especially in a time of inflation, they must base their decision on whether to proceed on a proposed project more on the time required for approval than on more justifiable considerations of physical and spatial design. Although those concerned with city planning have been aware of this serious regulatory delay for years, the average time for approval has not been reduced either by city councils establishing an absolute time limit without exception or by municipal departments revising or consolidating approval procedures. Nor have steps been taken to prevent circumventing legal time limits when they exist by threatening disapproval unless the applicant voluntarily requests an extension of time, permitting "further study.". . . As matters now stand, processing and review time will become longer and longer, until eventually desirable standards formulated over many years of trial and error are discarded in order to induce private enterprise to make the financial investment necessary for urban development and redevelopment.[4]

It is important for the planner to know the working capacities and present workloads of not only the planning department, but also the various other reviewers, such as the public works and health departments. One of the recurrent problems that delay projects is lack of integration between the various departments involved in project review. Perhaps the greatest management improvement of the development review process in most communities would be to put one person in charge of a project's progress through the review process. This could ensure that the project undergoes simultaneous review and skirts bureaucratic pitfalls. This expediter would need access to department heads and elected officials so that people who unnecessarily delay a project will know they can get burned. Clear lines of authority and decision making are critical to such a process, to avoid having decisions overturned as an application moves up the line.

Required Forms and Data

The developer wants to know what he must submit to have an application approved and reach the public hearing stage. It is important to establish by the preapplication conference the maps and information that the developer will have to submit. This should be put in writing. Moreover, the agency should have instruction sheets on how to submit project maps. For instance, these instructions should state what the contour interval for grading plans will be, at what scale the site plans should be drawn, and the type of architectural drawings that will be needed.

Policies, Guidelines, and Standards

What are the policies, guidelines, and standards that will be applied to the project? These issues should be ironed out in the preapplication process. It has been said that a project never looks as good as it does in the early stages. However, it is important to remember that elements of projects get locked in fast because it is in the early phases that projects are approved for financing by banks and other lenders. To the degree possible, problems with the development should be ironed out during the preapplication process. The developer should be informed of the problems his staff will have to solve and of the precedents that have been set in similar projects (e.g., dedications, exactions, grading).

Costs

What are the application and processing costs? What consultant expertise is needed? The applicant should know what the review process is going to cost before filing an application.

Developers also should not be asked to redesign a project midway through the public hearing process. This is the cruelest form of delay, and yet it is very common for a planning commission, badly advised by staff, to say, "Well, we couldn't vote for something that looks like that, but we'll give you time to fix it up and bring back something that we can approve." Such action is not conditioning; it really asks the developer to be a mind reader. Developers complain most bitterly about review processes that are a series of karate chops to their budgets, that require more and more experts to be poured in and on to analyze before-unseen problems, and that foster the need to use several designers to help guess at a design that will win approval.

Developers say again and again, "We need to be told what it is we have to do to get approval." The worst kind of planning professional is one who allows the requirements for submission to be decided based on the level of controversy in public hearings. For example, residents in one community decided that there might be flooding problems if the development went in as presented. The staff recommended on the spot that the developer do a special study of the hydrology and bring it back before the project could receive any further review.

This kind of detour is often the kind of crowd pleaser a politician will order, with comments such as, "I'm not gonna leave any of my good constituents wondering about whether or not the water will run off this development and flood their backyards. We're gonna want proof before we go any further that every drop will reach a culvert. Therefore I move that we continue this hearing indefinitely until they bring us the right kind of hydrologic study that these good folks that have come to the meeting tonight can understand."

Staff Quality/Fair Play

Developers want to know how good the staff is. Can staff members work fast on big projects or do they need to be spoon-fed? What is the staff's batting average with the planning commission and the elected politicos? Are staff members taken seriously or do they just write ex post facto resolutions? How deep and sophisticated is their analysis of a project? How do they play the regs?

Planners should avoid the sin of fixing things up with conditions. Very often it is better to go for a denial than try to "mitigate negative impacts" by conditioning the project until it is no longer financially feasible. More and more project approvals have become contingent on lengthening lists of specific conditions that developers must meet before the all-important certificate of occupancy is granted. As Melville Branch notes:

> These conditions are in addition to the many provisions of design and construction contained in building, safety, and health codes. Not long ago land development requirements were limited to the dedication of land for future streets and street widening, installation of sewers or in lieu of sewer fees and easements of public utilities. To these reasonable requirements have been added in Los Angeles, California, street improvement, including surfacing curbs and gutters, installation of sidewalks, street lights and trees,

fire hydrants, flood control facilities, land dedication or, in lieu, fees for neighborhood parks, earthen berms, or other physical installations, aesthetic design features, and most recently, provision of a percentage of low-income dwelling units in residential projects. The land developer may be also required to construct or pay for off-site improvements linking the project with streets or utility systems some distance away. Not only are more and more improvements demanded, but lately there is a move to require that they be built to such exacting engineering standards that the developer is being forced in effect to assume, in addition to the cost of construction of public facilities, some of the normal expenses of future maintenance which have historically been a responsibility of government. . . . [5]

Recently, the developer of a large residential subdivision up for governmental approval was requested to contribute a bookmobile to the community. There seems no limit to local government's desire to saddle on the private developer as many improvements and facilities as possible in the "public interest." What now is the case mostly in larger cities will undoubtedly become the precedent for smaller cities. Local planning officials sometimes deliberately substitute unacceptable conditions for an outright denial that they expect or want to avoid for some reason. If a special condition is overturned on appeal, it is possible to modify the requirement only slightly and thereby force another round of time-consuming, costly, and fruitless litigation. Interim zoning or moratoriums on zone changes can be employed as tactics of deliberate delay instead of for the stated purpose of providing time for legitimate study. This allows zone designations for the future that are not currently possible or maintains the lower market value of land zoned for low-density development until it is used as the planners desired or is acquired by eminent domain.

There are other "techniques" planners can use to block developers and plans which they oppose. For example, to prevent the introduction of mobile manufactured homes in established residential neighborhoods as authorized by recent legislation in California, city planners may deliberately impose requirements to achieve compatibility with existing homes that are so rigorous and impractical that the practice is in effect denied. Similarly, a municipality can define a family so as to nullify, at least for a time, a recent California Supreme Court decision allowing unrelated persons to live together as a family in a single-family residential zone. Or a design review committee in city hall can improperly attach conditions to a proposed specific plan in private session, rather than by the proper process of public hearings and open decision. Or a planning department can improperly recommend denial of a proposed residential subdivision on undeveloped land, despite the absence of a current master plan, because the site is designated on a state mineral resources map as having undetermined deposits of gravel.[6]

The Power Bases

Finally, developers want to know who cuts deals with whom and how. They want to know what the backing of the council is: homeowners, business, other developers, or other groups and what their attitudes are toward development. They want to know the attitudes of the neighborhoods. They want to know if there will be reappointments or elections to the planning commission or city council during the review period. Generally, developers will have to obtain such information on their own. It is dangerous for planners to gossip about their employers and clients, but planners can help guide the developer on what style to use. Is the commission a deliberative body that will want all the facts reviewed and put into the record or do the members prefer highlights only, with time left to focus on the parts that are of most interest? Are the commissioners unsophisticated about maps, design, drawings, models, and so forth, or do they have a good grasp of such project elements?

Letting the Developer In

The planner has considerable perceived power. To retain credibility in this respect, the planner should be competent, professional, knowledgeable, tactful, and nonabrasive. Any fairly intelligent developer will know that planners have information the developer can get without paying for expensive lawyers and experts. Robert Tennenbaum cited five things that the planners can do to establish good relationships between themselves and developers:

1. *Be consistent over the long haul.* Every change, no matter how small it may seem, costs the developer time and money. Remember that when you are changing plans or regulations, the developer may be in the approval process with his plans based on your existing plans and regulations.

2. *Review the plans in detail.* Be consistent in reviewing and make sure you understand the positions other agencies or departments have on an issue. The planner may conceptually approve a certain plan element, only to have the approval denied later on by some other department (the continual chopping process). Make sure that your review is thorough at each stage of approval. Do not try to do a quickie this time and catch your oversight later on. This response to your error will cost the developer time and money. . . .

3. *Encourage the developer.* When you see something good in the plans, go to bat for the developer.

4. *Consider results.* Spend more top-level time with the developer whose project will have a major effect on the environment. This may not necessarily be the largest project, but it may be the most visible or on some more difficult land, or some other priority characteristic.

5. *Share education.* Take the time to educate the unsophisticated developer about doing it better and the rationale behind zoning and subdivision regulations, assuming that the reasons are valid in the first place. Education should be a part of every planner's role in the development process. Mutual education and understanding is the formal approach toward closing the gap.[7]

Planners should allow the developer to fully explain what his development is all about. They should develop the art of listening, with only a simple question here or there.

NEGOTIATIONS

When it comes to cutting deals, planners should negotiate with the developer himself, not his architect or attorney, and they should *never* make deals, promises, or commitments beyond their areas of discretionary authority. It is very important for a planner to know exactly what his or her discretionary authority encompasses. When in doubt, the planner should ask for direction and pull in superiors. The planner should not go on ego trips or commit the cardinal sin of trying to build an extralegal power base by imposing personal preferences on the developer's design solutions and site plans. Use of the discretionary power to hold up development by requiring redesign or otherwise detouring of a development is not the same as acting in the public interest. Nor will it be long tolerated by the employer, or by the courts.

If a planner must say no, he or she should say no at the beginning and should be sure that there is support for the no all the way up the line to the director's chair.

Planners should negotiate for something better than the minimum requirements. However, it is better to spend time making a mediocre project a good project than to take a good project and try to make it excellent just because

the talent is there. It should be remembered that some of the people who will bring projects in for approval have neither the sophistication nor the desire for good projects. In these cases, it is critical for planners to be very specific about what will make the project better. Precedents, examples, and policies that have been adopted in general plans, area plans, and design guidelines (if any) can be used to explain.

Trying to play catch up with a single project is not wise. It is not fair and is probably not legal to require a single project to make up for the omissions of everyone else in an area; e.g., to require a new business to provide off-street parking that will accommodate the customers of neighboring enterprises that did not provide their own adequate parking. Planners should try to reach closure in preapplication negotiations, even if closure is only agreement on what will be of disagreement before the planning commission.

Planners can call them as they see them, but should leave the judgment calls to judges. It is interesting to note that planning commissioners and other quasi-judicial judges of development have been compared to baseball umpires. There are three types of baseball umpires:

1. One type says: "I calls some of 'em balls and some of 'em strikes, but I calls them as I sees them."

2. Another type says: "I calls some of 'em balls and some of 'em strikes, but I calls them as they are."

3. A third type says: "I calls some of 'em balls and some of 'em strikes, but they're nothin' until I calls 'em."

Planners should not depend on the developer's attorney for legal advice or the drafting of agreements or memos. If a planner finds that he or she is getting into deep legal waters, the planning department's attorneys should be used to work with the developer's attorney, and if legal business is to be done at the negotiating table, the planners' attorney should be there as well as the developer's.

Requests for an exaction or a dedication or an expensive piece of analysis and research should be made early. Hidden agendas are to be avoided and the planner should watch out for people who use zingers, such as "although we didn't discuss this, I've put this clause in our agreement. . . ."

There are many "shoulds" and "should nots" involved in negotiating with developers. Practicing planners usually find William Claire's accompanying tongue-in-check commandments for planners negotiating with developers of interest. Perhaps they ought to be included in every planner's notebook on negotiating.

The Ten Commandments of Negotiating

I.   Thou shalt negotiate in good faith and sincerity and try to meet thy opposite party's "bottom line."

II.   Thou shalt not skin thy opposite party when a sandpapering is enough to achieve thy objective.

III. Thou shalt do thy homework, organize and anticipate issues in thy negotiations.

IV.   Thou shalt remember thou art not dealing across the table with creatures of logic—but of emotions—bristling with prejudices, motivated by pride and vanity.

V.   If thou intends to ask for something, thou shalt ask for it early in the negotiations.

VI.   Thou shalt say "no" on an issue at the beginning if thou can't say anything else and thou shalt not ask for that which thee already has.

VII. Thou shalt not become angry, red of face, or loud of voice unless it is intentional on thy part.

VIII. Thou shalt know thy limits and go no further. Thou shalt have "deal makers" at the table whenever possible.

IX.   Thou shalt observe the attorney-to-attorney respect rule.

X.   Thou shalt know thine own "bottom line" and shall keep thy negotiating package intact.

Source: From a paper by William Claire III, BCL Associates, Long Beach, California, 1983.

WRAPPING UP THE PACKAGE

The planner's work involves constructing a complete package, with the involvement of many others. But specific to the planner are the following responsibilities.

Writing the Staff Report

In reviewing a project proposal, the following checklist for compliance with planning criteria is suggested.

1. Is the use proposed compatible with surrounding zoning and development? This may often be a more imagined than real issue. For example, very often townhouses in a single-family neighborhood are objectionable for social rather than planning reasons.

2. Does the project conform to the plan and purposes of the zoning for the area? Objections to look for are:

a. The project is premature and would open up an area to development before the intervening areas have developed (e.g., sprawl, leapfrogging, overbuilding).

b. It may be out of scale with surrounding development.

c. It simply doesn't conform to the adopted general plan. At this point, either the general plan or the project ought to be amended.

3. Does the possible development of the property as requested do anything detrimental to the health, safety, and welfare of the people or environment in the surrounding area? Where environmental impact reports are required, the negative impacts should be fully described, as well as the mitigating measures to diminish or cancel out these impacts. The alternatives and costs should also be described. For example, increased traffic might be mitigated by providing for additional public transit or changing the width of the roads, or even redesigning the access to the district (e.g., signals, channelization, pedestrian overpasses).

4. Has the area changed so that the existing zoning or plan designation is no longer applicable?

5. Will the proposed development adversely affect the functioning of public facilities in the area, overburdening the roads, schools, police and fire services, sewer and water facilities?

6. Is there a real public need for this project within the area proposed at this time? This is a very good ace to play if growth management is part of the policy of the community.

7. Is there a better alternative than the project as proposed (e.g., different density or use mix, different phasing, different design, and so forth)?

Using the General Plan As a Project Review Tool

The general plan of a community should contain the language supporting the reason for many recommendations in zoning and development review staff reports. To be useful, however, a general plan should meet the following criteria as cited in *The Job of the Planning Commissioner*:[8]

1. It shows how the community can keep and improve its liveability in the face of change. The definition of liveability lies in the minds of residents, something it would be well for planners to check out first, so they'll know what the plan is in terms of what people value.

2. It should provide clear guidance for day-to-day decisions, including how any single piece of development fits in with the rest. This means that urbaniza-

ble land should be clearly identified and separated from rural land and open space. It should be precise enough so that plans for sewage collection and treatment, water supply, police and fire service levels, and new school enrollments can be competently and accurately derived from the plan.

3. An excellent plan should give everyone a good focus on solving some present problems. In one western city, the plan consisted of a status quo map of the built-up areas and a series of growth management lines showing how far utilities would be extended beyond the "fringe" in five-year increments. At one public hearing, a grizzled old apple farmer demolished the city team's smugness by observing, "How am I supposed to believe everything's going to be hunky-dory in the areas you annex beyond those lines when everything now inside them is planned to continue to go to Hell in a handbasket?".

4. It shows how to get from here to there. Each proposal in the plan should be backed up with measures which will make it happen. These measures, especially the ones that require money, should be substantiated by factual knowledge of the real world. Thus, a plan proposal to involve the local school district in expanding playgrounds won't touch base with reality if for the foreseeable future the district will be closing many of its schools and paring its budget in the face of declining enrollments and available funds. A more realistic and workable plan would deal with the problems of school site and building recycling.

5. It should deal with visual concerns in a three-dimensional way. For example, in one city the plan was overhauled to allow add-a-rentals, row housing, and mobile homes in formerly pure single-family districts. People were naturally apprehensive about what they had not yet experienced. Eye-level illustrations of precisely what was being proposed and how it would benignly fit in with what existed were badly needed. Instead, the people got disconnected fuzzy policy statements like "X city needs to attain its housing goals by diversification within the existing neighborhood framework," and assurances that every departure from the status quo would require at least one public hearing and two levels of review.

6. It should deal with how things will work as well as where they will go. Nowhere has the validity of this

principle been more clearly demonstrated than the literally thousands of mismatches between highways and land use. The scenario is often played out in as little as a decade and it goes like this:

Stage 1: Ricky-tick Road connects Sapsucker City with Babbotville passing through the pleasant farmland of Petitpoint County.

Stage 2: Babbotville has zoned part of its road as solid strip commercial and soon it takes longer and longer to get through the congestion and in to Sapsucker City.

Stage 3: Meanwhile, Sapsucker's downtown is dying because the country has allowed a giant shopping centre and industrial park mobile home retirement village to be built just beyond the city limits with lots of free parking, but there's no improvement in the two-lane width of Ricky-tick Road, so traffic jams in the peak hours and weekends are miles long.

Stage 4: Everyone agrees that traffic is a mess. The state draws up a plan for a freeway with clover-leaf exits to the centers of Babbotville, Sapsucker City, and lots of places in between.

Stage 5: The freeway eats out the heart of both cities and explosive growth takes place in the new commuter corridor. Within three to five years the journey between the two places takes longer on the new freeway than it does on old Ricky-tick Road, because every interchange along the freeway route was zoned shopping center commercial or planned industrial and is intensively developed because of "easy access."

Stage 6: The freeway, commonly known as Blood Alley because of the hazardous conditions created at the ramps which discharge into narrow old farm roads, is restudied for potential conversion to a $4 billion light rail corridor known as ABORT (Alternative Babbotville Overhead Rapid Transit).

7. The plan should have a strategy for positive change for older built-up areas. While Europe has enchanted tourists with city areas hundreds of years old, the older urban areas of the United States have become blighted and in many cases nearly abandoned. One magazine predicts that these inner city problems will be exported to the suburbs in the 1980s. So very few urban plans have begun to shift away from urban renewal and gentrification programs to proposals that deal with problems of the push-outs (e.g., condominium conversion ordinances protecting low- and moderate-income tenants, such as found in San Francisco, Santa Monica, and other humane-minded cities).

8. The plan should have a timing strategy that does such things as balance supply with demand for services and facilities. An excellent plan will pace as well as place new development.

9. It should capture local policy in a way that is clear and comprehensible to the average citizen, so that in the future average citizens can defend the plan effectively and intelligently. The goals and policies in a plan should be explicit enough to allow the "making of findings" by future commissions reviewing development proposals.

10. The plan should be clearly understood to be an obligation and commitment on the part of both elected officials and commissioners who adopt the plan and those who succeed them. This requires the combing out of weasel words and phrases such as "critical environmental features shall be preserved, if feasible" or "affordable housing shall be provided as the opportunities to do so arise." It requires that the plan point in a single direction, rather than being a compendium of incompatible alternatives. If the direction originally chosen needs adjustment, then the changes should be made in public with due process, rather than picking a different page of the plan to justify a shift from previous decisions. This is a good place to stop reading and check out your community's general plan against these simple criteria.[8]

Other Criteria for Judging Projects

The following also may be of use to the practicing planner.

1. The project should leave open future options for the development of the community. For example, the economic development program of the community may be looking for a high tech industrial development. Does the proposal to put in an apartment project in the middle of one of the last large parcels in the community leave this future option open?

2. The proposed project should not be destabilizing to public functions. For example, would the proposed mobile home park in the approach zone of the municipal airport allow the airport to operate according to its future growth plan?

3. The development should not be growth-inducing, particularly in communities that are trying to control the demand for more capital improvements and public services in outlying areas.

4. The development obviously should not be detrimental to existing property values.

5. The project should be realistic and should be able to reach full development within a reasonable amount of time. One thing to remember in phased development is not to nail everything down for the next 20 years. Approval for future phases should allow options so that changes in market demand, technology, and business climate can be accommodated within the overall framework of the full project plan.

6. The project should not have displacement effects on low- and moderate-income housing occupants or remove special businesses and facilities from sites that cannot be duplicated. In one western city, a major office development was defeated because of the detrimental effects it would have on existing small downtown businesses that could not relocate within the downtown. The city decided there were other places for office towers to go, but there was no other place for the little businesses that had been a feature of the downtown and gave it much of its vitality.

7. The project should be checked to see whether it will disrupt agricultural or rural uses. Very often a subdivision placed in the midst of farming uses will so restrict those farming uses that it becomes impracticable to continue them (e.g., spraying, nuisance effects

of livestock, and constant complaints from suburban residents).

8. The development should be free from hazards such as landslides, redirection of water, and creation of fire hazards. Many of the disasters of recent years occurred from developments being built in very hazardous areas. Southern California is filled with such developments, where houses slide off cliffs or burn down because they are built in brush-filled box canyons.

9. The project should not pollute, cause congestion, or attract nuisances in an area. For example, sex businesses and bars with live music have been shown to have a deleterious effect on residential areas, churches, and schools in the nearby vicinity and are very often not permitted to be neighbors to such uses.

OVERVIEW

The scope of working with the developer and the project has changed over the years. Today, planners often need to overcome a general distrust of developers, identify the "good guy" developers, and work to ensure projects are in the public's—though not necessarily the planner's—best interest.

Developers need to be treated fairly, both for fiscal and public interest reasons. Meeting the developer's needs after assessing the quality of the developer should only benefit the planner's community. The planner can help by letting the developer in on ways to quickly and effectively move a project through the review process.

Negotiations involve several "should" and "should nots," and experience also is a guide in this area. Finishing the entire process without setback depends on the planner's skill and thoroughness from the start. Checklists can help keep the path smooth.

NOTES

1. Robert Tennenbaum, "The Developers Are Not the Enemy," *Practicing Planner*, March 1979, pp. 45-46.

2. Tennenbaum, pp. 45-46.

3. From course notes of University of California, Irvine, Extension Course, September 1982.

4. Melville C. Branch, "Sins of City Planners," in *Public Administration Review*, January-February 1982.

5. Branch.

6. Branch.

7. Tennenbaum, p. 46.

8. Albert Solnit, *The Job of the Planning Commissioner*, third edition (revised), American Planning Association, Chicago, 1987, pp. 44-48.

Appendix 4.A

Materials That Must Accompany Applications

City of Mountain View

Site Plan and Architectural Review applications must be filed with the Planning Department not later than Friday preceding the Thursday meeting of the Architectural Committee at which you wish consideration. Applications other than Architectural Review must be filed with the Planning Department not later than 15 days prior to the regular Administrative Zoning Hearing at which you wish consideration. Make all checks payable to the City of Mountain View. Fees are not refundable. You or your representative must be present at the meeting for which the application is set.

I. Site Plan and Architectural Review
   A. Six (6) copies of a fully dimensioned Site Plan drawn to a common engineering scale suitable to the size of the project showing:
      1. Subject property and abutting properties and streets (showing centerline).
      2. Location of structures on subject property.
      3. Location of parking, driveways and loading areas (indicate surfacing material).
      4. Location, size and type of all existing trees.
      5. Landscape areas, fences, retaining walls, and trash facilities.
      6. Location of signs and type of yard lighting.
      7. Grade differences exceeding 18 inches from top of curb (including sections).
   B. Three (3) copies of fully dimensioned Elevations drawn to a common architectural scale of all sides of all structures including buildings, accessory structures, fences, and signs showing building heights and heights of all floors from the proposed finish grade at that side of the building. Elevations of buildings adjacent to a street shall show the building in reference to the grade at top of curb. Elevations must indicate building materials and colors and lighting, if any.
   C. Three (3) copies of fully dimensioned Floor Plans plus any other details necessary to show balco-

nies or other features for which open-space credit is being claimed or which otherwise needs additional explanation not found on the Site Plan and elevations (e.g., roof gardens, cabanas, etc.).
   D. Calculation sheets and graphic displays showing calculations and methods of calculating the percentage of land used for automobile access and open parking, for buildings and for open space.
   E. Filing fee according to the following schedule:
      $ 0 Applications involving no structural change or addition, including existing sign-copy change (no increase in size).
      $10 Structures under 1,000 square feet (including equipment, fences, tanks, etc.).
      $30 Structures 1,000 square feet to 3,000 square feet.
      $40 New signs.
      $50 Structures over 3,000 square feet or in excess of one story.

II. Variance
   A. See required drawings for Site Plan and Architectural Review.
   B. Additional drawings as needed to explain and/or document the particular features of proposed project which necessitate or justify the requested variance (e.g., distance to buildings on adjacent lots).
   C. Filing fee of $25 or the fee for the Site Plan and Architectural Review, whichever is higher.

III. Conditional-Use Permit
   A. See required drawings for Site Plan and Architectural Review.
   B. Additional drawings as needed to explain and/or document the particular features of the proposed project which would bear on the application (e.g., uses on surrounding property and their locations).

C. Filing fee of $50 if no new structure or signs only are involved or $100 if new structures are proposed.

IV. Planned-Community Permit
   A. See required drawings for Site Plan and Architectural Review.
   B. Additional drawings as needed to demonstrate any particular features of the proposed development (e.g., building usages, sign programs, circulation patterns, etc.).
   C. Additional drawings as needed to demonstrate compliance with precise area plans which cover the proposed development.
   D. Agent must file written authorization from the owner.
   E. Filing fee of $100.

V. Planned-Unit Development
   A. Seven (7) copies of development plans and architectural drawings to common engineering and architectural scale respectively showing:
      1. Location of subject property and all abutting properties and streets.
      2. Location and size of streets and pedestrian ways within the development.
      3. Location, design and character of proposed uses and physical relationships of uses within the development.
      4. Location, dimensions, and elevations of proposed structures within the development.
      5. Location, size and types of public facilities (schools, parks, playgrounds, etc.).
      6. Parking, driveways and loading areas.
      7. Location of open spaces indicating ownership.
      8. Signs, fences and landscaping (showing existing trees).
      9. Any proposed land subdivision.
   B. Two (2) copies of any proposed deed restriction or covenants which will apply to this project or any portion thereof.
   C. Filing fee of $100.

VI. Planned-Residential-District Development (R3P)
   A. Seven (7) copies of a fully dimensional Site Plan conforming to the requirements for drawings for Site Plan and Architectural Review, containing in addition the following information:
      1. All the contiguous land within the ownership or control of the developer indicating proposed uses and structures.
      2. All existing streets and development within 500 feet.
      3. Proposed lot lines.
      4. Public and private roadways, driveways and parking areas.
      5. Open spaces, recreation areas, pedestrian greenways and landscaped areas.
      6. Relations to adopted precise or specific plans pertaining to the property.
   B. Three (3) copies of elevation drawings for all structures conforming to the requirements for drawings for Site Plan and Architectural Review.
   C. Three (3) copies of typical floor plans and any other details as needed to adequately describe the project.
   D. Two (2) copies of any proposed deed restrictions or covenants.
   E. Filing fee of $100.

Appendix 4.B

Instructions for an Application for a Comprehensive Plan Amendment or Zone Change

---

Multnomah County, Oregon

---

1. *Fill in* the information requested on the general application form. *Please type or print clearly.*
2. Submit *owner verification*. Submit a copy of recorded deed. If applicant is not the owner of record submit a copy of the recorded contract or a letter of authorization from the legal owner. If an authorized representative is applying for the applicant submit a letter of authorization from applicant.
3. Submit a detailed *Site Plan*. Must be an 8½″ × 11″ size, original black-ink drawing. Include engineer's scale, north arrow, property lines, buildings, fences or landscaping, access points, vehicular access, parking and circulation, public streets adjoining the property (by name and width), signs, use areas as necessary, utilities (sewer, water, etc.), location of easements, if any, and any natural features (drainage swale, trees, rock outcroppings, etc.). Dimension all lines, buildings, setbacks, etc., and include building height. Submit three copies. Show by using different kinds of lines or words whether the above items are existing or proposed.
4. *Submit a peripheral area map.* This can be an 8½″ × 11″ sized original or larger if necessary. Include scale, north arrow, property lines of yours and immediately adjacent property. Show fences, landscaping, buildings, use, and access points *on adjacent property.* Dimension all lines and setbacks. Submit two copies.
5. *Describe how and why your request meets or complies with each of the following criteria:*
   A. Granting the request is in the public interest: (Show how your request is providing healthful, safe, and aesthetic surroundings; how it is meeting the public need and interest; e.g., a very low vacancy rate would justify a change of land use to a higher residential density because it is in the public interest to have adequate housing opportunities).
   B. There is a public need for the requested change and that need will be best served by changing the classification of the property in question as compared with other available property: (e.g., why should the proposal occur on this land as opposed to other land in the areas that are already zoned for the use). To respond to this criteria, you may have to inventory the land within a reasonable radius of your site to determine whether there is any developable land already zoned for the proposed use and to describe whether that property is available (i.e., vacant) and if so why it is not suitable for the proposed use. See the public information series publication on Market Studies for assistance.
   C. The proposed action fully accords with the applicable elements of the Comprehensive Plan (refer to #6).
   D. Proof of change in a neighborhood or community or mistake in the planning or zoning for the property under construction. (This criteria is optional.)
6. *Describe* how your request meets or complies with each of the following *Comprehensive Plan Policies:* Nos. 13, 14, 16, 22, 37, 38, and _____.

   The burden is upon the applicant to justify that the proposal meets the Ordinance Criteria. All information/evidence concerning the request must be presented in the applications because if there is a subsequent appeal, hearing information will not be admissible unless it could not have been available at the prior hearing.
7. *Describe your request in detail,* including information on the following items as well as any other details necessary to describe your proposed use.
   A. Use: Kind, public served, units of operation, number of employees and users.
   B. Building: Floor area, specific uses, materials, orientation, height.
   C. Parking: Number of spaces, truck-loading area, types of vehicles expected.

D. Outdoor Storage: Nature of stored material, screening.

8. *For Comprehensive Plan Amendments Only.* If you are claiming that there is a mistake, error, or oversight by the Plan as it relates to your property, ask the staff for "Procedure Regarding Identification and Correction of Potential Errors in the Community Plans." There are limited circumstances when this ground can be claimed.

9. *Sign* and notarize application. (We have a free notary public at 2115 SE Morrison Street.)

10. *Return application* with a $30.00 fee for a pre-filing conference with staff. The pre-filing conference with staff is intended to assist the applicant with substantive and procedural questions as well as to ensure a complete and adequate application. Make amendments to your application as directed by the staff at the pre-filing conference and return it for further review as directed by the staff. Later, when the application is determined to be adequate and complete, you can then return completed application with the filing fee specified by the staff.

Hearings are held the first Monday of every month. To apply for any given hearing, your completed application must be filed at least five weeks before the hearing date. Applications will only be accepted after the pre-filing (pre-app) conference is satisfactorily completed.

Appendix 4.C

Checklists

Summary of Submittal Requirements for Land-Use Approvals	Submittal Requirements																	
	Vicinity Map	Legal Description of Property	Environmental Checklist (if environmental review required)	Plot Plan (also show existing structures)	State of Purpose or Justification	Building Elevations	Parking Plan (may be part of plot plan)	Topographic Map (may be part of plot plan)	Floor Plans	Calculation of Lot Coverage	Calculation of Building Tower Bulk	Floor-area Calculation	Height Calculation	Average-grade Calculation	Block Front Plan (RS zone only)	Landscaping Plans (may be part of plot plan)	Proposed Dedications	Designation of Usable Open Space
City Council Actions																		
1. Rezones	•	•	•	○	•													
2. Council Cond. Uses	•	•	•	•		○	•	○	○	•	○							
3. Full Subdivisions	•	•	•	○													•	
4. Planned Unit Dev.	•	•	•	•	•	•	•	•		•		•	○	○		•	•	
5. Street Vacations	•	•			•													
6. Skybridges	•	•	•		•	•												
Citizen Board & Design Reviews[2]																		
1. RM-MD	•	•	•	•		•	•	○				•						
2. Townhouse	•	•	•	•		•	•	•	•	•			○	○		•	•	•
3. Review District	•	○	•	○	•	○		○								○		
Environmental Reviews on above	•		•	•	○	•	•				○					•		
Master Use Permit[3]																		
1. Establish New Use	•	•	•	•	•	•	•	•	•	•	○		○	○	○		•	○
2. Change of Use	•	•	•	○	•		•		•									
3. Variances	•	•	•	•	•	○	○	○				○	○	○	○			
4. Conditional Use	•	•	•	•		○	•	○	○	•	○				○			
5. Special Exception	•	•	•	•	•	○	•	○	○	•					○			
6. Shoreline Permit	•	•	•	•	○	•	○	•										
7. Shore Subdivision	•	•	•	○													•	
8. Street Use																		
a. Curb Cuts	•																	
b. Sidewalk Cafes	•	•	•	•	•													
c. Overhangs	•	•		•	•	•												
9. Environmental Reviews	•		•	•	○	•	•	•			○						•	

[1] Elevations should show skybridge connections to adjacent buildings and height of structure.

[2] If demolition is part of the proposed activity, the review board will want to review the information provided as part of the demolition permit.

[3] A number of additional materials are available on Master-Use-Permit Application requirements.

Appendix 4.C

Checklists

(Continued)

Submittal Requirements

List of Other Permits Applied for	Plan of Existing & Proposed Streets & Alleys	Proposed Use on Public Property	Plans for Structure on Public Property	Area of Public R-O-W for Vacation	Dump-site Designation	Grading Plan (including final topography)	Proposed Zoning	Subdivision Map	Certificate of Divided Lands	Exterior Building Design Detail	Interior Alteration Plan	Description of Major Physiography (canals,railroads,etc)	Petitioner's Interest in Property	Tide-level Plan/Description	General Site Plan	Shoreline Site Plan	Shoreline Cross-Sections	For Further Information Contact:
						•							•					DCLU
																		DCLU
	•							•	•									DCLU
	•					•						•						DCLU
			•															ENG
		•																ENG
																		DCD
○	•							•	○									
		•			○	○												DCLU
																		DCLU
															○			
•														•		•	•	
	•							•	•									
		•	•															
		•	•															
		•	•															
•					○	○												

Department Contacts

Department of Construction and Land Use
- Land-Use Counter
- Technical Review Section (including Environmental Review)
- Land-Use Information Center
- Zoning Plans Examination
- Permit Counter

Department of Community Development
- Office of Urban Conservation (landmark, historic & special review districts)

Engineering Department Municipal Building
- Street Use
- General Information

Key
- • Mandatory submittal
- ○ May be required depending on application

Source: City of Seattle, Department of Construction and Land Use

CHAPTER

5

How to Red-Pencil Preliminary Subdivision Plats

Charles Reed

Errors and mistakes in subdivision development are reduced by making a complete review of all development proposals when they are submitted to your planning office. The completeness of the review can start with your own in-office checklist.

Few planning offices have – or use – such a checklist. And as a result, subtle (and not so subtle) aggravating errors end up permanently on the ground – errors that could have been caught in the paper stage in the office.

To produce better subdivisions start with this chapter's checklist; modify it, copy it, but use it to make up your own in-office plat checklist.

We cover plat boilerplate, the layout of lots and blocks, streets, natural resource protection, and technical review of utilities and improvements proposed by the developer in this chapter. Appendixes 5.A, 5.B, and 5.C provide more information on preliminary subdivision plat development.

This checklist will not fit your specific situation. Moreover, our terminology may differ from yours. Many communities include these checklist items in their sketch subdivision plan, their final plat, or in improvement plans separate from the preliminary plat.

In preparing your own checklist, department heads and experts involved in your plat review process must review this – and your draft – checklists. The checklists will undoubtedly generate revisions to your subdivision regulations.

The categories and their subcategories in our

checklist follow a logical review sequence. The earlier items in the sequence guide the review of later items. This consistency will help organize the redraft of your own in-office checklist.

This checklist is for urban residential subdivisions. This includes PUDs, cluster subdivisions, subdivisions with performance zoning and land use intensity ratings, subdivisions platted and sold in stages, and zero lot line subdivisions. Excluded are condominium subdivisions, industrial park and commercial subdivisions, resort rural subdivisions, replats and reorganization of existing subdivisions, large lot estate subdivisions, rural strip residential subdivisions platted from farms along highways and county roads, and lot splits and minor subdivisions.

The written text provided by the developer is similar in appearance to a legal brief. It consolidates notes, engineering specifications, plat covenants and legal statements provided from land planners, engineers, lawyers and other professionals hired by the developer to prepare and design the plat. Many agencies require the written text to be provided as one or more plat sheets bound into each copy of the plat.

CHECKLIST OF ITEMS TO BE INCLUDED ON PRELIMINARY PLATS

Notes on Face of Plat and Its Attached Brief

Legal descriptions
• *Legal description of land to be subdivided.* Is the legal description correct, or are metes and bounds traverse properly described? Are plat boundaries tied to existing survey monuments and adjoining surveys? Are section lines, range, and township survey descriptions shown?
• *Legal description of lots and blocks after being subdivided.* The plat must provide correct legal descriptions for each lot. Count all block num-

bers to ensure that all blocks are consecutively numbered and that there is a logical numbering system for all blocks. Then, in each block, count all lot numbers, starting with number 1 for each new block, with each lot numbered consecutively.
• *Numbering of outlots* should be checked for lot and block numbering; outlot blocks should be legally separate from the numbering sequence of adjacent single-family blocks.
• *Landowners of the plat property* and their legal interests in the property should be identified, along with landownership encumbrances, clouds, and liens.
• *Mineral and mining rights* should be released, consistent with state law, after the final plat is recorded.

Subdivision name
Name of subdivision should not duplicate or will not be confused with existing recorded plats.

Plat reference information
• *Plat prints* are provided as black-line or blueline prints, with sepia or ozalid reproducibles provided if required. The correct number of plat sets have been submitted to your office for distribution to reviewers and to your plat review committee members.
• *All required sheets are bound within the plat set:* title sheet, the plat itself, notes sheet or brief, grading plan, planting plans, construction and improvements engineering sheets, cross-section sheets and profit section sheets for all rights-of-way (ROW) and sewers.
• *Plat sheets are of proper page size,* and the plat plan is drawn to the proper scale.
• *Nomenclature of lines and symbols* used on the plat follow conventional practice or are as required in your subdivision regulations.
• *Title block* is prepared properly and includes all required information: north arrow; graphic scale bar at required scale; date; name, address, and phone number of developer and

person preparing plat; seal and signature of registered professionals preparing the plat; legal corporate name of developer for this plat.

• *Vicinity map* must be provided on proper plat sheet. Is the subdivision located properly on the vicinity map? Does vicinity map include required information: scale, north arrow, location of major streets, watercourses, topographic features and land uses?

• *Variances and waivers* from subdivision and zoning regulations being requested by the developer for the subdivision and for his draft of the homes association charter must be listed in the brief.

• *Soils and geology information* is provided: soil types identified, with hydrologic, permeability, and percolation information and analyses; interpretation of soil types by qualified soils analyst.

Multisheet plats

• *Key map* is provided on first of each sheet of plats that are larger in area than that which can be shown on one sheet, or if the subdivision is to be platted in two or more stages. All sheets or stages of development are properly located on the plat key map.

• *Matchlines* on all sheets must match properly so that lots are not duplicated, left out, or numbered incorrectly in blocks bifurcated onto two or more plat sheets.

Table of statistics

• *Your definition of gross and net area* is understood by the developer, as evidenced in his statistical tables. Gross area of land to be subdivided and gross area of stages to be platted are included in the statistical table.

• *Land use statistics* include: gross and net areas of land uses proposed in the plat and on land to be dedicated; lineal feet and total acreage of street ROW; net acreage of dedicated parks and school sites (including park and school land in flood hazard areas), by site and total net acreage; gross acreage of flood hazard areas (including land to be dedicated for park and school land), within flood fringe area and within floodway.

• *Lot statistics* include, for each of the developer's proposed land uses and for each proposed zoning district, number and average of net area and size of lots, in acres or square feet as required by your subdivision and zoning regulations, and net proposed dwelling unit densities, and average net dwelling unit density for hillside zoning districts. Check that access to flag lots is excluded from net lot area calculations.

• *Performance zoning and land use intensity statistics (LUI) include: LUI rating and associated ratios of open space, impervious surface, floor area, and other measures required by your PUD, cluster, and performance zoning ordinances.*

• *Excess ROW to be dedicated:* net acreage of ROW in excess of that attributable to the subdivision. Estimate of compensation to the developer for value of excess ROW dedication (usually excess width of arterial streets and freeways beyond local and collector ROW width).

• *Engineering data* includes, for example, storm drainage runoff flow calculations.

Required insurance

• *Statement of fire class rating limitation* for the subdivision, if subdivision is below standards of fire underwriters for your jurisdiction's water system, for water lines that cannot be looped or sustain adequate hydrant pressure for water flow for fire fighting.

• *Title insurance and title abstract* is provided by the developer for the property included within the plat, and name of insurer.

• *Insurance against perils of construction* is provided by the developer covering all contractors, the amount of protection, deductibles, and name of insurance company.

• *Maintenance insurance or bond* is posted by developer to repair or replace defective improvements in the subdivision one to three years after acceptance by jurisdiction.

Options for assuring completion of improvements Which optional method does the developer choose for assuring completion of all improvements? If your subdivision regulations give the developer a choice of methods for posting bond, has the public works engineer approved the choice and adequacy of the dollar amount of the bond, and has legal counsel approved the correct form of bond?

Excess capacity of oversized streets and utilities Payment or charges to and from public revolving accounts are made for the value of land and cost of installing excess capacity of oversized streets and improvements provided beyond the needs of the subdivision. Payments are made by the developer to the fund for his share of oversize facilities of other subdivisions already built that benefit this plat; conversely, the developer receives compensation or a credit from the fund for the value of oversize facilities this plat provides that will benefit other subdivisions built later. Approval is needed by the accounting/finance agency for such charges.

Cash in lieu of park and school land dedication Developer will deposit cash into a special public account equal to an estimate of land value in lieu of land otherwise dedicated as park, and according to formulas set forth in your subdivision regulations or by the park department. Funds are deposited with the school agency in lieu of the subdivision's share of the cost of schools or with a fund for acquiring school sites outside the subdivision.

Protective covenants
• *Covenants required by your long-range plans and by government agencies* include: the comprehensive plan, precise land use and area plans, state or regional environmental plans or agencies, and those covenants required by the zoning districts proposed by the developer for the plat or required by your subdivision regulations.

• *Homeowners association covenants* which create the association and summarize its rights and duties. Reference to standard language for association charter and bylaws, as required by state or local law, or reference to model codes, with the developer's proposed modifications for this subdivision.
• *Minimum floor area covenants* must conform to the requirements of the developer's proposed zoning districts for minimum floor area of houses.
• *Flood hazard covenants* include limitation on development in flood fringe areas and prohibition and limitation on development in floodways, and prohibition by homeowners to connect roof and driveway drains to sanitary and storm sewers.
• *Architectural design covenants* require all buildings, including houses and garages, to have a common architectural style, such as all exterior walls must be adobe or earthtone stucco, or roofs must be covered with specified Spanish tile.
• *Architectural variety covenants* require that no two adjacent houses shall look alike, have the same floor plan, orientation, or mirror reverse plan, or have identical architectural design of adjacent houses.
• *Restrictions on front yard obstructions* and maintenance of landscaping and buildings. These covenants prohibit fences, walls, structures, and hedges in front yard of lots. No parking of trucks, campers, or other vehicles is allowed in front yard or on streets. Home owners must maintain and trim trees and shrubs within those parts of the site distance triangle on their lots at street intersection.

Legally mandated clauses
• *Civil rights nondiscrimination clauses* to be required for lot purchase or home ownership, and subsequent sales by home owners; to be provided as required by law.
• *Set-aside clauses* to be required of the de-

veloper for setting aside a required portion of construction contracts for hiring of minority contractors.

• *Nondiscrimination clauses* to be required of individual contractors constructing the subdivision in the hiring of employees.

• *Provisions for handicapped* to be provided as required by law, or by public works department specification for design of ramps, rails, and other assists for the handicapped.

Dedications

Schools

Is adequate acreage provided in sites for elementary schools for review by school board? Is land provided for, by dedication or purchase, in full or part, for junior and senior high school sites, per school board, in accordance with criteria in master school plan or your comprehensive plan?

Parks and open space

• *Your definition of parks* is understood by the developer. Does this definition include neighborhood and community parks? Can such parks include all or part of flood hazard areas and open space medians at street intersections, wyes, and circles?

• *Required acreage for park land* is provided by the developer in his plat, based on your jurisdiction's park land dedication formula. Acreage in each dedicated park site must meet your minimum site size requirement for such dedications. Which agency takes title to dedicated park lands?

Rights of Way

• *Which ROW are public and which are private?* Locate existing ROW and streets in areas adjoining the plat and in the plat area. Locate proposed private streets, access easements, and spite strips to be privately owned located on plat. To whom will rights of way be dedicated—municipality, borough, township, or county?

• *Access easements* for flag lots, for landlocked lots, and for stub-end rights-of-way connecting from interior streets to plat boundary as connections to streets in future adjacent plats to be held back from dedication on the final plat. Check for temporary reservation for ROW from adjacent lots at stub-end streets, to accommodate temporary turnarounds needed until connection is made with through street in adjoining subdivision.

• *Excess dedication of ROW* of nonlocal streets such as collectors, arterials and freeway rights of way. Are ROW dedications provided for right-turn flare-outs on arterial intersections and flare-outs for ramps at freeway interchanges? Are freeway interchange dedications approved in shape and amount of land dedicated by appropriate freeway public agency?

• *Subdivision entrances* may require extra width of ROW. Is this ROW reserved or dedicated to the jurisdiction or the home owners association? Developer will provide street entrance median strip, signs, and gate houses that meet your subdivision regulations.

• *Access to and within outlots:* for proposed apartment and commercial complexes. Will streets be private or dedicated to the public and require conformance to public works improvement standards?

• *Proposed street names* must conform to jurisdiction's street naming ordinance or regulations. Avoid street names with different spellings but same pronunciations and long and complex names that are difficult or confusing to fire and emergency services. Check street names for proper use of avenue, street, drive, court, terrace, place, way, manor, and approval to use special names, such as "Camino." Check street addresses with your street address plan and with the post office.

Other uses

• *Reservation of sites for other private land uses:*

for churches, golf courses, and other private community-related uses. Can reserved sites be platted into lots if sites are not sold for their reserved usage? Are reserved sites numbered as outlots or they are assigned the last lot numbers within the block in case of replat and renumbering of additional lots as part of the existing sequence of lot numbers in the block?
• *Other dedications* provided by the developer to home owners association or jurisdiction for bikeways, trails, and jogging or bridle paths. Can the receiver of the dedication avoid excessive maintenance cost based on developer's design for the improvement within the ROW proposed by the developer?

Layout of Lots and Blocks

Conforming to proposed zoning
• *Minimum lot area, width, and depth* required under the proposed zoning must be met for all lots. Red-pencil all lots that do not meet your zoning requirements. Check especially lots fronting on cul-de-sacs at the front building line. For PUDs, does the average lot area and size for all lots meet requirements of the proposed PUD, cluster zone requirements, and for hillside zoning average dwelling unit density formulas? Check minimum lot width for conformance to lot yard requirements for special housing types within PUDs and clusters (for example, lots with zero lot lines). Check flag lots for conformance to front yards as defined for flag lots and for proper width of access to public right-of-way.
• *Confirm lot measurements on plat with those listed in the statistical table.* Does the count of lots and dwelling units meet density requirements or requirements of land use intensity and associated ratios or other required measures of performance zoning as shown in developer's statistical table?
• *Cluster zoned areas* are clearly defined on the plat. Count all lots in each cluster for dwelling unit count and allowable housing type, and determine square footage of cluster, then average land area for each dwelling unit, and minimum size of cluster lot for each dwelling unit.

Conforming to subdivision regulations
• *Ratio of lot width to depth* must conform to your subdivision regulations for conventional subdivisions, PUDs, or cluster subdivisions.
• *Building lines* if required on preliminary plats, must be checked for each lot.
• *Block length,* as defined in the subdivision regulations, should not be excessive for any block. Pedestrian and bicycle accesses should be provided across blocks to the next street where such accesses lead directly to schools, parks, and other through streets (reasonable short cuts for pedestrian/bicycle usage).
• *Length of dead-end streets,* including cul-de-sacs, do not exceed maximum length required by your subdivision regulations.

Reserve sites for community facilities
• *Check your long-range plans for community facilities* that should be located in the plat area. Your plans include: community master plan, precise land use and area plans, long-range capital improvements program, and siting and community spacing standards for such community facilities as libraries, fire and police stations, and city/county services satellite offices.
• *Sites reserved for community facilities* should be red-pencilled onto the plat. Appropriate agencies must be contacted immediately. Purchase agreements and purchase prices for reserved sites need to be agreed upon by the developer and appropriate agencies. Such agreements may require developer to reserve those sites for a period of time before sale. If these agencies do not acquire the sites within the time period (usually one to three years), the sites are released to the developer for private development.

Design of lots and blocks

- *Review overall layout of lots and blocks* to optimize natural amenities and open space on the site. The lot and block pattern in the plat should coordinate with the pattern in the surrounding neighborhood, and coordinate with soils and geology analyses submitted in the developer's brief. Perhaps yellow-tissue overlays need to be prepared by the planner suggesting to the developer a redraft of lots, blocks, and street pattern. If too many lots are to be eliminated in the yellow-tissue redraft, the planner needs to provide approximate equal number of lots in his redraft and try to provide shorter utility runs and streets, for cost savings to the developer.
- *Double-frontage lots* should be checked for lots backing onto arterials and limited-access highways.
- *Key lots* should be deleted from the plat as often as possible. Key lots are lots on the ends of blocks on cross streets. Houses on key lots front onto cross streets and do not face any other houses on the block except an opposite key-lot house. Key lots are acceptable when they face a row of houses on the opposite block face; this obstructs the view of rear yards behind the house on the key lot.
- *Extra deep or wide lots* should be provided for corner lots, double-frontage lots, and lots backing onto ravines, streams, railroads, and major utility easements.
- *Flag lots (or panhandle lots)* should be checked for reasonable usage, for efficient use of otherwise landlocked areas. Flag lots should not form into a third tier of lots on a block to avoid providing additional streets.
- *Awkwardly shaped lots* should be redrawn. No lot lines should be curved; excessive acute-angle intersections of lot lines with ROW lines and with other lot lines should be red-pencilled by reshaping the lots in question.
- *Public shoreline access* to beaches, and to ocean, lake, river, and reservoir shorelines, required by state and local laws, must be observed by the developer. The rear lot lines of waterfront lots backing onto lakes, rivers, canals, flood areas, and wetlands should be red-pencilled if not located properly in relation to high tide lines, high flood pools of reservoirs, and dock and water navigation lines.

Layout and design of easements

- *Local utility service to all lots* must be provided as easements for electrical, gas, telephone, and cable TV utilities. These easements should be at lot edges as often as possible, and split between adjacent lots. Check flow of easements from block to block to allow reasonably straight runs of utility services throughout the subdivision and connecting to similar easements in adjacent subdivisions.
- *Major utility easements* must be accommodated by layout of lots and blocks in the plat for storm drainage, high-voltage power lines and towers, and nonlocal pressure pipelines, such as large gas lines. Lots that include such easements must have adequate depth to provide usable building sites for houses. Rear yards in such lots are not within storm drainage cuts or are under power lines. Check that electrical substation sites and gas-pumping and pressure stations are provided in the plat as required by utility companies.
- *Easements for pedestrian trails and bikeways* must have a reasonable overall layout throughout the subdivision connecting to schools, parks, libraries, and linear ravine parks; such connections should conform to your local/regional trail and bikeway plans.

Utilities

Sanitary sewerage

- *Conforming to your sanitary sewerage system plan*: The general layout of lots and blocks in the preliminary plat and the layout of the developer's proposed sanitary sewerage system must result in a logical drainage pattern that conforms to your jurisdiction's sanitary sewerage and treatment plan. All lots must be served by sanitary sewers. Abrupt or awkward changes in direction of sewers that would impede the natural gravity flow of effluent should be avoided. Clean outs should be provided at points of directional change. The diameters of all sewers must be indicated on the plat.

• *Force mains* and associated pumping stations to pump effluent uphill through the mains should be avoided. Determine if force mains are proposed for permanent or temporary installation. The overall layout of lots and blocks may need to be redesigned to reduce or eliminate force mains.

• *Profiles* for all sewers are to be shown on the plat. The profiles must have adequate gradients for dry weather flow. Gradients in the profiles must conform to the grades set by proposed contours on the grading plan. Sewers must have adequate underground depth. Composition of pipe materials, the design and method of connecting pipe joints, and the method of ditching and backfilling for laying the pipes must be approved by the public works department.

• *Package sewage treatment systems,* their outfalls, and their percolation fields must have adequate capacity, be designed to meet public health standards, and be designed for reliable maintenance, by construction drawings and specifications. Review the layout of lots adjacent to the system for undesirability. Determine who will own and maintain the treatment plant after the final plat is accepted by jurisdiction.

• *Sanitary sewers and watermains* in same easements or next to each other in ROW must be avoided to avoid contamination of potable water by poorly located sewerage mains. Watermains crossing over sewers must meet public works crossover standards.

• *Combined storm and sanitary sewers* located downslope below the subdivision must have sufficient capacity to serve additional sanitary loads of this plat during storms.

Septic systems

Soil analyses and maps must show adequacy of soils, hydrology, and sufficient depth of water table to serve the septic systems proposed for the plat. Check the developer's brief for performance of percolation tests. Each lot that contains a septic system should not have its septic drainage field too close to building sites on adjacent lots. Size of lots with septic systems must equal the minimum lot size required by your zoning ordinance for lots with septic systems, and by public health agencies.

Storm drainage

• *Conforming to your storm drainage plan*: The overall layout of the storm drainage system for the plat must tie in to storm drainage systems upslope and downslope outside and adjacent to proposed subdivision in accordance with your jurisdiction's storm drainage plan. The capacity and design of the storm drainage system in the preliminary plat must be able to contain local storm water under typical local area storm circumstances.

• *Storm water flow across buildable lots* and building sites must avoid localized flooding. Cross-sections of streets and ROW must show that all driveway and sidewalk curb-cuts slope toward the street and sidewalk to reduce storm drainage from streets onto individual lots. Drainage swales should not overload any lots with storm runoff and cul-de-sacs should not drain storm water onto end lots.

• *Culverts, lined drainage ditches, and swales* must have reasonable engineering design for storm drainage, including specifications for culverts, box culverts, catchments, and surfacing materials for drainage ditches (sod, riprap, concrete, or other material).

Water

Overall layout of watermains in the entire plat must provide water service to all lots and be looped with very few lots served by stub waterlines. These stubs must be looped by later stages of platting on the same parcel of land or by future adjacent subdivision plats. Composition of materials in pipes to be used (plastic and type, or metal and type), and method of ditching, backfilling, and laying pipes, and sealing pipe joints and fittings must be approved by the water agency.

Fire hydrants and firefighting services

• *Fire hydrants* shown on the plat must conform to local standards for spacing and adequate diameter capacity of water lines. Location of hydrants in relation to street and curbs must provide adequate access by fire trucks as required by the fire department.

• *Turnaround diameter* of street pavements at street intersections and at dead-end and stub streets must be able to accommodate fire trucks.

• *Ponds, retention, and surcharge basins* planned by the developer as backup sources for water for fire fighting should be checked; adequate access needs to be provided to such ponds by fire pumper trucks.

Street lighting, street signs, postal box stanchions

• *General layout of proposed street lighting* must include location and spacing of light poles, approved design of standards and luminares, location and layout of conduits and electrical circuitry to provide the required level of street lighting in foot candles.

• *Street signs and postal box stanchions* must meet public works department requirements. Postal box stanchions that group post boxes for several houses in one location should be installed by the developer, and also must meet post office specifications—and should not interfere with sight distance triangles, bus stops, or other street geometrics.

Design of Streets

Conforming to your general transportation plan

• *Functional classification of streets.* All streets in the developer's preliminary plat must conform to the community's functional classification of street types set forth in your general transportation plan. These street classes usually include: local, collector, minor arterial, major arterial, expressway, parkway, boulevard, and freeway. Streets in apartment complexes and industrial and commercial subdivisions may have different functional street classifications. The functional classification of streets in the plat must be reasonable in terms of street layout.

• *ROW cross-sections for each functional street class* used in the plat must be in agreement with those provided in your general transportation plan. For each cross section, check all dimensions, notes and description of construction methods and materials used. Typical cross section includes: sod or planter strip between ROW line and sidewalk; sidewalk; boulevard planter strip if sidewalks are not integral with curbs; curb and details of curb cross section and footings; street, including typical layering section of street construction from rock base through finished wearing surface; and street centerline.

• *Solar access for building sites* should be optimized by a street layout with a general east-west orientation. Each lot should be able to provide unobstructed solar space if required by your zoning ordinance. Check orientation of streets and lots to optimize potentials for earth-contact houses.

• *Street profiles* must be provided for all streets on the ROW centerline. Each profile is drawn to vertical and horizontal scales acceptable to the public works engineer. The profiles must show street gradient, vertical curves, and leveling of streets at intersections according to engineering standards to avoid blind intersections. Profiles should be also be shown for sewers in street ROW; culverts, drain sewers and other pipes crossing under the street centerline should be shown in the street profile. Profiles must be confirmed by contours proposed by the developer on the grading plan.

• *Excessive grades* on dead-end and cul-de-sac streets should be avoided to reduce excessive water runoff onto end lots and avoid cutting off access from lots on dead-end streets to through streets due to excessive ice and snow.

General pattern of circulation and layout

• *General layout of streets* in the plat must not be confusing for emergency access and for residents. Local streets should channel traffic to collector streets; intersections with arterial streets should be minimized. All streets should intersect at approximate right angles to optimize site distance at intersections.

• *Tee intersection offsets* should be avoided. Offsets of adjacent tee intersections should not form street jogs of less than minimum standard (usually 125 feet).

• *Flow of arterial street traffic* should not be significantly impeded. Local street intersections should be spaced along arterial streets relative to traffic signals and stop signs to minimize interruptions of arterial traffic flow.

Connections to streets adjoining the plat

• *Streets must align with streets in adjacent subdivisions* at intersections on peripheral streets common to both the adjacent subdivision and this preliminary plat along the plat boundary. This alignment creates four-way intersections rather than twice the number of off-set tee intersections.

• *Half streets adjoining plat boundaries* in adjacent subdivisions are matched by the developer in his plat to form complete streets. Where half streets are proposed by the developer, make sure that the brief describes how (and who) will pave half streets.

• *Spite strips* must not be permitted. Spite strips are narrow strips about a foot wide not dedicated and retained by developer on half-streets shared with future adjacent subdivisions; developer sells spite strip at high price to adjacent subdivider who must have matching half street.

Street geometrics

• *Vehicular movement at design speed* must be assured. All streets must have proper widths of ROW, curb-to-curb width, and radius of curvature of horizontal and vertical curves for required level of service. Check for variations on cul-de-sac, eyebrows, court, and court-stub streets.

• *Design of cul-de-sacs* should meet specifications of the subdivision regulations and the public works engineer, especially for width of cul-de-sac ROW and the paved street turnaround circle. Center planter circles proposed by the developer should be added or deleted as required by your regulations or fire department preferences.

Sidewalks, curbs, and driveways

• *Location of sidewalks along streets.* If sidewalks are to be shown in plan view on the plat, sidewalks should be provided according to your community's sidewalk plan or policies. If only one side of the street needs to be served by sidewalks, make sure there is a reasonable layout leading to schools and parks to minimize the need for children using sidewalks to cross and recross streets. Check for sidewalks required on both sides of collectors and arterials, and adjacent to schools and parks.

• *Relationship of curbs and gutters to sidewalks.* If your subdivision regulations allow the developer to choose to integrate or separate the sidewalk from the curb and to choose vertical versus rolled curb, check the plat for his choice of options. Check that sidewalk geometrics at street intersections conform to public works standards. Vertical curbs should be rolled where a sidewalk meets a street to allow pedestrian wheelchair access.

• *Driveways* should conform to typical driveway standards, including the slope of driveway to curb valley for storm drainage, and the radius of the driveway at curb to reduce wheel ruts next to curbs.

Grading Plan

General layout of proposed grades
The plat must contain a plan showing existing contours at contour intervals appropriate for on-site slopes and showing the developer's proposed changes in contours by regrading of earth. Proposed contours on the grading plan must provide usable building sites for all lots, schools, churches, parks, automobile parking areas, recreational areas, and athletic fields. There should be a minimal regrading of desirable topography; the grading plan should indicate the total amount of earth fill and removal, sources for obtaining or disposing of earth fill on site, and disposal of unacceptable earth fill (grubbed tree trunks, shrubbery, and debris). Grades indicated by proposed contours on the grading plan must confirm gradients shown in street and sewer profiles. The developer's brief should indicate his proposed method for compacting and stabilizing raw earth after grading.

Wetland and water recharge area preservation
The grading plan must maintain, preserve, or drain lowlands, wetlands, or areas adjacent to wetlands, acquifer recharge areas, and artesian wells in accordance with your state, regional, or local coastal, water, or wetlands plan.

Hillside and slopes in grading plan
• *Earth grading.* Proposed contours shown on the grading plan should not create excessive: grading of earth, depth of earth fill, terracing along hillside streets, cuts into hillsides to create terraces, or use of retaining walls and abutments. To provide building sites on hillside lots, the plat or its brief must show appropriate waivers of yards, lot width, and distance of building lines from ROW lines.

• *Building load stability of soils.* Developer must provide soils and geologic analyses of hillside stability against slippage, earthquake potential, mudslide, settling, slump potential, and failure of subsoil base under building load on hillsides.

Flood Control

In designated flood hazard areas
The developer's preliminary plat must show boundaries mapped on your jurisdiction's official flood hazard maps of flood fringe areas and floodways for defined-year floods (10-, 100-, and/or 500-year calculated flood elevations), and the relocation of such boundaries adjusted by the grading plan. Changes in the volume of flood water stored in flood fringe areas and changes in flood water flow in floodways must be in accordance with standards and procedures of the flood hazard ordinance. Proposed land use and layout of lots and streets should reduce the need to adjust flood hazard boundaries and to reduce flooding of lots in or adjacent to flood hazard areas. Questionable lots near or in flood hazard areas should have covenants requiring floodproofing below calculated flood stages or be graded so that the grade level of houses, schools, and other habitable buildings are above flood stage elevation.

In designated but unmapped flood hazard areas
Lots and street layout in designated flood hazard areas that are not mapped with flood hazard boundaries (generally smaller streams and creeks) must be acceptable to appropriate public agency engineers for estimated flood flows and flood water storage for base-year floods (often, 10-year floods).

For obstructions to flood water flow in floodway
Piers and abutments of proposed bridges, culverts, docks, marinas, and seawalls should be designed to minimize interference with obstructions to floodwater flow and to avoid snagging flood water debris that would create obstructions to flood water flow. Brush and debris should be removed from floodways by the developer as required under flood hazard ordinances or as authorized by public works department or flood control agency. Stream channel changes and streams closed over with storm culverts should be reviewed for their impact on storm drainage and flooding.

Natural Resource Protection

Environmental impact review
Under your state or local environmental assessment procedures, provide a finding of no undue impact, subject to public review and comment. Otherwise, review the assessment findings, public comments and the plat for the necessity of requiring the developer to go through your community's environmental impact analysis and review procedure.

Preservation of trees and woodlands
The developer's plat should show the location and identification of any existing individual trees of required or larger caliper/diameter, and stands of trees to be preserved. Locally valuable or rare tree species on site should be preserved.

Preservation of ravines and stream valleys
Ravine and wetlands vegetation should be preserved in an undisturbed state for erosion control, stream bank stabilization, and for preservation of wildlife habitats.

Planting plans and screens
The developer's planting plans should show trees, stands of trees, bushes, shrubs, and ground cover to be added. The plan must iden-

tify trees, shrubs, and ground cover to determine if the proposed species are appropriate for their ecological or functional use (e.g., ornamental flowering trees versus shade trees as street trees). The location of planting screens and proposed street trees must meet any requirements of zoning districts proposed by the developer for land uses in his plat. Other zoning requirements in particular zone districts might include species to be planted and size of specimens to be planted to meet vegetative height requirements and requirements for full visual screen block based on crown height of mature trees and shrubs. Check for walls, fences, and berms to be used in lieu of vegetative screening.

Maintenance and landscaping
The developer's brief should show how planting screens and street trees will be maintained until public agencies (or the home owners association) assume their maintenance.

Erosion, Sedimentation, and Dust Control

Subdivision design and layout to minimize erosion/sedimentation
Review the developer's grading plan for locations indicating removal of natural surface vegetation and where potential for surface erosion can occur. Examine streams and watercourses for erosion into rivers and for potential silt buildup in reservoirs. Spot these areas for on-site periodic inspection by erosion control officer. Possible review of plans by the Bureau of Land Management or other reservoir authorities.

Soil usage and stabilization
Check the developer's brief for his method of saving and reusing high-quality topsoils existing on site. Check developer's plan to stabilize or use problem soils, subject to slippage, swelling, or shrinkage based on site soil characteristics.

Erosion and dust control during construction
The developer's brief must describe his plan for minimizing soil erosion and controlling airborne dust during construction and before landscaping and ground cover has rooted and grown sufficiently to retard erosion.

Appendix 5.A

An Applicant's Guide to Procedures: Tentative Map

Community Development Department   City of Walnut Creek, California

---

Purpose

State Law authorizes local governmental agencies to regulate and control the design and improvement of subdivisions. A subdivision is defined as the division of any improved or unimproved land for the purpose of sale, lease, or financing. A subdivision also includes the conversion of a structure to condominiums. The State Subdivision Map Act provides general regulations and procedures that local governments must follow in the regulation of subdivisions. The City also has a Subdivision Ordinance which provides specific City guidelines and standards for the regulation and control of subdivisions. Subdivision regulations which encompass a division of property into five or more lots (requiring tentative map approval), and minor subdivisions of four or less lots (requiring parcel map approval). This guideline only covers the procedures for major subdivisions requiring tentative map approval.

The tentative map review procedure is designed to insure that such things as street alignments, grades and widths, drainage and sanitary facilities, location and size of easements and rights-of-way, fire roads, trees, lot sizes and configurations, traffic access, grading and numerous other features conform to city regulations and policies and are arranged in the best possible manner to serve the public.

The tentative map is evaluated for its consistency with the General Plan and zoning designation and the compatibility of site plan and public improvements with surrounding development. Special attention is focused on the preservation of natural topographic features of value and the integration of the development to existing terrain and land forms.

Process

Step 1—Project Consideration
Early in the consideration of a potential subdivision, the applicant should carefully review what the City's General Plan and zoning calls for in the location or area affected.

It is important that the proposed subdivision be consistent with both the zoning regulations and the General Plan, or the application cannot be accepted. In addition, local utilities and other special agencies should be contacted regarding requirements for future development in the area.

Step 2—Preapplication Conference
It is recommended that the applicant submit a preliminary proposal to the Planning Staff prior to submission of the formal application. This will allow the Planning and Engineering staffs to review the plans and to provide input to the applicant at a subsequent preapplication staff conference on possible environmental concerns, General Plan and engineering requirements, traffic, siting, and design criteria. This early review and input by staff could save the applicant possible delay and expensive plan revisions. Later in the process, staff can also review the history of other development proposals on the site and review the required data and procedures to be followed through the process.

Step 3—Filing of Application
The applicant should submit the completed application to the Permit Center of the Community Development Department. A staff planner will review the materials to make sure all the required information is provided. Following completion of the environmental review process, the applicant shall be notified with 30 days as to whether the application is complete or if any additional information is required. The applicant will also be required to make a deposit at the time of submittal for processing the application. The final charge will be based upon the actual cost of staff time required to process the application to final action.

Step 4—Environmental Review
All subdivision requests are required to have an environmental assessment to determine if it will be necessary to have an Environmental Impact Report prepared. In-

formation on timing and sequence of this process is contained in "An Applicant's Guide to Procedures for Environmental Review," which will be provided to the applicant during the preapplication conference.

Step 5—Design Review Commission Recommendation
Subsequent to the Environmental Review process, subdivision applications are required to be reviewed on a preliminary basis by the Design Review Commission (DRC) for their recommendation on any design considerations for use by the Planning Commission in their application review. The applicant may submit either a preliminary map or the actual Tentative Map at this stage. The Design Review staff will analyze the project and prepare a written report giving recommendations for conditions of approval. The applicant will receive a copy of the staff report with the meeting notice. DRC review of applications are open to the public but are not public hearings. At the meeting, staff will present its report and recommendation. A presentation can then be made by the applicant. The DRC then analyzes the site plan, grading, landscaping, and building design. The DRC will then forward to the Planning Commission any comments it desires to make and any changes to the proposed plan it deems appropriate as a result of its preliminary review. Upon receipt of the DRC recommendations, the applicant must then have the actual Tentative Subdivision Map prepared and submitted in accordance with the mitigating measures called for in the ND or EIR and with changes requested by the DRC. Whether or not a revised tentative map is submitted, the application is not considered accepted until this time.

Step 6—Community Development Department Subdivision Conference
Following the DRC recommendation and the submittal of the final Tentative Map, the Community Development Department will send a copy of the Map to all affected public agencies, utilities, school districts, and other City departments for their comments. The staff may then hold a subdivision conference with the subdivider and invite all the affected agencies to review their comments and suggested changes or conditions.

Step 7—Staff Review for Planning Commission
Following the subdivision conference and receipt of any comments from other agencies, the Planning Staff will study the application by reviewing the relationship of the request to the City's General Plan and analyze the environmental, land use, traffic, site plan, design, and other impacts or concerns of the proposed development. A written staff report will be prepared for the Planning Commission which will analyze the Tentative Map and include the DRC and other government agencies' recommendations as well as staff recommendations. A copy of this report will be sent to the applicant prior to the Planning Commission review of the Tentative Map.

Step 8—Planning Commission Review
Following the subdivision conference, the Tentative Subdivision Map is scheduled for review by the Planning Commission. The Planning Commission will hold a hearing, with notice to the applicant (subdivider), to review the Tentative Map. The Planning Commission must review and take action on the Tentative Map and report its decision to the City Council and the subdivider within 50 days after the Tentative Map has been accepted for filing. At the hearing, staff first will present its report and recommendations. This presentation will be followed by testimony from the applicant and, if permitted by the Commission, any interested persons who may wish to comment on the application. A decision will be made by the Planning Commission after evaluating the applicant's testimony, the staff report, and the environmental information. The Commission may then close the hearing and make its decision (1) approving, (2) conditionally approving, or (3) denying the request or postponing it to a later date. They may also continue the hearing to a specified time, date, and place.

Step 9—City Council Review
If the Tentative Map is approved, the staff will forward the decision of the Planning Commission to the City Council. Within 10 days or at its next regular meeting, the City Council has the option to review the application and the condition imposed by the Planning Commission. If the Council decides to review the Tentative Map, written notice of the hearing date will be sent to the applicant (subdivider) and Planning Commission. The City Council must review the Tentative Map within 15 days or at its next regular meeting unless the subdivider consents to a continuance. After hearing testimony from the applicant, staff, and other interested citizens, the Council may add, delete, or modify the Plan-

ning Commission's conditions of approval or deny the Map based upon the appropriate findings. If the Council does not act to review the Tentative Map within the required time limit, the application is deemed approved as set forth by the Planning Commission. The decision of approval or denial by the City Council is final.

Appeals to City Council
If the Tentative Map is denied by the Planning Commission or if the applicant (subdivider) disagrees with any conditions of approval imposed by the Planning Commission, an appeal may be filed with the City Clerk within 15 days of the decision. The Council will then hear the appeal within 30 days of the filing with notices sent to the subdivider and Planning Commission. After the hearing, the Council has 10 days to declare its findings, whereby it may sustain, modify, or reject the rulings of the Planning Commission subject to the same limitations that are placed on the Commission. Any affected person may also file a complaint with the City Clerk within 15 days of the Planning Commission decision, whereby the Council may reject the complaint or set the matter for hearing in the same manner as previously mentioned.

Other Required Actions
Following approval of the Tentative Map, the Design Review Commission must review and approve final plans for the dwelling units and other structures. Information on the timing and sequence of this process is contained in "An Applicant's Guide to Procedures for Design Review."

The applicant (subdivider) must complete and have approved by the City Engineer the final map and related improvement plans within 18 months or the approved map expires. An extension of this time period up to one additional year may be granted upon approval of the Planning Commission. The application for an extension must be filed not less than 45 days before the tentative map is to expire.

Estimated Time of Process
The estimated time for the processing of a Tentative Map application will vary depending upon the complexity and magnitude of the proposal and staff workload, but is generally estimated as follows:

A. From application to DRC review	−ND -		6 weeks
	−EIR -		14 weeks
B. From DRC review to PC review	−		4 weeks
Estimated Process Time	−	10 -	18 weeks

Application Submittal Requirements
The specific submittal requirements are listed on a separate page which will be provided to the applicant at the preapplication conference.

Appendix 5.B

An Applicant's Guide to Submittal Requirements: Tentative Map

---

Community Development Department   City of Walnut Creek, California

---

I. Application Forms—Completed and signed.

II. $_____ Deposit (actual fee is based on the amount of time spent by staff reviewing the application utilizing a standard charge rate. If the fee is less than the deposit, the remainder will be refunded, if more, the balance must be paid before building permits will be issued). Checks payable to the City of Walnut Creek.

III. Site photos (Polaroid OK) showing topography, vegetation, existing and adjacent structures, views of and from the site.

IV. *Preliminary Map* (optional) for review by the Design Review Commission. Actual Map (Step 5) may be utilized if preferred:

    Plans: 10 copies required (these must be folded to approximately 9" × 11"). Required data:

        A. Existing boundary lines, trees, waterways, structures, contours, streets, and easements

        B. Proposed grading, street layout, lot lines, open space, and recreation and building sites

        C. North arrow, scale, and contour interval

        D. Vicinity map showing nearby cross streets.

V. *Tentative Map* (must be prepared by a Registered Civil Engineer):

    Plans: 35 copies (25, if Preliminary Map was submitted), folded to approximately 9" × 11" (all but 5 copies may be reduced to 11" × 17" if permitted by staff). The map must be legibly drawn on one sheet of paper containing the following:

        A. A title containing the subdivision number, subdivision name, and type of subdivision

        B. Name and address of legal owner, subdivider, and person preparing the map (including registration number)

        C. Sufficient legal description to define the boundary of the proposed subdivision

        D. Date, north arrow, scale, and contour interval

        E. Existing and proposed land use

        F. A vicinity map showing roads, adjoining subdivisions, towns, creeks, railroads, and other data sufficient to locate the proposed subdivision and show its relation to the community

        G. Existing topography of the proposed site and at least 100 feet beyond its boundary including:

            1. Existing contours at 2-ft. intervals if the existing ground slope is less than 10 percent and at not less than 5-ft. intervals for existing ground slopes greater than or equal to 10 percent. Contour intervals should not be spread more than 150 feet apart. Existing contours should be represented by dashed lines or by screened lines.

            2. Type, location, and dripline of existing trees over 28" in circumference. Any trees proposed to be removed should be so indicated.

            3. The approximate location and outline of existing structures identified by type. Buildings to be removed should be so marked.

            4. The approximate location of all areas subject to inundation or storm-water overflow and the location, width, and direction of flow of each water course.

5. The location, pavement, and right-of-way width, grade, and name of existing streets or highways.
6. The widths, locations, and identity of all existing easements.
7. The location and size of existing sanitary sewers, water mains, and storm drains. The approximate slope of existing sewers and storm drains should be indicated.
8. The approximate location of the 60, 65, and 70 CNEL (Community Noise Equivalent Level) contours, if any.

H. Proposed improvements, including:
1. The location, grade, centerline radius, and arc length of curves, pavement and right-of-way width, and names of all streets. Typical section of all streets must be shown.
2. The location and radius of all curb returns and cul-de-sacs.
3. The location, width, and purpose of all easements.
4. The angle of intersecting streets if such angle deviates from a right angle by more than four degrees.
5. The approximate lot layout and the approximate dimensions of each lot and of each building site. Engineering data must show the approximate finished grading of each lot, the preliminary design of all grading, the elevation of proposed building pads, the top and toe of cut-and-fill slopes to scale, and the number of each lot.
6. Proposed contours at 2-ft. intervals must be shown if the existing ground slope is less than 10 percent and not at less than 5-ft. intervals for existing ground slopes greater than or equal to 10 percent. A separate grading plan may be submitted.
7. Proposed recreation sites, trails, and parks for private or public use.
8. Proposed common areas and areas to be dedicated to public open space.
9. The location and size of sanitary sewers, water mains, and storm drains. Proposed slopes and approximate elevations of sanitary sewers and storm drains must be indicated.

I. The name or names or any geologist or soils engineer whose services were required in the preparation of the tentative map.

J. The source and date of existing contours.

K. All lettering must be ⅛″ minimum

L. Certificates for execution by the Secretary of the Planning Commission indicating the approval by the City Council if the map was reviewed by the City Council.

M. If it is planned to develop the site as shown on the tentative map in units, then the proposed units and their proposed sequence of construction should be shown on the tentative map.

VI. *Accompanying Data and Reports.* The Tentative Map must be accompanied by the following data or reports:

A. *Soils Report.* A preliminary soils report prepared in accordance with the City's Grading Ordinance must be submitted. If the preliminary soils report indicates the presence of critically expansive soils or other soil problems which, if not corrected, would lead to structural defects, the soils report accompanying the final map must contain an investigation of each lot within the subdivision.

B. *Title Report.* A preliminary title report, prepared within 3 months prior to filing the Tentative Map.

C. *Engineering, Geology, and/or Seismic Safety Report.* If the subdivision lies within a "medium risk" or "high risk" geologic hazard area, as shown on the maps on file in the Community Development Department, a preliminary engineering, geology, and seismic safety report, prepared in accordance with guidelines established by the Community Development Department. If the preliminary engineering, geology, and/or seismic safety report must accompany the final map, it shall contain an investigation of each lot within the subdivision.

D. *School Site.* The subdivider must obtain from the school districts involved their intentions, in writing, concerning the necessity for a school site, if any, within

the subdivision and must present this information to the Community Development Director prior to the consideration of the Tentative Map by the Planning Commission.

E. *Utility Certification.* Certification in writing from all utilities that the proposed subdivision can be adequately served.

F. *Other Reports.* Any other data or reports deemed necessary by the Community Development Director.

Appendix 5.C

Learning to Read Plans

---

*Reprinted with permission from League of California Cities
Planning Commission Handbook*

Maps, plans, and drawings are the tools of planners and developers. Over time, planners and architects have developed a specialized language of contour lines, symbols and abbreviations to more uniformly describe development projects. While extremely efficient, the language of planning is not common knowledge among the lay public, and many planning commissioners must learn to interpret maps and plans from scratch.

Contour Lines

Contour lines are the primary two-dimensional graphic vehicle used to express three-dimensional ground form.

A contour line connects all points of equal elevation above or below a known or assumed reference point or plane. Therefore, all points on the contour line have the same elevation.

Contour lines are used to study proposed changes in land form, and eventually to guide and direct the work of earthmoving contractors in executing a grading project.

Contours show land forms, i.e., a hill, a valley, ridge, hogback, etc. They show the relationship of land forms—this hill to that valley, to this stream and finally to the ocean, etc. As contours are shown two-dimensionally, the scaled distance between them is ex-

actly the same as in the field.

All contour plans have a contour interval which remains the same over the entire drawing. This interval stands for the vertical distance between contours, and is always indicated somewhere on the plan.

Proposed and existing contours are both shown on the same drawing. By showing both on the same drawing, it is possible to understand the exact location of work to be performed and the exact amount of work to be done. Existing contours are shown by a light dashed line (usually ¼" long, spaced about 1/16" apart). Every fifth contour is shown slightly darker for easy legibility. Proposed contours are shown as a solid light line. This solid line begins where you propose to make a grading change, and moves away from the existing (dashed) contour, returning to the existing (dashed) contour at the end of the proposed grading change. It is therefore possible to "read" the change by studying the area between proposed contours and existing contours.

Contour lines are labeled with the number on the high side of the contour. Contour lines correspond to a selected interval which may be 1', 2', 10', etc. Generally, all contour lines on a map indicate the same interval and the interval should be labeled somewhere on the map.

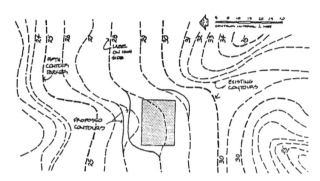

In an area of slight relief or generally flat and level country, the vertical interval may be as low as one foot, whereas in an area of marked relief it may be as large as 500, 250, or 100 feet. It sometimes happens that the relief changes from slight to marked within the limits of a map. When this is the case, intermediate contours are dropped or the vertical interval is changed from a small to a much larger one for the areas of marked relief.

"Reading" changes in contours is tricky, but can be mastered with practice. Basically, proposed grading changes either add earth (filling) or remove earth (cutting). A proposed contour which moves in the direction of a lower contour is adding earth (filling). For instance (see diagram), proposed Contour 7 moves in the direction of a lower Contour (6) and indicates filling. Conversely, a proposed contour which moves in the direction of a higher contour is removing earth (cutting). This can be seen where Contour 8 moves in the direction of Contour 9—and is removing earth (cutting). The amount of earth to be added or removed can be determined by comparing the proposed contour with the existing contours it crosses.

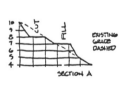

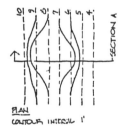

Profiles or sections can be constructed from contours

and conversely, contour locations can be determined from profiles. A freehand construction of a cross-section is the best way to understand what the contours are doing. The following are most typical forms found in grading.

A valley is represented by contours which point uphill. To construct the section, draw first the place where the section is to be taken. (Labeled A), then project up, parallel lines at each place a contour crosses 'A'. Somewhere above, draw lines parallel to 'A' and scaled according to the contour interval. Where the two lines cross becomes the section line, and one has only to connect these points to complete the section.

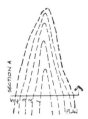

A summit is indicated by concentric closed contours, and adequate contour labeling to distinguish it from a depression. Depressions are often labeled with hachures and both forms should include spot elevations at the highest or lowest point.

A ridge is shown similar to a valley, but with the contours pointing downhill. Note carefully the contour labeling, for this is the easiest way to determine if it is a ridge or valley. Ridges and valleys often are very wide, and difficult to distinguish on a large scale map.

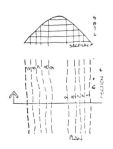
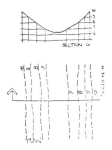

A convex slope is shown with parallel contours, each spaced further apart with the closer contours at the lower contours. Convex and concave landforms are the most common forms found in nature and should be well understood by landscape architects.

Drainage always occurs perpendicular (at right angles) to the contours. The perpendicular line is the shortest distance between contours, and hence the steepest route (see Diagram 1). Water naturally seeks the easiest (steepest) route as it travels downhill in runoff. Channels, ditches, and valleys are indicated by contours which point uphill, and are sometimes made obvious by drawing an arrow in the direction of drainage, or labeling it a SWALE (Diagram 2).

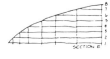
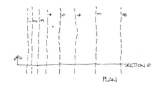

Conversely, a concave slope is shown with parallel contours, each spaced further apart starting with the closely spaced contours at the top.

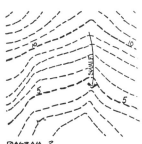

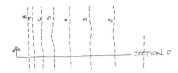

Characteristics of Contours

1. All points on a contour line have the same elevation. A contour line connects points of equal elevation.

2. Every contour closes on itself within or beyond the limits of the map. In the latter case, the contour will not end on the map but will run to the edges.

Two adjacent contours with the same numbers indicate either the top of a ridge or the bottom of a valley. Again, the numbering indicates which it is, so check carefully.

3. A contour which closes on itself within the limits of a map is either a summit or a depression. A depression is usually indicated by the elevation at the lowest point, a spot elevation, or the letter "D" placed there. A depression is also indicated by placing short hachure marks on the low side of the contour line (See No. 3 for depression and 3a. for summit)

4. Contour lines never cross other contours except where there is an overhanging cliff, natural bridge, or pierced or arched rock.

5. Contours which are equally spaced indicate a uniform sloping surface (see No. 5).

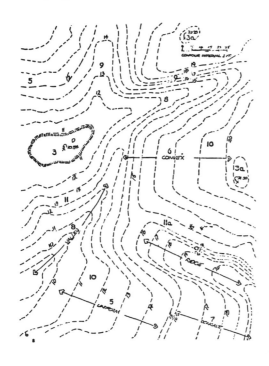

6. On a convex slope, contours are spaced at increasing intervals going up a hill; the higher contours are spaced further apart than the lower contour lines (See No. 6).

7. On a concave slope, the contours are spaced at increasing intervals with the lower contour lines spaced further apart than the higher ones (See No. 7).

8. Valleys are indicated by contours that point uphill (see No. 8). In crossing a valley, the contour lines run up the valley on one side, turn at the stream and run back the other side.

9. Generally contours which are close together indicate a steep slope (see No. 9).

10. Contours which are spaced far apart indicate a relatively level or slight grade (see No. 10).

11. Contours never split; however, you will occasionally see two contours numbered the same and side by side. This indicates either a high area, or a low area. It will be high (see No. 11) if the numbers of both contours fall in the same interval, and a low area (see No. 11a) if the numbers don't.

12. The steepest area of a slope runs perpendicular to the contours (water also drains this way).

Variations in Slope

In the proceeding examples we have talked about 2 to 1, or 3 to 1 slope and have described the manner to depict this by using contours. These slopes are necessary as it is not possible to pile earth, sand, soil, clay, etc., vertically, so we must slope these materials and the slope becomes either a 2 to 1, 3 to 1, 4 to 1, etc., slope (typically show 3:1). By 3:1 we mean three feet horizontal space is required for each one foot vertical change in elevation. As contours are shown in plan view, to maintain 3:1 slope the contours (assuming 1' contour interval) would have to be spaced 3 feet apart.

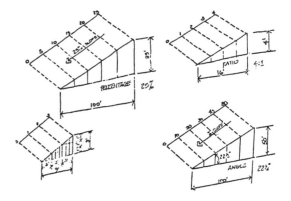

Slope proportion can be expressed as a ratio, in percentage, or as an angle. When expressed in percentages, a 3:1 slope becomes 33⅓, a 4:1 becomes 25, etc. Percentage slope is easiest to understand if you think of the slope being 100 feet long (measure horizontally). Then the vertical distance becomes the percent. To determine the percentage of any slope, divide the vertical distance by the horizontal distance (a 3:1 slope would be ⅓ or 33⅓).

Vertical Distance
_____
Horizontal Distance

Angles are seldom used to described slopes as mathematical conversion of ratios to angles is difficult. Angles can be measured with a protractor, or converted from direct reading tables. To set the bounds, a 90 degree angle is straight up (0:1 ratio), a 45 degree angle is a 1:1 ratio, a 22½ degree angle is 2:1 ratio, etc.

It may be worth noting that the ratio is expressed by some with the rise first. Thereby a slope which I would designate 3:1 would be designated 1:3. If the ratio seems excessive, check to see if it is backwards.

CHAPTER

6

How to
Red-Pencil
Site Plans

Charles Reed

To obtain better development, prepare your own site plan review checklist. Use the checklist provided in this chapter to stimulate your thinking as to what you need to include in your checklist.

Consider preparing checklists for zoning applications, special PUD/cluster housing projects, historic/architectural district applications, and for building permits and zoning clearance certificates. Prepare short checklists for routine one-family detached house permits, and extensive checklists for large multi-use, multibuilding site plans.

Keep in mind the difference between subdivisions and site plans in preparing your checklists. Subdivisions relate to the layout of lots and blocks, platting of lots and parcels, and the provision of public facilities necessary to build the subdivision to your community's development standards. (See Chapter 5.) Site plans relate to the layout, design, and con-

struction of buildings, and structures on a site to protect the public's interest in safety, economy, and from the adverse consequences of site development.

Parcels being developed that require site plans most likely have already been rezoned and platted for development,. But some of these sites are platted as subdivision outlots and may need further plats to carry out the site plan.

Much of the information for reviewing site plans and subdivisions will be the same. As the size of sites gets larger, information needed for site plan review becomes more extensive, becoming similar to that needed for subdivision review.

This checklist may use different terminology than that used in your community. This checklist also probably includes more items than you would review in your most complex site plan. A logical sequence of items is followed in this

81

checklist. Earlier items in the checklist guide the review of later items. Sort checklist items so your field review of site plans is in the same sequence as in your checklist.

Boilerplate, materials needed in site plan applications, analysis of site plans, and information the developer should provide on site plans for physical design and construction on the site for each major type of use, for buildings, structures, site furniture and public facilities is included in this chapter. Examples of other checklists for project and site plan reviews are shown in Exhibits 6.1 and 6.2. See also Appendix 6.A for another example of a checklist that can help ensure better development.

Exhibit 6.1
Project Review Check List,
Simi Valley, California

1. Is the project in accordance with the general plan?
   Land use
   Density
   Latest general plan revisions.

2. Is the project zoned correctly?
   Is a planned unit development (PUD) ordinance required?
   Is the use permitted or is a special use permit (SUP) required?
   Is an SUP in force on the project now?
   Is a PUD presently on file in the planning office?

3. Is a zone change required or requested?

4. Is a land division or subdivision required or requested?

5. Are special ordinances or policies applicable?
   Hillside Ordinance*
   Combining Freeway Zone*
   Other overlay zone
   Tree preservation policy
   Service Station Resolution*
   Other _____

6. Are neighboring properties used for a compatible purpose?

What will the neighborhood's reaction be?
Will the requested use be materially detrimental to enjoyment or valuation of property of other persons located in the vicinity of the site?

7. Is the proposed site adequately served by highways or streets of sufficient width and improved as necessary to carry the traffic such use would generate?
   Does the street width meet police and fire protection district criteria?
   Will the streets be dedicated or private?

8. Is the proposed site adequately served by other public or private service facilities?
   Freeways
   Railways
   Airport
   Bus line(s)

9. Is a right-of-way dedication required? If so, how much and where?

10. Are there enough parking spaces?
    For maximum expected employees?
    For customers?
    Is a drop-off area planned?
    Are parking spaces well planned?
    Are all parking spaces accessible?

11. Is the on-site, off-site circulation adequate?
    Are traffic bottlenecks created?
    Is pedestrian circulation adequate?
    Is the structure an aviation hazard?
    Are there any four-way intersections?
    Are horse trails required?
    Are bicycle trails required?
    Is vehicle circulation separated from pedestrian traffic?

12. Is the concept plan adequate for the city's landscape architect to make an evaluation?
    Can the status of live trees be determined?
    Are planters wide enough?
    What size plants will be installed?
    Are electric outlets provided in the planters for present or future lighting?

13. Will municipal demands be greatly affected?
    Police
    Fire

Liquid wastes
Sewage
Water
Parks and recreation
Schools
Trash collection
Other utilities

14. Will the development landlock another property?
Is an easement in effect?
Will an easement be required (i.e., for access to recreation areas)?
Is the property next to a flood control channel?

15. Does the structure show design excellence?
Is the structure facing the correct street?
Is variation in front yard setback provided?
Are side yards for recreational vehicle storage provided?
Is there horizontal and vertical relief?
Are structures shown clearly? Are they sited well?
Can colors, materials be determined?
Are there any existing structures? Do they need refurbishing?
Are setbacks correct?
Is the design proposed for the structure sensitive to its surroundings?
Do second story windows overlook other people's private spaces?
Are all elevations shown?
Has a sign or identification for the building and the site been considered in the design?

16. Is the environment enriched? Does it include:
Trees, landscaping, common open green spaces?
Walkways, meandering sidewalks?
Curvilinear streets?
Landscaped parkway (perimeter as well as internal)?
Berms?
Flood control channel treatment?
Amenities such as tot lots, pools, tennis courts?
Mature trees?

17. Will fencing/walls be required? If so, are they adequate?
Has lot height difference been considered in

fencing?
Are there decorative block walls?

18. Will it be possible to underground existing above ground utilities as part of this project?

19. Has an environmental assessment been made?
Is a noise study required?
Are liquefaction tests required?
Are soil borings required?
Are other special studies needed?
Is the project within the 100-year flood plain?

20. Have cuts and fills been evaulated? Is there a grading plan to indicate grade differentials?
How are grades to be treated?
Has drainage been evaluated?

21. Have all agencies responded and provided conditions for the project?

22. Have conservation devices been provided?
Pilotless ignition for ranges and furnaces
Thermostat with night setback feature
Exhaust hood with automatic dampers
Insulated hot water pipes
Low flow toilets
Water control devices on showers and faucets

23. Are there contracts, covenants, and restrictions for attorney review?
Homeowners association
Assessment district

24. Have other models been applied?

25. Has the Simi Valley net benefit model been applied?[1]

26. Has the Kevin Lynch model been applied?[2]
Pathways
Edges, barriers
Interest nodes, focal nodes
Linkages
Sense of entry
Movement through
Graphics, signs
A sense of hereness and thereness
Major open space

27. Has structure quality been maintained?
Diversity
Colors

Texture
Scale
Material
Shape

28. Is scale appropriate?
Site (largest)
Node
Personal (human scale)

29. Behavioral support
Rain shelter
Noise
Seating

30. Basic rules
Linkages 80 feet in length without nodes
are boring
Blocks should not be greater than 150 feet
Cul-de-sacs should not be longer than 800
feet

*Simi Valley ordinances.

1. *Net-Benefit Elevation Process: Balancing the Impacts of Development in the City of Simi Valley.* Prepared with John Blayney Associates, San Francisco. Available from Department of Environmental Affairs, 3200 Cochran St., Simi Valley, CA 93065 (805/522-1333). 1976. 115 pp. Appendixes include a "Check List for Preliminary Review and Net Benefit Assessment" and a "Simi Valley Cost Benefit Study Project Evaluation Form."

2. A "Check List of Site Data" appears on pp. 91-94 of Kevin Lynch's *Site Planning.* The Simi Valley check list is based in part upon the Lynch model. However, there are some differences. For instance, while Simi Valley seems to use "linkage" to designate physical connection of activity areas, Lynch defines linkages as "movements of people, goods, and wastes or communication of information. They may be based upon amenity, such as the view afforded by a park, or they may be negative repulsions due to nuisance effects. The links connect units that are distributed in time as well as space."

Exhibit 6.2
Site Plan Review Check List
Schaumburg, Illinois, Planning Department

1. *Application*
   ☐ Current zoning determined
   ☐ Zoning requested
   ☐ Variations requested
   ☐ Correct fee paid
   ☐ Proof of ownership submitted

☐ Plat of survey submitted
☐ Foundation landscape plan submitted
☐ Application correctly submitted
☐ Tax impact study submitted
☐ Traffic study submitted
☐ Elevations and floor plans submitted
☐ Preliminary utility plan submitted
☐ Covenants and easements declared
☐ Overall landscape plan submitted

2. *General*
   ☐ Northpoint and scale drawn
   ☐ Floodplain status determined
   ☐ Number of phases
   ☐ Type of housing unit noted
   ☐ Price range noted
   ☐ Construction date noted
   ☐ Building materials specified
   ☐ Compliance with master plan
   ☐ Density of development
   ☐ Number of acres
   ☐ Surrounding land uses
   ☐ Rental prices
   ☐ Completion date set
   ☐ Provisions for garbage collection

3. *Bulk Regulations:*
   ☐ Proper yards provided
   ☐ Proper setbacks shown
   ☐ Correct land coverages shown
   ☐ Building height
   ☐ Floor area ratio (FAR) correct
   ☐ Minimum distance between buildings

4. *Utilities*
   ☐ All easements shown with proper width
   ☐ Sewer available
   ☐ Underground along street right-of-way (ROW)
   ☐ Depth and size of retention and detention facilities shown
   ☐ Village water available
   ☐ Storm drainage satisfactory
   ☐ Telephone and electric underground in rear line easement
   ☐ Maintenance of fish life

5. *Streets and Traffic*
   ☐ Proper ROW width
   ☐ Proper cul-de-sac radius maintained
   ☐ Street names provided
   ☐ Required sidewalks provided
   ☐ Streets and ROW aligned with existing ones

☐ Pedestrian walkways provided
☐ Effect on external traffic noted
☐ Served by mass transit
☐ Traffic signal needed
☐ Donation toward traffic signal made
☐ Existing traffic pattern
☐ Proper ROW dedicated for future streets and street widening
☐ Unnecessary street jogs eliminated
☐ Proper block lengths
☐ Proper street length within cul-de-sac
☐ Proper street width shown
☐ Access for emergency equipment
☐ Adequate internal traffic flow
☐ Minimum 30-foot return radius
☐ Acceleration and deceleration lanes needed
☐ Bypass lane needed

6. Landscaping
   ☐ Trees and shrubs properly dimensioned
   ☐ Trees and shrubs properly labeled
   ☐ Fencing or berming needed
   ☐ Escrow account required
   ☐ Landscape budget per unit set
   ☐ Existing trees shown
   ☐ Minimum 30-foot landscaped perimeter
   ☐ Trash dumpster shown and screened
   ☐ Low maintenance landscaping provided

7. *Parking*
   ☐ Required number of spaces provided
   ☐ Separate parking for boats and recreational vehicles
   ☐ Parking lot properly screened
   ☐ Landscaped isles provided
   ☐ 9-foot by 20-foot stalls for 90 degree parking
   ☐ 12-foot aisle width for one-way
   ☐ Additional guest parking provided
   ☐ Spaces and aisles drawn to scale
   ☐ Adequate parking by recreational facilities
   ☐ Parking spaces located in close proximity to buildings
   ☐ 24-foot aisle width for two-way

8. *Maintenance of Open Space and Buildings*
   ☐ PUD guidelines met in declaration of covenants and easements
   ☐ One-year homeowners association (HOA) budget submitted
   ☐ Meeting facilities provided
   ☐ Review of sales brochure

☐ Escrow fund for private streets and utilities established
☐ 10-year HOA budget submitted
☐ Dates for HOA control set
☐ Buyers' guide available

9. *Recreational Facilities*
   ☐ What facilities are proposed?
   ☐ Will they be adequate?
   ☐ Publicly dedicated facilities, if any
   ☐ Financial burden on HOA determined
   ☐ Tot lots provided
   ☐ Recreational walkways provided
   ☐ School site, if needed
   ☐ Agreement with park district submitted

10. *Tax Impact Study*
    ☐ Correct population generation figures shown
    ☐ Correct village income shown
    ☐ Correct village expenditures shown
    ☐ Proposed assessed valuation feasible
    ☐ Correct school district income shown
    ☐ Correct school district expenditures shown

11. *Development Donations*
    ☐ Cultural center
    ☐ Medical facility
    ☐ Park district
    ☐ Fire and police departments
    ☐ School district

12. *Single Family Detached Subdivisions*
    ☐ Correct lot size
    ☐ Correct corner lot size
    ☐ Correct minimum frontage
    ☐ Side lot lines at right angle to straight street lines
    ☐ Correct minimum width
    ☐ Correct minimum depth
    ☐ Correct building lines shown
    ☐ Variations needed

13. *R-6 Cluster Subdivisions*
    ☐ Minimum lot size 8,750 square feet
    ☐ Minimum lot depth 100 feet
    ☐ Minimum lot width 70 feet
    ☐ Minimum building line
    ☐ Variations needed
    ☐ Minimum open space 12.5 per cent
    ☐ Provisions for publicly dedicating open space
    ☐ Maintenance of private open space

CHECKLIST OF ITEMS TO BE INCLUDED ON SITE PLANS

Administration

Each type of development approval may need a site plan checklist

• *Zoning approvals* that generally may require site plans include rezoning applications, variances, special exceptions, conditional use permits, design and appearance certificates, permits to develop along specific boulevards and streets identified in your zoning ordinance, environmental permits, and preannexation zoning agreements.

• *Zoning approvals for planned projects* include applications that your zoning ordinance defines as requiring major site plan review regardless of any other special planned site requirement; planned sites and projects for unified development projects for: PUDs, cluster zones, zero lot line projects, mobile home parks, manufactured housing subdivisions; industrial and research parks; office parks; shopping centers; mixed-use developments; and historical-architecural district reviews.

• *Development within special mandatory overlay districts* whose boundaries were previously mapped or defined—airport approach, flood hazard, hillside, wetlands, beach and dunes, tidal line, and harbor lines.

• *Permit approvals* include site plans for various types of permits—demolition, temporary use, grading, design, foundation, building, remodeling, occupancy, parking, and property maintenance.

• *State-mandated approvals* include site plans that must be submitted to state or regional agencies and commissions, such as development of regional impact, development of environmental significance, state-defined sensitive areas (usually soil, estuarine, farming, forest, wetlands, wilderness, hillside, and mountain areas), and coastal zones. Local agencies would follow state agency guidelines that describe principles, standards, and criteria that site plans must meet.

Process for reviewing and approving site plans

• *How process is described.* For each type of development approval, the process for submitting, reviewing, and approving site plans is described in writing, as an ordinance, or as agency regulations, manuals, handbooks, or guidelines.

• *Sequence of steps* must be described in each process as a flow chart or listing of steps in order of review and approval. The description of the approval process includes the number of days, calendar dates, or day of the month each step occurs; sequence of docketing for meetings; advertising, public notice, site plan review sequence; public hearings; ordinance approval procedure.

• *Procedural descriptions* include preapplication procedures, including meetings by applicant with neighborhood groups and abutting property owners; public notice procedure and requirements for hearings; procedure as to how meetings are to be conducted, providing due process; number of days community has to approve/deny application.

Information to Be Provided on Materials Submitted

On site plans

• *Title page* information includes date of site plan, name of development, name and address of land owners and major leasees, applicant(s) and which person is lead applicant, general developer, collaborating developers and consultants, architects, design counsel, legal counsel, financial counsel, economic feasibility consultant, real estate broker, and financing institutions/general syndicate partner. Address/general location of project, legal description of project, small location map orienting project property to general surrounding area also should be included.

• *Boilerplate information required on each plan sheet* is drafted on specified size of page (usually 24″ by 36″ or 30″ by 42″, with short dimensions as binding edge); has page borders drafted as specified, contains required title block information (page number, date of drafting, date of last edit to plan, name of development, name of developer, legend of information shown on site plan, official seal or signature of professional licensed to prepare site plan information), has north arrow (always to top of page), and has scale (graphic scale preferred).

• *Basic physical construction and site design information* contained on site plan includes boundaries, rights-of-ways and easements, contours existing and proposed, use of all parts of the site, buildings and structures, parking lots and areas, landscaped areas, pedestrian areas (walks, arcades, plazas), vehicular streets, drives and aisles, loading and other service areas, utility service areas and major utility lines, drainage and water runoff, water bodies, barriers (berms, landscape screens, fences and walls), signs, and major street and site furniture.

Supporting maps, plot plans, and site plans

• *Surveys and ownerships* include survey and certification by registered surveyor and ownership map if multiple separate ownerships are involved.

• *Site inventory maps* include soils map, map showing location of soil/geologic test borings, with evaluation of soils types to support site development; geological and hydrological conditions map; existing and proposed contours/grading plan; vegetation map; map showing specific trees of large caliper.

• *Site analysis maps* include map showing location of problems and opportunities relating to development and changes to the natural ecology of the site and a description of each

such problem and opportunity on the site. Examples of problems and opportunities include: excellent natural contours for solar orientation of buildings, certain locations on the site provide excellent views of downtown skyline or a forested valley, high embankment of adjacent railroad with many noisy trains going by the site.

• *Site plan maps* detail secondary information that would be too confusing if shown on the general site plan. These plans include a planting and landscaping plan and list of plant materials showing size, height, or caliper of materials at time of planting (this information is especially critical since trees are often shown on the site plan under the impression of full mature growth when trees actually planted often are very small and twiglike and create an unattractive barren site appearance); a utilities plan showing location of existing and proposed utilities; a plan showing phasing and timing of development of the site if site is to be developed over a build-out period exceeding three to five years; a map showing disposition of individual parcels for proposed use, ownership, and development in a multiparcel development proposal such as a redevelopment plan or a plan for development of a historic preservation district.

Engineering specifications and drawings

• *Cross sections* of streets either for each street or by functional use of streets and drives for the site or portions of site explaining/clarifying extensive site improvements or multistory structures.

• *Profiles*, existing and proposed, for earth grading of slopes, streets, utilities, and stream courses.

• *Demarcation boundaries or lines* beyond which development is not allowed for beach lines at appropriate tide levels, dune lines and beach vegetation lines, harbor and navigational lines for pier limits, shorelines for lakes, reservoirs,

and storm drainage holding ponds, hillside lines, and embankment and steep slope lines.
• *Working drawings and specifications* for buildings, structures, public works, and site furniture either by providing construction drawings or by reference to standard drawings or national/regional engineering association construction/performance standards for specific items required by public works engineers, by name of professional standards association and its reference identity, or by specified manufacturer, model number, including any optional add-ons for specified items.

Written information
• *Legal information* includes legal description of existing and proposed outlots, portions of the site proposed for sale or long-term lease; existing and proposed covenants and restrictions on the site.
• *The development program* includes explanations, justifications, and policies governing design, construction, and phasing of site development and proposed sharing of construction costs by the developer and public bodies for facilities that serve the project or are required off site due to the impact of the project.
• *Financing methods* and programs including federal, state, and local financing programs, special private developer eminent domain programs, tax abatement programs, tax increment financing, lease-purchase programs, government revenue bonds, special tax assessment abatement districts, and financial schedules for sharing of development costs among the applicant, tenants, and public bodies.
• *Property management* structure and operating policies, including description of property owners or home owners association organization, duties, enforcement, and financing/dues regulations and covenants.
• *Relocation plan* for relocating occupants of existing uses and households on the site, including number of persons displaced needing relocation assistance by type of relocation characteristic, method and timing of notice to vacate premises, amount and method of payment for relocation expenses, including moving and rent adjustment for new quarters, and availability of existing housing or tenancy space elsewhere in the community at similar rents for displacees.
• *Environmental impacts* caused by proposals in the site plan or identified by environmental assessment.

Calculations, data, and statistics
• *Calculation of permit fees* includes square footage and valuation of structures needing permits.
• *Usage of site* includes tables of proposed land use for density and intensity of use, gross and net square footage or acreage occupied by each use on the site before and after dedications, and date of occupancy.
• *Land use intensity ratios* required by zoning ordinance—open space ratio, hard surface/impervious surface ratio, floor area ratios, recreational usage ratios.
• *Parking* to be provided must meet zoning requirements for each type of use. This includes number of parking spaces to be provided for each use to meet requirements of zoning ordinance. The type of parking spaces to be provided (regular sized spaces and special spaces for compact cars, handicapped persons, buses, RVs and bicycles) also should be included.
• *Housing information,* including total number of dwelling units, by dwelling type, per multifamily building (each building keyed by letter symbol to the site plan), mix of apartment sizes with each size indicating number of bedrooms and average square footage per apartment; special populations expected to be housed that influence site development needs, e.g., school-age children, elderly, handi-

capped, developmentally disabled, low-/moderate-income households.

• *Economic development information* includes market feasibility analysis (includes description of trade areas and methodology for analysis), proposed tenant mix for commercial occupancy, and taxes estimated to be generated by site uses.

• *Calculations required for engineering analyses* include storm water runoff and surcharge needs, water supply, cut and fill calculations, building construction and structural/load bearing analyses, build-out and phasing of construction.

Fees to be paid by applicant

• *Development impact fees* to be paid to public bodies for the developer's share of communitywide streets, schools, parks, and other major public facilities needed to accommodate future community growth; method of fee payment and developer's calculations supporting his proposed amount of impact fees if different from required formulas.

• *Administrative fees*, including application fees for permits, rezonings, variances, subdivisions, surety and performance bonds, and fees and charges for expenses of public agencies. Also fees for legal notices, advertising and posting of notice signs, plan review and checking, and for duplicating plans and materials required by public agencies.

• *Form of fee payment* should explain calculations showing conformance to required size of fee—such as number of lots, total project acreage, square footage of buildings, linear footage of streets, and how to pay fee (by check, certified/cashiers check, letter of credit).

Analysis of Site Plan

Measures to be used to analyze site plans

• *Density* includes the number of units per unit size of land (such as persons per net acre)

for total population, population by specific type (such as school-age children, elderly, low-/moderate-income households); employees by type of land use or by occupation; spatial density—number of square feet of the ground area of buildings and structures under roof per net acre.

• *Coverage of site* is expressed by various ratios of net site area covered by various types of surfaces. These include floor area ratios, ratios of total site to impervious surfaces, hard surfaces open space, and permeability (to determine effects of storm water runoff and absorption of storm water into site soils and to determine amount of land available for passive open space and recreational use), ratios and density calculations for cluster/PUD development (total square footage of buildings, number of housing units for the entire site, and for private land use areas).

• *Efficiency of site design* for optimizing the use of public-serving needs of the site. Getting the most use of public facilities by the site's private land uses could be obtained by mixing tenants to share facilities at complementary times (such as shared parking areas and staggered rush hours to reduce total needed capacity of drives for the site), multiple use of site facilities (parking areas used for plazas, pedestrian and open space areas designed as fire lanes, loading areas used as parking areas during business hours), indoor lighting located to serve also as exterior security lighting, and berms and grades for landscaped passive open space used to retard storm water runoff.

• *Minimizing need of public-serving facilities* on the site is also a measure of the efficiency of site design. This is measured as the linear feet of streets, drives, driveways, sidewalks for access among site buildings and major uses on the site that functionally relate to one another; the reduction of movement of earth by grading (cut and fill) in relation to alternative possible plans for street and building site locations.

• *Vehicular trip generation/attraction* by uses planned for the site to determine how well existing and planned streets can serve the site. Trip generation data is often provided, at cost, to local governments by regional planning agencies that are the area's official transportation planning agency under federal aid highway acts. This information is almost always applied to major site proposals such as shopping centers, large apartment complexes, and office and industrial parks. Smaller sites also use trip generation information to analyze uses with very high unit rates of trip generation, such as medical/dental centers, 7-11-type convenience stores, gas stations, taverns, bowling alleys, multiscreen movie theaters, private racquetball and soccer buildings, fast-food outlets, and high schools and junior colleges.

• *Performance measures of land use* identify side effects generated by land uses that are adverse to other uses. These measures often relate to manufacturing activities of industrial uses that generate smoke, noise, glare, vibration, and other industrial performance measures near nonindustrial uses. But adverse side effects also relate to commercial, office, residential, and recreational uses. Examples typically include the intensity of noise and crime from taverns, noise and rowdiness from drag stips, restaurants with live entertainment in very late night hours, and take-out, fast-food restaurants, with the accompanying cooking odors and food wrappers and garbage blown about the neighborhood.

Analysis of site to off-site environs

• *Absorption of the off-site capacity of public facilities.* Site analysis determines how much capacity of major capital facilities the proposed activities on the site will absorb at full site development. Otherwise, portions of the service area of capital facilities may be without adequate levels of service. For smaller sites under review, you need to determine what precedents are being set by design aspects of the site plan that will allow similar physical site design for other sites in the service area of affected capital facilities. The capacity of major capital facilities is invariably established through regional plans: freeways, freeway ramps and interchanges, arterials, arterial intersections and turning lanes, transit routes and corridors; parks, greenbelts, parkways, bikeways and trails; and plans for water, sewerage, sewage treatment, and storm drainage system.

• *Effect of site plans on the natural capacity of sensitive environmental elements.* Assess site plans to determine how much the capacity of sensitive environmental elements is being absorbed, changed, severed, or destroyed—and what alteration in site design can be made to mitigate this damage. Major environmental problems often include excessive hard surface construction over acquifer recharge areas, drainage of wetlands, blockage of sheet water flows in wetlands, drawing-down of water tables that allows salt water intrusion, or loss of water supply to rest of the service area or subsidence of ground surface, hillside and steep slope construction that creates unstable slopes, disturbance of shorelines and beach environments, loss of migratory waterfowl nesting and resting areas, or severing of natural land migratory routes of wild animals.

• *Changes in the type, direction, or character of community growth and development* need to be analyzed for site plans. Land use impacts for major proposed major sites—usually nonresidential usage that generates new urban growth or competes with other existing urban areas in the region or neighborhood for expected future economic growth include shopping centers, single-plant industrial sites, industrial parks, and office parks.

• *Relationship of the site to adjacent uses and land parcels* is analyzed in terms of plans and policy statements for land use, housing, open space, recreation, public facilities, and other local plan elements such as seismic and earthquake activity or hurricane disaster plans. These plans include community comprehensive plans and policy guides, neighborhood area plans, detailed master plans and precise plans for multiparcel/multiblock portions of neighborhoods. If the site is in an urban area, additional analysis is needed for zoning guides prepared for hot spots in your community if the site is located in or near such a hot spot, for renewal plans, and CDBG policy guides and plans, for housing assistance plans, for fair-share housing plans and guides for your community and region, and for CPC/BZA policies for land development or variances for applicant's proposals.

Conformance to required special overlay districts These districts include airport height envelopes over the site, flood hazard boundaries mapped for the site and how development will affect changes in flood levels in the flood fringe areas, architectural/historical districts, special fire insurance rating districts, enterprise zones, foreign trade zones and subzones, and districts affected by regulations, guidelines, and rulings by state-authorized regulatory commissions and agencies (e.g., state welfare department, state air/water quality control commissions).

On-site relationships
• *Permanence of site uses.* The design and layout of site design elements fix the range of alternative potential uses of the site. If the site's uses have little permanence, the site design needs to consider alternative potential uses to retain the economic viability on the site. For example, drive-up uses (such as a gas station or fast-food restaurant) require strong commitment of the layout and design of site elements to that type of use. Failure of drive-up usage of the site could require domolition of all site structures to enable site reuse. Site uses can

change through failure of the market to support site uses, changes in the ownership of the site after approval is obtained, failure or error in site design that causes failure of site uses to be successful, and unanticipated changes in markets that require site management to change the tenant mix to meet new markets.
• *Circulation among on-site uses.* Uses and major activities on the site link to one another by circulation corridors and routes. These routes are for vehicles, pedestrians, or commodities. The type, location, and size of these routes is analyzed for effective use of capacity, avoidance of conflict between circulation system elements where they intersect, location of routes to retain the cohesiveness of use areas that should not be divided or crossed by circulation routes (e.g., a proposed arterial street cutting through a residential neighborhood), and determination of shortest routes linking on-site activities.
• *Relationship of site uses and circulation system to natural characteristics of the site.* Are developer's proposals that change or disturb natural site characteristics—either on the site itself or as part of an accumulative impact that changes the natural characteristics of the site and its surrounding area—acceptable? What are the environmental risks created by site development for changes in site topography and use of slopes and hillsides for development? For proposed creation of new slopes that could create later problems for uses proposed on or near such slopes? How do the developer's proposals relate to characteristics and possible future behavior of site soils, such as soil shrink and swell, slippage of wet soils, absorption rate of soils, especially in relation to height of water table and proposed extractive and underground uses? How will site development alter the location and flood potential of existing water courses on the site?
• *Spacing and orientation of buildings and other structures.* Poor building location, orientation,

and spacing can destroy amenity, property values, and neighborhood cohesiveness as much as an improper zoning. Analysis includes checking for the creation of monotonous or barrackslike visual effect; blocking of views due to the location, height and mass of buildings and structures near property lines; movement of light and air to adjacent uses; reduction of legitimate commercial visibility of adjacent commercial uses or reduction of liveability of adjacent residential uses.

• *Logical relationship of building groups.* This is done for parking, trafficways, service areas, recreational, and open space (e.g., can the buildings in a group be rearranged to provide common parking areas or, vice-versa, should illogically related uses have separate parking/traffic areas, such as commercial and multifamily residential parking areas). Do apartments face each other in adjacent buildings with loss of privacy and view to open space? Are buildings oriented for solar gain potential? Are buildings oriented to avoid unnecessary exposure of outdoor recreational areas and major building entrances to cold northern winds and winter snows? Are courtyard areas formed by building groups logical to the use of the building group?

Boundaries, Rights-of-Way, and Easements

• *Site boundaries.* Make sure that the site plan shows the site parcel boundary completely in its correct location. Also check that the written legal description of the boundary coincides with the boundary mapped on the site plan. Boundaries of each development stage for multistage site development plans (or at least for the current development stage) and boundaries of outlots and outparcels to be sold or leased long-term must be correctly located on the site plan and must coincide with their written legal description. Boundaries of adjacent parcels and lines of platted lots abutting the site are shown where they intersect with site plan parcel boundary. For abutting subdivisions, show subdivision name and the numbers of abutting blocks and lots. Existing and proposed zone district boundaries are mapped on the site plan in their correct locations, with existing zoning classified to the correct district.

• *Easements.* All existing and proposed easements on, abutting, or near site parcel and within the first 100 to 500 feet on adjacent parcels of ROW adjacent to site parcel must be shown correctly on the site plan. Purposes and uses of easements should be indicated, along with the names of companies and agencies for whom easements are provided. Within easements, show location of all utility lines and poles, indicating capacity/size of lines—for waterlines, sewers, electricity, telephone, gas, slurry pipelines, railroads, fiber optic and other telecommunications lines.

• *Rights-of-way.* All existing and proposed street and railroad rights-of-way and street lines of private streets must be shown on the site plan. Also show ROW setback lines, special ROW setbacks for portions of site located along boulevards and streets named specifically in zoning regulations requiring special setbacks. Within ROW, show all street, curb lines, driveways, sidewalks, crosswalks, street moving lanes, left-right turning lanes, railroad tracks and switches, ganged postal box stanchions, and location of traffic signals—all properly scaled and dimensioned.

Need for Subdivision Plat

After you have completed your analysis of the site plan, determine if a preliminary plat must be submitted for the site, even if the entire site is to be treated as a single parcel. Consider requiring subdivision plats for commercial site plans with long-lease and sale parcels. The platting process allows the community to obtain necessary dedications and public improvements, especially if the site is in your extraterritorial subdivision review/approval area but outside the purview of your zoning regulations.

Land Use Information Shown On Site Plans

Residential uses

• *Density and intensity of usage.* Suggest changes on the site plan that reduce overcrowding of structures or population on the site while maintaining floor area ratio (FAR), by increasing the number of stories in buildings while reducing structural coverage of site by buildings (building footprints). Change spatial density and population density by changing the housing type or floor area of individual dwelling units.

• *Layout of living areas with in dwellings* and from dwelling to dwelling should be analyzed on the site plan for problems of liveability within dwelling units. Analyze multifamily dwellings for the relationship of living areas separated by party walls and common walls. Check the site plan for quiet areas (sleeping areas, bedrooms) abutting family rooms/living rooms (higher noise areas); privacy of views from active living and entertainment areas (living room picture windows/dining area sliding doors view of landscaped open space areas rather than parking lots and blank walls of poorly located buildings next door); kitchen/laundry/entertainment areas abutting living/sleeping areas of nearby dwellings. Apartment trash collection areas should be separated from dwelling areas.

• *Relationship of residential buildings to other buildings* on and off the site. For adjacent buildings containing different housing types, the usual problem is that taller, larger, and bulk-ier multifamily dwellings can loom over single-family dwellings either across the street or abutting back yards. The solution is to reduce the height of multifamily buildings, shift the location of buildings to increase spacing buffer, and plant more mature landscaping at time of development combined with decorative walls or fences.

• *Use of utility easements* on the site. No part of utility easements can be occupied by permanent buildings. Allowable land uses on easements and underneath overhead wires include outdoor recreational uses, such as tennis, paddleball, racquetball, handball, tot lots, gardens (landscaped areas except certain species of trees and shrubs that would grow into overhead wires or cause excessive damage to utility lines in ice storms, and outdoor service areas, such as dog runs, clothes drying areas, parking areas, and trash and service areas.

• *Dwelling uses and housing types.* Check that they are permitted in the zone district proposed for the site. Developers often propose incorrect housing types for the proposed site zoning, e.g., attached single-family dwellings—garden apartments or patio houses—in zones allowing only detached single-family dwelling.

• *Correct number of dwelling units.* Count all dwelling units shown on the site plan. Examine the basement floor plans of multifamily buildings to find extra dwelling units near laundry/furnace service areas as manager's apartment on site plan. Make sure the site plan dwelling count matches the count of dwellings listed in all other materials that accompany the site plan in tables and statistical data, especially for each type of residential zoning proposed on the site plan. Make sure that the total number of dwellings for each dwelling/housing unit type is at or below allowable density for the zoning for which the site plan is to be developed. Check that the count of extra density and dwelling units allowed for bonus incentives for design and open space amenity are correct.

• *The ability to convert group living quarters to individual dwelling units* needs to be checked on site plans for nursing homes, rooming and boarding houses, motels and hotels, fraternities, dormitories, and other group quarters housing occupants in individual sleeping rooms. Check that living/sleeping rooms with individual bathrooms do not have kitchen facilities or stub-in wiring and plumbing for de facto conversion later to complete apartment dwelling units. Require applicants for these uses to submit floor plans of buildings, including basements, showing configuration of rooms; require a note on site plans that states no kitchen, eating or sink facilities (no electric/plumbing rough-in service) are to be provided in rooms (unless your community approves). Otherwise, site owner could later informally convert each living quarter to a permanent apartment unit. These informal dwelling units probably would violate various development codes of the community such as permitted uses, residential density, off-set parking per unit, open space per unit, bulk envelope yards (zoning ordinance), minimum size of unit (health code), minimum fenestration, number and location of entries, and floor layout (life safety code, fire code or health codes).

• *Each building site must meet zoning dimensional requirements.* Examine each lot/building site one at a time for lot size, frontage on streets, lot width, lot depth, ratio of lot width to depth (commonly in error on many site plans), setbacks lines and minimum yards to meet minimum zoning requirements for these items. Each lot on curving and cul-de-sac streets must have required street frontage. Each dwelling shown on the site plan must meet minimum floor area requirements for the housing type,

per bedroom. Applicant must redraft site plan to eliminate substandard lots.

• *Additional building site requirements for flexible planned zones* for PUDs, cluster subdivisions, and zero lot line developments and zones. For all lots on the site plan and for each development stage in the plan, the applicant's proposals must meet average mean area and width of lots for flexible development zones. Each such lot also must meet absolute minimum dimensional requirements for lot area, width and depth for such flexible zones. Each lot must contain a reasonably level and well-drained building site.

• *Parking requirement:* The correct number of parking spaces for each dwelling unit and for each housing type with different parking standards includes spaces required for dwelling occupants and for visitors. Required parking must be provided for each parcel for separate parcels for each single- and two-family unit, or for all multifamily units on the site plan. Each parking space must meet dimensional requirements of length and width for the parking space angle provided; aisle width must be properly dimensioned; bumper blocks and distance of parking spaces from barriers and property lines must meet minimum requirements; and vehicle turnaround areas at the ends of parking aisles must be of required shape and dimension.

• *Open space* must be provided as required in PUD and cluster flexible zoning districts. Measure total number of housing sites/lots provided and total public or association/common space provided, and take ratio of private space to common space to determine if this ratio meets your PUD/cluster zoning requirements. Check that recreational areas—tennis courts, swimming pools, tot lots, playgrounds, and clubhouses—are (or are not) part of required open space as defined by your zoning ordinance.

• *Buildings containing dwellings must meet zoning requirements for such buildings.* Each building must meet the height requirement defined by your zoning ordinance for the type of roof proposed by applicant for buildings (e.g., mansard, gambrel, gable, hip, flat roof). Dwelling units are allowed or prohibited on the lowest defined floor level in buildings (cellar, basement, walk-out basement). All buildings must meet yard requirements for each yard for all lots and zone lots on the site plan; check carefully for double-frontage lots, corner yards, and street side yards. Buildings should meet architectural requirements for variety and avoidance of monotony, or for conformance to a defined architectural style and design.

• *More than one building allowable on single-building sites:* Buildings in multiple building groups allowed on individual lots must meet spacing standards between buildings and for light- and -air clearance planes in front of windows facing other buildings, walls, berms, and window wells. Check for conformance to spacing between buildings provided in special courtyard requirements for building groups.

• *Accessory uses and buildings and ancillary nonresidential uses* proposed by the applicant must be permitted by the site's zoning. All accessory buildings and structures should be at or below maximum size allowable for accessory buildings; accessory buildings must meet all accessory yards. Accessory structures (such as satellite dishes, air conditioning compressors, treehouses, gazebos, play lot apparatus, swimming pools) must meet accessory yard requirements.

• *Perimeter of large-scale developments* must meet yard, width, screening, and landscaping requirements for setbacks, buffers, and barriers (wall, fences, berms). Check that site ROW, streets, walkways, and easements connect continuously to corresponding stubs on abutting platted parcels and subdivisions.

• *Fences and walls* must meet requirements of opacity, decorative design, and maximum height for fences for the yards in which they are shown.

• *Sight distance areas.* Examine each street and driveway intersection for conformance to sight distance triangles and clear-view distances by potential obstructions (trees, poles, fences, signs, walls, landscaping, and accessory buildings and structures).

• *Signs* for nonresidential uses, such as schools and churches, must meet specific sign requirements. Residential entrance signs, project signs, model dwelling signs, and traffic control signs on-site should meet zone requirements for such signs.

• *Driveways* must meet minimum spacing standards from each other, from property lines, and from intersecting streets and alleys. Driveways are of adequate length to provide safe clearance for vehicles parked or leaving drives to streets. Driveways in single-family and two-family zones can accommodate required number of off-street parking spaces. Driveways are of permitted width, provide correct radius from drive to curb/gutter, intersect curb at allowable angle, prevent drainage of storm water from street to site at the curb, gutter or sidewalk, and meet the design standards of local public works agencies and of the state highway department where driveways connect to state highways.

• *Landscaping requirements* should be met for allowable species of landscaping and street trees, spacing requirements of individual trees, required number of trees provided per dwelling in front yard or along streets, caliper and size of landscaping specified at time of planting. Landscaping as drafted onto the site plan and as shown in artist's illustration is routinely depicted as being more mature than what is actually planted on the ground—which often results in a disappointing barren appearance.

Community facilities, recreational and open space

• *Dedication of necessary sites for public use* in private applicant site plans: Are the physical characteristics of such dedicated sites adequate for buildings and structures? Are these sites sufficiently level and well-drained, with minimal soil and drainage problems (developers often propose undesirable building sites for dedication for public usage, saving best and most profitable sites for private development)? Site adequacy also includes: shape of site, whether the site is located next to functional types of streets that are best for such uses (e.g., fire and police sites along major arterials near/at intersection with crossing arterials to provide best accessibility to the largest possible service area).

• *Public uses for site provided by private applicant site plans.* Sites most commonly reserved for nonprofit organizations or dedicated for public uses by applicants on site plans are (in descending order): churches, neighborhood parks, public elementary schools, community centers, libraries, junior high schools, fire stations, and police stations. Each of these uses has its own particular needs. Heads of departments and agencies accepting these sites should analyze the site plan proposals for their needs. But keep in mind that these people may not recognize realistic development needs and cost relationships involved in their preferences for best sites.

Commercial and office land uses

• *Density and intensity of development:* Examine site plans for crowding of buildings on the site—density of structures on the site should be in keeping with the character of the neighborhood. Examine the site plan for excessive coverage of the site by buildings and paved surfaces (parking areas, service areas, plazas), lack of landscaped open space, trees, buffer screening, and poorly designed or defined use of site

perimeter.

• *Dominance of structures on the site* can change the perceived character of nearby residential neighborhoods. This occurs in three ways: trip generation is so large that it increases traffic congestion radically on nearby arterial and local streets; height of buildings pierce the tree-line or create a skyscraper effect that visually gives a commercial sense to residential areas; building mass and floor area is so much larger that the perception of the predominant character of land use in the neighborhood is changed.

• *Architecture of buildings and site element.* Which facades of commercial/office buildings have architecturally finished exteriors? Do all four facades of free-standing buildings have finished exterior walls? In there coordination of architectural styles, colors, materials, textures among multibuilding commercial/office buildings on a site? Does architectural style meet special community design guidelines (e.g., earthtone colors, Southwestern or colonial/Georgian architecture) to blend with or give unified design image to the community? Visibility and design of site furniture should relate to the image of the occupant on the site.

• *Relationship between primary and secondary site uses.* Secondary site uses are often located on separate sites. These separate sites are shown on the site plan as pads or locations in parking areas or are separate outparcels for uses such as: auto accessories and service, gas stations, banks and savings and loans, drive-up services, photo processing, bank ATMs, telephone booths, self-service postal service stations. Convenience-use functions of buildings on pads and outparcels should not conflict with primary function of site or with traffic circulation on or to the site.

• *Conformance to required yards and spacing between buildings.* Spacing between buildings must meet zoning and fire code requirements, including access by fire trucks and garbage trucks. Perimeter of site parcel must have required setbacks, yards, screening, and landscaping. Zoning conformance must be correct for setbacks and yards for buildings on outparcels or zone lots; height of all buildings and structures including poles, antennas and roof signs, gross floor area of buildings on main-use site parcel and on separate zone lots or outparcels, and gross leasable area must be clearly defined on floor plans of buildings to meet zoning requirements per parking area.

• *Fences and walls* must meet zoning ordinance requirements to screen the site from adjacent parcels and to screen service areas (trash areas, dumpsters, outdoor storage, parking of commercial vehicles, and loading and dock areas). Fences must meet height, opacity, allowable decoration requirements, outdoor lighting must not give glare off site, and site lighting provides required minimum intensity of lighting (in lumens) for parking areas, streets, and pedestrian areas.

• *Parking and loading* requirements. Site plans must have the legally required number of parking and loading spaces. Examine each parking space on plans for adequate length and width, and aisle width and length in relation to proposed angle of parking. Loading spaces must meet legally required dimensions. Wheel stop blocks at each parking space should not permit bumpers of vehicles to project over property lines or sidewalks, or touch fences, walls, and buildings. Vehicle turnarounds at ends of rows of parking aisles must be properly sized to allow vehicles to turn around without difficulty.

• *Access by emergency services.* The site plan must allow access by fire fighting vehicles to all parts of buildings. The location of fire lanes must be coordinated with the location of fire hydrants, and aisles and drives that pass under buildings and arcades and through tunnels must meet minimum clearance to allow passage of cars, trucks, and fire trucks.

• *Landscaping, signs, site furniture.* Proposed landscaping must be of legally allowable plant species in allowable sizes of caliper/plant height; percent coverage of site open space must be provided; each sign must meet sign area requirements for each individual sign and for all signs for each type of sign category; and freestanding pole and ground signs must meet setback, height, and yard requirements and sign distance triangle requirements at street and driveway intersections.

Industrial uses

• *Need for specialized assistance in the site plan review.* Planners and plan examiners often do not have the technical expertise to understand many industrial processes and analyze them for their development impact and conformance to development codes. You might require, through development regulation, additional fees to be paid by the applicant if the community needs to retain appropriate engineering consultants to analyze and interpret industrial processes. These consultants can also review your proposed site plan changes to conform to your development regulations.

• *Specialized site analysis information* may need to be supplied by the applicant at your request to allow public agencies to review the site plan at full physical development to determine the community's ability to service the site and meet off-site community needs. This information could include: number of employees at various shifts (for local streets to handle the site's rush hour traffic); volume and characteristics of freight and cargos and how they are transported to and from, and stored on, the site; volume of, and peak demand for, water usage from public water system; on-site reuse of water supply; on-site treatment of water and liquid wastes prior to drainage to public sewerage system; identification of chemicals, substances, liquid and solid wastes generated and used within industrial processes, and an explanation of their special adverse, toxic, corrosive, acidic/caustic properties; projected release and discharge of gasses and airborne pollutants regularly or an emergency basis, needing air quality regulation—perhaps by state and federal agencies; amount of storm runoff; and potential adverse chemical composition of storm runoff from residual on-site wastes drained from the site by rain.

• *Permitted uses.* Determine which potential industrial uses can occupy the site as implied by site design and layout. A common difficulty of industrial site plans is that the site can be designed to allow many uses not permitted by site zoning, either as an allowable use or by conformance to the performance standards of the zone district. Performance standards and regulatory requirements for permitted uses can vary considerably within an industrial zone. Proposed industrial zones can also vary considerably—from research park zones through warehouse zones, from light industrial through heavy industrial to mining-extraction zones. Site design and layout must bear a reasonable relationship to uses that the applicant intends to be accommodated on the site and for all other uses permitted in the site's zone district(s).

• *Adequacy of public transportation facilities* to support industrial development. Require the applicant to pay for the costs of the facilities needed to meet specialized traffic problems unique to the industrial use and to meet traffic volumes generated by the site use well beyond that normally generated by site development. Most commonly required is: additional off-site traffic control for streets nearby and adjacent to industrial sites to accommodate very high levels of rush hour traffic at shift changes; additional ROW to be dedicated to accommodate widened public streets to provide additional street capacity; traffic signals and control devices; traffic turning lanes from adjacent arterial streets; and rebuilding or constructing new streets serving the site to provide heavy industrial truck and freight load-bearing capacity.

• *Railroad tracks crossing public streets* to service the site. Applicant must obtain permission from appropriate state and local agencies and submit a written commitment by the railroad company to construct (and pay for) railroad spur tracks that cross public ROW and streets to the site—and provide crossing control signals. Agreements need to be concluded among applicant, railroad company, and public agencies to ascertain who pays for future maintenance of spur track street crossing and signals and who accepts liability for accidents at these crossings.

• *Adequacy of water and waste-related public facilities.* Industrial processes often use large quantities of water and generate waste water effluents that are much larger in volume than can be handled by public water supply and waste water treatment systems. Industrial processes may generate effluents that are not treatable by the community treatment system without great public cost. This may require the industrial applicant to provide additional community facilities to meet these needs, which include: on-site recovery, reuse, and recirculation of "grey" waste water (not containing sanitary wastes), to reduce draw-down of the public water supply, provide on-site pretreatment of sewage to remove industrial solvents, chemicals, substances, and solids; and provide additional capacity of public water supply distribution system serving the site.

• *Adequacy of emergency services serving the site.* Specialized capital facilities or equipment may need to be provided or paid for by the applicant. This includes providing additional water pressure for fire fighting at the site; supplying the site with additional on-site fire fighting and security service because of special needs that the public services are unable to provide to serve this one site without exceptional cost (e.g., special fire apparatus to suppress chemical fires and fires in radiation hazard areas); shifting location of buildings, storage tanks, and structures housing fireprone and other hazardous activities and materials away from other buildings, property lines, critical access routes, gas and utility lines, and public water supply lines; and changing site topography and grades to provide containment dikes surrounding large storage tanks.

• *Zoning bulk and development regulations* that must be met include minimum yards; additional yards if site abuts different zoning (such as residential, open space, or office zones); spacing between buildings on-site; special yards and spacing requirements for industrial uses determined to be dangerous by the zoning ordinance or interpretation by planning/zoning administrator; height of buildings and industrial apparatus and structures; and on-site dwelling units for caretakers and security staff.

• *Fencing and lighting.* Site plan must meet zone district fencing requirements for industrial sites, including security, safety, and screening fencing requirements, and fencing required for outdoor storage of automobiles, industrial equipment, and for junk yards. On-site industrial lighting must not create off-site glare at night.

• *Conformance to industrial performance standards.* Typical performance standards and siting solutions are: odor (change location or odor-producers on site plan, change volume of industrial process activity to reduce strength of odor, allow industrial process creating odor only to occur with downwind dispersal away from urban areas); smoke and air pollution (provide air scrubbers and bagging of pollutants, dispersal chimneys); glare (enclose weld-

ing and other glare-producing processes that are visible off the site); noise (enclose noise generators inside buildings, shift doors and windows to building walls facing away from noise-sensitive uses, shift noise-generating processes to daylight hours when noise standards may be less stringent, provide acoustic noise dampening, or change industrial process to reduce/eliminate adverse noise problem — frequency; pitch, beat); vibration (shift industrial process to alternative location on site where vibration is dampened by more favorable soil/subsoil, change design of foundations and structural load-bearing frame to dampen or absorb vibration, or increase distance to property line); eletromagnectic interference and nuclear radiation (adequate shielding or change in industrial processes to resolve interference/radiation, or dispersal to safe levels by relocation on-site).

Mixed Uses

• *Project is a genuine mixed-use project.* Applicant's proposed uses must meet the spirit and intent of mixed-use zone district objectives. Applicants commonly will propose mixed-use zoning but file a site plan with a few mixed uses, reserving for future development other mixed uses — this is often a hedge to allow developer to change site uses without filing for new zoning. Is the applicant's mixed-use site plan really a single-use site plan with individual uses separated from one another as outparcels and zone lots on separate lease-holds or building sites?

• *Conflict of amenity and liveability of mixed uses.* Analyze mixed-use plans to optimize liveability and amenity (which mixed-use projects seek to emphasize) among uses. This helps the project to achieve its potential and avoids later abandonment of one or more of the mixed uses adversely affected by poor site plan design or site design mistakes. Examples of conflicts are abutting incompatible activities (residential areas too close to restaurants—noise, cooking, odors, trash storage); views and aesthetics of two adjacent uses are incongruous (commercial parking lot abutting office high-image front yard open space), traffic circulation of various uses conflict with one another (office workers must walk through commercial store malls to get to their offices, outdoor use areas are not compatible with one another and with adjacent buildings (decorative high-jet water fountain blowing water mist onto busy pedestrian plaza); and unified and complementary architectural design control for site buildings with different uses and ownerships.

Site Infrastructure

Circulation

• *Community to supply adequate level of traffic service.* How will site plan affect size, location, and capacity of roads and streets that serve the proposed development? The measure of adequate service is analysis of trip generation to and from and on the site for a typical 24-hour period, and for seasonal characteristics of the use (commercial traffic at Christmas shopping season) that provide expected levels of traffic service.

• *Dedications and ownership of streets.* To meet desired level of traffic service, the applicant is commonly required to provide these site plan changes and design requirements: dedicated additional ROW for on-site industrial local streets, shift location of streets on the site; change ownership of streets, drives and aisles within site plan to/from private/public ownership to resolve questions of who, is to pay cost of street maintenance, accept liability for accidents in the ROW, and assure fire and security/police access on the site—especially if parts of the site are blocked off to public access.

• *Public transit access.* Applicant may need to provide pedestrian waiting shelters and

benches for mass transit/bus transit; provide turnarounds for mass transit buses, especially where public transit system will change its routes to serve the site; provide additional ROW for bus turnout areas to accommodate bus passenger loading areas; agree to subsidize the cost (or portion of each fare) of new bus transit route to serve the site.

• *Physical changes to traffic elements in site plans.* The applicant must provide or pay for these items (in descending order as commonly is required of applicants on site plans): changes to street gradients and profiles to accommodate storm drainage from the ROW and paved street surfaces; changes in street grades to adjust vertical/horizontal sight distances for safe design driving speeds; provide right-turn lanes onto the site from public streets; provide right-turn acceleration lane from the site to major abutting streets; provide additional traffic (moving) lanes on public streets abutting site; provide various conduits, drainage channels, culverts, swales, drain inlets, and box culverts for storm drainage in ROW along property lines of site abutting public streets; provide traffic signals at intersections of existing public streets intersecting near or abutting site, or with public street and entrance/exit drives/streets from the site.

Storm drainage

• *The storm drainage system is often inadequate* on site plans, especially from less experienced developers. Applicants often fail to recognize or understand storm drainage site needs or understand the local history of storm drainage problems peculiar to the site and neighborhood. But applicants also sometimes want to propose an inadequate storm drainage system; it is quite expensive to build and, if designed correctly, often dictates a less desirable site layout for location of buildings, parking areas, and drives.

• *Performance standard for site storm drainage.* In

recent years, many communities have greatly increased storm drainage site standards required for site development. Communities require that the site be designed so that the peak water discharge from the site by designated five- to ten-year storms not be increased by site development. To meet this standard, the developer often must provide extensive (and expensive) storm containment facilities on the site.

• *Drainage structures required.* The grading plan must provide at least a minimal slope for all flat surfaces exposed to open rain or that channel storm waters. These include parking areas, streets, drives, plazas, lawn, and landscaped areas, and sidewalks. Roof surfaces must also provide for site storm drainage. Ground surfaces must slope toward catchment inlets. Inlets are located along curbs, with gutters, or are located at designed low points in parking areas and wide pavements; they should connect with channels of sufficient storm capacity. Channels should empty out to either sur-face drainage swales and larger channels or to larger catchments as box culverts, perhaps after intervening travel in above-ground ditches or channels. These culverts eventually drain to ground surface channels and swales.

• *Design storm frequency must be correctly calculated.* The applicant may need to show his assumptions and calculations for the frequency, intensity, and seasonal characteristics of storms that typically occur in your community if the adequacy of his storm drainage system is questioned. His calculations must support the designed size and capacity of the site's storm drainage structures. Storms that are expected to occur once every five to ten years are most commonly provided for smaller site plans. Larger site plans, those of possibly 40-plus acres, may also be required (or contribute to the cost of) major drainage structures that are designed to accommodate 100-year storms, or provide dams and dikes overlooking other property to accommodate 500-year storm drainage.

Appendix 6.A

Building Placement Criteria

Manual: Design and Control of Land Development in Suburban Communities

---

John Seddon and Anthony Corkill   Institute of Rational Design, Inc.

Below is a list of criteria for determining building types and their location and orientation on a site. These are derived from basic principles of the effects of the environment on buildings and activities.

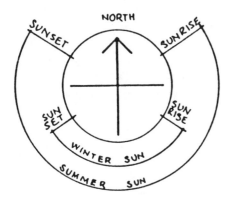

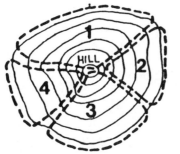

SUN

desirable slope orientation
- winter   morning and afternoon
          south-east to south-west
- summer   early morning and late
          afternoon east, west

undesirable slope orientation
- winter   west, north, east
- summer   south-east to south-west

aspects of the sides of a hill
1 cold side
2 cool side morning
3 hot side (summer)
4 warm side evening

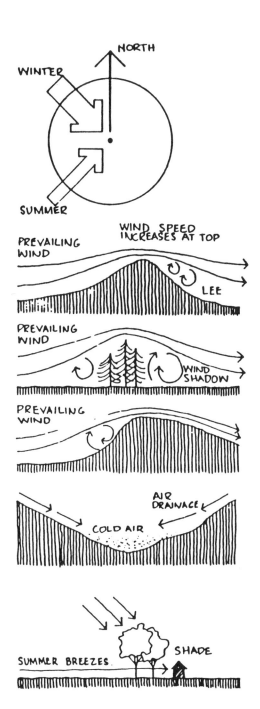

WIND

desirable   summer breezes
undesirable winter prevailing winds

buildings
insulate to protect from cold winds
and open to allow winds to cool
in summer

locate buildings on the lee side of
the hill to protect them from winter
prevailing winds

locate buildings or plant hedgerows
or tree buffers to protect them from
prevailing winter winds

the most desirable location for building with respect to wind and hills also
depends on the shape of the hill

cold air accumulates in valley floors
and then tends to move down the
valley   this is particularly a night-
time effect

plant trees to protect buildings from
summer sun but allow for breezes

deciduous trees are desirable as they
provide shade in summer while letting
the winter sun through

hot air rises causing the air from colder areas to move in under the rising hot air   this process causes a circular movement with air moving from cold areas to hot areas

design buildings and layouts to take into account the daytime and night-time direction of air movement

DRAINAGE

maintain natural, surface drainage system

provide storage for excess runoff in lakes and temporary ponds

avoid building in flood plains (conform to the national flood insurance program)

locate structures in areas that are not prone to natural disasters or build structures that can withstand the natural disaster (e.g. hurricanes, tornados, earthquakes, tidal inundation, mudslides, erosion, floods, subsidence, etc.)

SOILS

structural quality of the soils should determine type of construction

maintain soil as a fertile medium for plant growth

minimize earthmoving requirements

restrict construction areas and movement of heavy machinery to avoid
unnecessary soil compaction

stockpile topsoil from excavated areas
for reuse after construction is completed

provide subgrade drainage of all wet
soils, discharging into surface drainage
system

maintain water balance and water table
by avoiding compaction of soil, massive
regrading and high coverage (causing
excessive runoff)

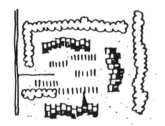

VEGETATION

utilize existing tree patterns
- lines
  maintain scale, rhythm and form of
  hedgerows and other linear elements

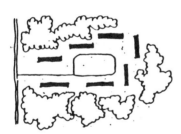

- areas
  large scale structures relate well to
  large masses of trees, woods or
  forests

  areas can be cleared creating tree
  masses to relate to building complexes

- points
  scattered clumps and individual trees
  relate well to single family houses

  build in woods rather than treeless
  fields

maintain visual continuity by avoiding
indiscriminate tree planting

maintain habitats for wildlife by insti-
gating a vegetation management program

new tree plantings should complement
existing trees to be preserved

TOPOGRAPHY

design and place buildings so that they
follow contour lines and relate to the
form of the terrain

build on the sides of hills not on the
top so that the form of the natural
feature will be protected

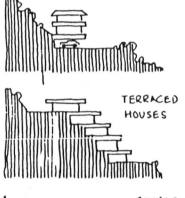

use slopes to create parking spaces
under buildings

TERRACED
HOUSES

on steep slopes design buildings for
that unique condition

imposed structures may hug the slope

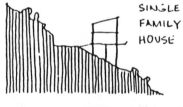

SINGLE
FAMILY
HOUSE

stand completely free

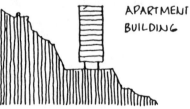

APARTMENT
BUILDING

rest on a platform

avoid high land coverage on rough, unique and/or steep terrain   it is possible to keep the same floor area ratio while minimizing the coverage by building multi-story structures

unique soil conditions or fragile eco- logical system such as sand dunes require designs that do not disturb the natural system

preserve natural features such as rock outcrops, trees, etc. rather than "improving" them for ease of construction

	SLOPE	CONDITION AND SITE IMPROVEMENTS	SUGGESTED TYPE OF RESIDENTIAL USE
	flat	requires regrading and underground drainage system	
	0%-5%	best left with no major development or construction	recreation open space
	gently sloping	most development can be sited with minor reshaping of land	all housing types
	3%-10%	generally good for building	single family houses
	rolling	low retaining walls may be required around roads and parking areas	
	5%-20%	generally good but less coverage	town houses
	steep	very high or tiered retaining walls may be necessary to accommodate grade changes - minimize	no parking lots
	15%-30%	land coverage	apartments
	very steep	foundations and retaining structures are usually prohibitive in cost	
	over 30%	avoid building and construction of all types	open space

note   the suggested residential use is only meant as a guide and is based on land coverage and access only - combinations and/or changes can be made

VISUAL

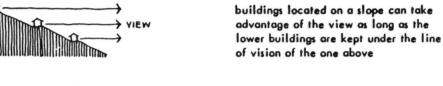

buildings located on a slope can take advantage of the view as long as the lower buildings are kept under the line of vision of the one above

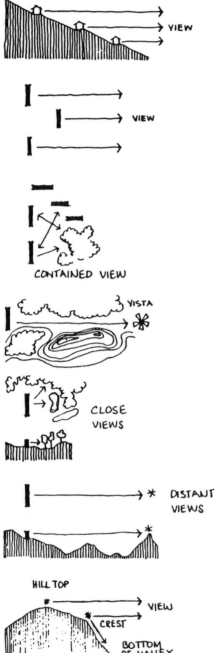

buildings on flat terrain have to be placed so they do not block the view

when the terrain offers no view the buildings should be placed so that an internal or contained view becomes significant

place buildings to take advantage of vistas or to create vistas

design and place buildings to take advantage of both close views and distant views

the brow or crest of a hill is a more critical location than the top of the hill as it offers views down the hill into the valley as well as distant views out

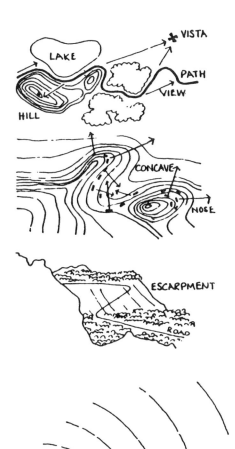

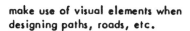

make use of visual elements when designing paths, roads, etc.

hollows or concave slopes are en- closed, sheltered, oriented internally or to a focused view

noses or convex slopes are exposed, expansive, oriented outward to a general view

avoid crossing prominent landforms with roads or other man-made structures there- fore maintaining the identity or integrity of the features

SOUND

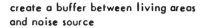

create a buffer between living areas and noise source

avoid prominent sites for projects that generate a lot of noise e.g. industry, highways, airports, etc.

noise reverberates through and along valleys

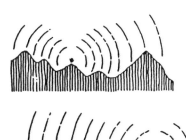

noise travels very well across water bodies

The design criteria below cover basic principles of organization of buildings and access into a coherent system or pattern for a site. These principles should be combined with the site derived from the previous pages in the design of a conceptual site plan.

MOVEMENT PATTERN

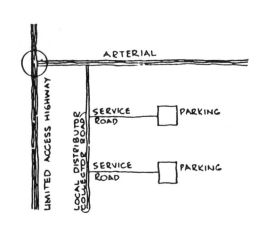

create a hierarchy of roads each
with a clearly defined function
- limited access highway (interstate)
  inter-city, high speed, no development, grade separated interchanges

- arterial (state)
  intra-city or county
  no development

- local distributor (county or town)
  slow moving
  sidewalks
  some frontage access

- service road (minor street)
  building access
  sidewalks
  no through traffic

avoid through traffic in residential
neighborhoods by the correct selection
of street pattern

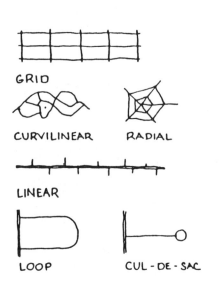

no hierarchy of roads created
through traffic is possible (except
within the pattern)

patterns o.k. for collector systems but
not so good for residential neighborhoods

hierarchy created but allow for too much
access i.e. causes strip development

through traffic not possible therefore
good for service roads in residential
neighborhoods

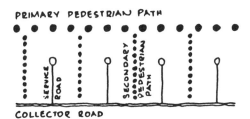

separate vehicular and pedestrian movements

separate the functional uses of roads and paths (trucks, busses, bicycles, children, idle strollers, etc.)

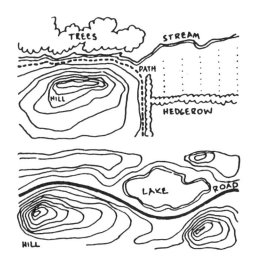

walkways and paths should follow natural and/or man-made edges and linear elements

roads and paths should follow contour lines and other natural features

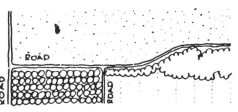

roads should follow established man-made or natural patterns, forms, edges and lines

DEVELOPMENT PATTERN

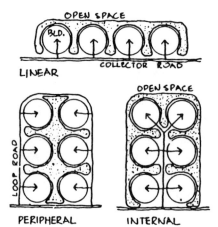

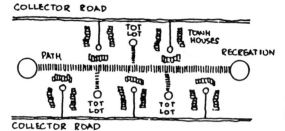

create an organized pattern of roads,
open space, paths, land use
and activities

distribute activities according to
proximity, location and linkage

create a compatible environment

cluster like uses

create an overall mixture of uses and
type of unit for variety

avoid a mixture of uses that are not
compatible – e.g. heavy industry
and residential

create an environment that is in sym-
pathy and harmony with the natural
and man-made resources of the area

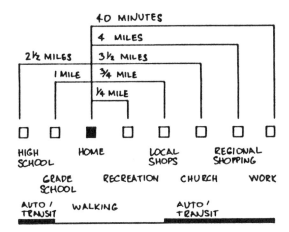

create residential developments with
identifiable neighborhoods with a good
relationship to all other activities

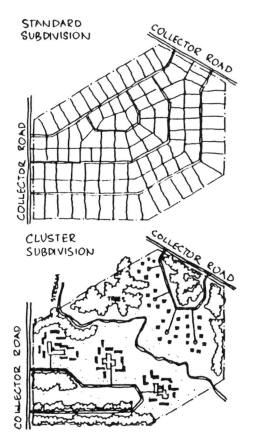

residential and other uses should be
clustered to preserve natural features
and to create a harmonious living and
working environment

7

Regulating Appearance

Text by Peggy Glassford
Drawings by Robert C. Ballou

Many towns and cities have taken tentative steps toward aesthetic control of new development through the adoption of landscaping ordinances or parking lot design regulations. Often these requirements are written into zoning ordinances and call for specific standards, such as a certain percentage of a parking area to be landscaped or landscaping of a certain height to screen a parking lot. Although much of what is contained in the standard zoning ordinance may be aesthetic in intent, zoning ordinances usually stop just short of design control. For example, they commonly dictate what size sign is permitted but do not address the design of the sign or its harmonious placement in the existing environment.

Frustrated with the limitations of traditional zoning requirements, some communities have sought to control design through an incentive approach. In Needham, Massachusetts, for example, eight "choiceful" guidelines have been

established for sign design. These guidelines cover such factors as compatibility with building design or enhancement of architectural elements. A sign committee appointed by the selectmen decides if the guidelines have been met. If four of the eight guidelines have been met by an applicant, the committee can vary certain zoning requirements. It may, for example, allow a larger sign than is normally permitted in order to obtain better design.

In some communities, community recognition for good design is an important incentive. In Myrtle Beach, South Carolina, for example, a community appearance board reviews all multifamily and commercial development. This board reportedly is successful in raising the collective consciousness of the town regarding good design. Two factors appear to give the board credibility within the community. First, more than half of its members are from the business community. Second, an annual design awards program conducted by the board has enhanced its visibility and importance. According to the local planning director, the awards now have a degree of prestige and are in the minds of architects and developers.

Many communities, however, have taken much stronger action to control their aesthetic future. In these cities and towns, boards and commissions have been established to review development for compliance with legislated standards for good design. Where design approval is not given, a building permit can be denied. Scottsdale, Arizona, has such a process for development within certain specified districts. Mono County, California, has created an independent design review authority that reviews commercial, public use, and multifamily projects for compliance with established design standards. Lawrence, Massachusetts, has created a design review board to review signs and facade renovation in the downtown area. The Lawrence board has the right to deny an application if it does not meet the established standards. For eight years, the Edmonds, Washington, design board has reviewed all development for compliance with legislated criteria for landscaping, signs, and architecture. An applicant must get approval from the Edmonds Design Review Board before the building permit is issued.

Municipalities across the country have begun to accept the challenge of controlling design for better quality in the built environment. The approach taken by a group of suburban Chicago communities is typical. These communities have taken on the formidable task of legislating for aesthetic quality through the adoption of appearance codes—local ordinances that regulate the exterior design features of commercial, multifamily, or industrial structures in the community. Usually an appointed public body referred to as an appearance commission is given the authority to determine if there is compliance with the appearance code. Appearance commission members thus become the arbiters of good taste for the community.

"Variation of detail, form, and siting shall be used to provide visual interest."

"The orientation of buildings to provide access through rear entrances is encouraged."

APPEARANCE REVIEW PROCEDURES

Perhaps the easiest way to understand the appearance review required by a typical appearance code is to take a walk through the process. Single-family uses usually are exempt from appearance regulation, although they may be covered by some other architectural regulation in the community. Generally, new or remodeled exterior designs for any use except single-family homes are subject to regulation by the appearance code. A merchant who wants to remodel his storefront, for example, would need appearance approval to get a building permit.

The first step is usually a discussion with the municipal staff member, usually a planner, who administers the appearance code. At this point, the merchant and his architect are advised of code requirements. They are given a copy of the code itself and a list of the documents that are required. After the merchant and his designer have had an opportunity to digest the requirements, they may ask the planning staff to answer questions, give help with time lines, or, in some cases, assist in design suggestions. Usually, a specific deadline will be set several days before the appearance commission meeting for submittal of documents. This allows staff lead time for reviewing the proposal, making comments, asking for more information if necessary, and distributing the proposal to commission members prior to the meeting.

Required documents vary depending on the project, but they must contain sufficient detail to explain the physical change to the site. An elevation may be required along with a site plan showing landscaping and all details of the site. Usually one of the elevations must be in color. Photographs are often required to illustrate adjoining properties or the site itself. A sample of the materials to be used in construction would be required.

Many communities allow preliminary and final hearings for a project. The preliminary hearing gives the applicant an opportunity to discuss the proposal with the commission before going on to final design. Preliminary hearings are optional; the final hearing before the commission is required and will result in approval or denial of the proposal. However, this hearing may continue for several commission meetings, during which petitioner and commission negotiate a design that commission members deem in compliance with the appearance code. Once approved, the proposal is given a certificate of approval, which instructs the building department to issue a building permit if all other municipal code requirements are met. After the building permit is issued, all design elements must be completed as approved in order for an occupancy certificate to be issued. Many appearance codes require continuing maintenance of the design that has been approved. Usually this requirement is used to ensure that landscaping materials will be maintained after an occupancy permit is issued.

Procedural requirements for appearance review vary. For example, some communities require a formal public hearing with the attendant legal notification. Some do not provide a preliminary hearing. For others, there is no provision for continuing maintenance.

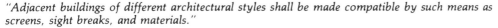

"Adjacent buildings of different architectural styles shall be made compatible by such means as screens, sight breaks, and materials."

THE TYPICAL CODE

The appearance codes of the many communities are basically similar. Appearance code requirements that must be met are performance standards, not specific requirements. For example, rather than requiring a certain number of trees of a particular kind based on the area of the site, the code may state that, "Landscape treatment shall be provided to enhance architectural features, strengthen vistas and important axes, and...provide shade." Or, businesses would not have to confine their storefronts to wood or metal or glass, but would have to use materials that would have "good architectural character and shall be selected for harmony with the building and adjoining buildings." Similiarly, a code may not require a wall sign used on a new facade to be ivory and back-lighted but "the colors, materials, and lighting of the sign shall be restrained and harmonious with the building and site to which it principally relates." Such are the standards of appearance codes. The introduction to the Highland Park, Illinois, appearance code justifies performance requirements as follows:

> The problem with any quest for precise standards in design review is simply that there are some varieties of "aesthetic" regulation for which sensible details are impossible to prescribe without defeating the very purpose of the regulation....Precise standards direct the attention of design communities to the superficialities of style instead of to the basic aspects of design that are likely to affect community life.[1]

The typical appearance code is divided into several sections. First, there generally is an introductory comment stating the intent and purpose of the code. Nearly every municipality is careful to mention some aspect of the police powers so that the code is said to promote the public health, safety, and welfare. Usually some economic objective is also mentioned, such as enhancement or preservation of property values. This language is meant to justify municipal involvement in aesthetic matters. The importance of establishing these purposes should be discussed with the municipal attorney.

The code also usually includes a section that describes the geographic area involved. Most codes include all zoning districts except single-family residential.

A third section of an appearance code usually is devoted to definitions. Some definitions are architectural in nature. "Logic of design," for example, is defined in one ordinance as "accepted principles and criteria of validity in the solution of the problems of design." Other definitions delimit the nature of a catch-all phrase. Utility hardware, in the same code, for example, is defined as "Devices, such as poles, crossarms, transformers and vaults, gas pressure regulating assemblies, hydrants, and buffalo boxes that are used for water, gas, oil sewer, and electrical services to a building or project." Some definitions confront the sublime. One, for example, defines attractive as "having qualities that arouse interest and pleasure in the observer." See Appendix 7.A for an example of a definitions section.

The heart of any appearance code is the section that establishes the criteria for appearance (see Appendix 7.B for an example). It is here that the performance standards are set. In order to help the applicant understand the criteria, a few codes use graphics within the text of the code. The elements that are addressed in the appearance criteria section may include all or any of the following:
• Building design
• Relationship of building to site
• Relationship of project to adjoining area
• Landscape and site treatment
• Signs
• Lighting

- Street hardware
- Miscellaneous structures
- Maintenance

Many of the appearance criteria deal with good scale and proportion for harmony and compatibility. Some, such as requirements for screening mechanical equipment, are more prosaic. Overall, the standards depend heavily on the subjective judgment of those who apply them. It is at this point that aesthetic legislation is most vulnerable. Who can say what is beautiful? And isn't beauty, after all, in the eye of the beholder? A recently conducted survey indicates that the appearance commission "beholders" in eight selected communities are meeting the challenge with great aplomb.[2]

THE SURVEY

Staff members of eight selected communities responded to a questionnaire that was designed to obtain factual information concerning appearance codes and opinions on the value of the appearance review process to the municipalities involved.

Several survey questions were included that were intended to disclose the impact of appearance review in the various municipalities. When asked if the adoption of an appearance code has improved the quality of development in the community, seven communities responded affirmatively. The remaining municipality had only recently adopted a code and believed it was too early to make a judg-

"Monotony of design in single or multiple building projects shall be avoided. Variation of detail, form, and siting shall be used to provide visual interest."

ment. The municipality's staff did comment, however, that many applicants thought they had a better project as a result of appearance commission review.

When asked to elaborate concerning "success stories," many communities responded that they had had great success in dealing with franchised businesses. The appearance review of a pastry outlet in one community resulted in a change of color for the tile roof; the change has since been adopted by the company for all its new installations. In other cases, communities report Kentucky Fried Chicken stores without buckets and McDonald's restaurants without arches. Such successes may help put to rest the notion that a company with a logo or trademark will go elsewhere if the community wants modification of its signs. According to the survey, other appearance review successes resulted in better design, more landscaping, more harmonious exteriors for downtown development, and generally better signage. One community reported that a proposed condominium development with too large an asphalt parking area came away from appearance review with underground parking, green areas, and patios for all units.

Many survey respondents commented that the review process becomes a kind of creative negotiation between petitioner and commission. With this kind of give-and-take, commissioners can be persuasive without threatening the developer. Occasionally, however, no middle ground can be reached, and an application will be denied.

When asked what they saw as the major benefits of appearance review, five of the eight communities referred to the advantage of design continuity, particularly for the central business district, when old and new buildings are blended. Several mentioned the development of community awareness and desire to improve the quality of the environment. Ad-

ditional benefits, of course, were more attractive buildings, landscaping, and signs. One interesting benefit listed by two communities was that the review process provided free professional advice to small businesses.

In response to a question regarding the problems of appearance review, three communities suggested that appearance review requirements be well advertised among developers and the business community because it is difficult to obtain conformity to the code if plans are already drawn. Awareness of an appearance code helps developers in two ways: they more realistically can predict how long the development process will take, and they can learn the ground rules before the design is started.

The extended time required for project approval was listed as a problem in one village. Occasionally, it was reported, developers have gone elsewhere to avoid the community's sometimes time-consuming review process. Several communities have attempted to prevent unnecessary time delays by providing detailed guides to the process. (See Appendixes 7.C and 7.D for examples.) Commissions also try to accommodate schedules by meeting twice, rather than once, a month. In some communities, building department review is required to occur concurrently with appearance review. Certainly, municipalities are aware of the potential for delay in the approval process.

Another problem has been the lack of qualified people willing to donate the time necessary to serve on the commissions. Nearly all staff members agreed that some degree of expertise among commissioners is desirable. Since many of the standards in appearance codes are subjective, it is necessary that a person with design experience guide the commission in its deliberations; otherwise, judgments are likely to be capricious and unreasonable, or may be viewed as such. If there are no commission members with "aesthetic credentials," it is more difficult to garner the respect of the business community or developers who are affected by the commission's decisions. In some communities it may be necessary to hire a consultant to provide guidance or to hire staff with design backgrounds. In some communities where there is strong enthusiasm for appearance review, an architect serves as staff liaison to the commission. One such community has a department of urban design with two full-time staff members and some part-time personnel, and meetings between staff and developers are likely to result in actual sketches to help solve design problems. Where staff expertise is lacking, a preliminary conference with the commission can establish the same rapport and assistance, provided that some member or members of the commission have the desired credentials.

Although not listed as a serious problem, one administrator mentioned the potential for appearance reviews to result in the kind of conformity that may, in effect, destroy individual creativity. Too many signs with ivory letters or dark brown backgrounds could quash the charm of individuality. The fact that most codes stress the desire for creative design seems to signal an awareness among communities of a potential problem. A number of codes, for example, include statements such as, "These criteria are not intended to restrict imagination, innovations, or variety, but rather to assist in focusing on design principles that can result in creative solutions. . . ."

In those communities where continued maintenance is required, compliance can sometimes be difficult to achieve. In one village, the local K mart decided that maintenance of landscaping materials was not on its agenda, despite repeated requests by the village. Since the business existed as a result

of special use approval, a legal notice was published as the first step to consider the revocation of the special use. K mart officials had a change of heart after seeing the legal notice, and the landscaping was restored to the condition required by the appearance certificate of approval. In another case, the same community revoked an occupancy permit and turned off the water in order to achieve compliance.

Finally, one community mentioned a problem caused by conflict between the plan commission and the appearance commission. Not much can be done if such conflict is political, but care should be taken to eliminate procedural conflict by a clear delineation of the duties of each appointed body. Another solution to this problem may be to give the appearance commission function to an advisory committee of the plan commission. Such an arrangement may, however, give nonexperts on the plan commission an opportunity to veto recommendations of the committee.

CAUTIONS AND COMMENTS

The communities that have adopted appearance codes have been gathering experience in successful administration and enforcement of aesthetic legislation. The survey focused, in part, on the collected wisdom of those staff members who responded to survey questions. The information and advice drawn from the survey, from personal interviews, and from the writings of others experienced in aesthetic regulations have been combined to produce the following guide to good appearance code regulations:

1. *Develop and adopt a code of standards for appearance review.* Although difficult to create, a code of standards gives guidance to applicants and avoids the charge that the community is totally arbitrary in appearance and design

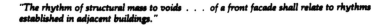

review.

2. *Develop clear procedural guidelines to give to every applicant.* Step-by-step instructions help developers and business people understand procedures, time lines, and the necessary submittals. The whole process is much smoother if there is clear communication from the beginning.

3. *Make sure that the commission (or other design review body) includes people who have expertise in making aesthetic judgments; architects are particularly valuable.* This is not an area in which the lay person can operate as effectively as the expert. There are judgments involved that call for education and background in the principles of design. If no experts are available for the commission, an expert staff member or a consultant must be involved.

4. *Provide some procedure for conferring with staff and/or commission before final design.* A preapplication conference with staff and/or preliminary hearing before the commission gives the applicant an opportunity to discuss plans before a great deal of time or money is expended. If a certain design is inappropriate, the applicant will know beforehand. Guidance is also available to help ensure a speedy recovery at the final hearing.

5. *Keep time delays to a minimum.* One of the biggest objections by developers and business people to appearance review is the extra time required to get a building permit. Items 1 through 4 on this list will help to avoid delays. In addition, the commission should be prepared to hold extra meetings if necessary to speed up an approval.

6. *Be careful not to restrict creativity.* It would be unfortunate indeed if plans were denied simply because they were unusual. Uniformity in design review should mean application of basic design principles, not conformity in design.

7. *Efforts should be made to publicize the appearance review codes and procedures.* Two benefits should derive from this: first, developers will be aware of the requirements; and, second, the community will benefit from an awareness of the built environment. Both developer and community should be able to take pride in their product. A practical suggestion for publicizing the process is to give awards yearly for the best design effort.

Certainly this list is not inclusive, but adherence to these guidelines should result in excellent beginnings for the fledgling appearance code community.

NOTES

1. Highland Park, Illinois, *Appearance Code,* p. 3.

2. The survey was conducted in 1983 by the author of this chapter.

Appendix 7.A

Definitions

Libertyville, Illinois

Appearance The outward aspect visible to the public.

Appropriate Sympathetic, or fitting, to the context of the site and the whole community.

Appurtenances The visible, functional objects accessory to and part of buildings.

Architectural concept The basic aesthetic idea of a building, or group of buildings or structures, including the site and landscape development, that produces the architectural character.

Architectural feature A prominent or significant part or element of a building, structure, or site.

Architectural style The characteristic form and detail, as of buildings of a particular historic period.

Attractive Having qualitites that arouse interest and pleasure in the observer.

Berm A raised form of earth to provide screening or to improve the aesthetic character.

Code The Libertyville Municipal Code (Ordinance No. 77-0-61).

Cohesiveness Unity of composition between design elements of a building or a group of buildings and the landscape development.

Compatability Harmony in the appearance of two or more external design features in the same vicinity.

Conservation The protection and care that prevent destruction or deterioration of historical or otherwise significant structures, buildings, or natural resources.

Exterior building component An essential and visible part of the exterior of a building.

External design feature The general arrangement of any portion of a building, sign, landscaping, or structure and including the kind, color, and texture of the materials of such portion, and the types of roof, windows, doors, lights, attached or ground signs, or other fixtures appurtenant to such portions as will be open to public view from any street, place, or way.

Graphic element A letter, illustration, symbol, figure, insignia, or other device employed to express and illustrate a message or part thereof.

Harmony A quality that represent an appropriate and congruent arrangement of parts, as in an arrangement of varied architectural and landscape elements.

Landscape Plant materials, topography, and other natural physical elements combined in relation to one another and to man-made structures.

Light cut-off angle An angle from vertical, extending downward from a luminaire, which defines the maximum range of incident illumination outward at the ground plane.

Logic of design Accepted principles and criteria of validity in the solution of the problem of design.

Mechanical equipment Equipment, devices, and accessories, the use of which relates to water supply, drainage, heating, ventilating, air conditioning, and similar purposes.

Miscellaneous structures Structures, other than buildings, visible from public ways. Examples are: memorials, stagings, antennas, water tanks and towers, sheds, shelters, fences and walls, kennels, transformers, drive-up facilities.

Plant materials. Trees, shrubs, vines, ground covers, grass, perennials, annuals, bulbs.

Proportion Balanced relationship of the size of parts to each other and to the whole.

Scale Proportional relationship of the size of parts to one another and to the human figure.

Screening Structure of planting that conceals from view from public ways the area behind such structure or planting.

Shrub A multistemmed woody plant other than a tree.

Site break A structural or landscape device to interrupt long vistas and create visual interest in a site development.

Street hardware Man-made objects other than buildings that are part of the streetscape. Examples are: lamp posts, utility poles, traffic lights, traffic signs, benches, litter containers, planting containers, litter boxes, fire hydrants.

Streetscape The scene as may be observed along a public street or way composed of natural and man-made components, including buildings, paving, planting, street hardware, and miscellaneous structures.

Structure Anything constructed or erected, the use of which requires permanent or temporary location on or in the ground.

Utilitarian structure A structure or enclosure relating to mechanical or electrical services to a building or development.

Utility hardware Devices such as poles, crossarms, transformers, and vaults, gas pressure regulating assemblies, hydrants, and buffalo boxes that are used for water, gas, oil, sewer, and electrical services to a building or a project.

Utility service Any device, including wire, pipe, and conduit, which carries gas, water, electricity, oil, and communications into a building or development.

Village The Village of Libertyville, Illinois.

Appendix 7.B

Criteria for Appearance Codes

Highland Park, Illinois

The purpose of these criteria is to establish a checklist of those items that affect the physical aspect of Highland Park's environment. Pertinent to appearance is the design of the site, building and structures, planting, signs, street hardware, and miscellaneous other objects that are observed by the public.

These criteria are not intended to restrict imagination, innovation, or variety, but rather to assist in focusing on design principles, which can result in creative solutions that will develop a satisfactory visual appearance within the city, preserve taxable values, and promote the public health, safety, and welfare.

1. Relationship of Buildings to Site

a. The site shall be planned to accomplish a desirable transition with the streetscape and to provide for ade-quate planting, safe pedestrian movement, and parking areas.

b. Site planning in which setbacks and yards are in excess of zoning restrictions is encouraged to provide an interesting relationship between buildings.

c. Parking areas shall be treated with decorative elements, building wall extensions, plantings, berms, or other innovative means so as to screen parking areas from view from public ways.

d. Without restricting the permissible limits of the applicable zoning district, the height and scale of each building shall be compatible with its site and existing (or anticipated) adjoining buildings.

e. Newly installed utility services, and service revisions necessitated by exterior alterations, shall be underground.

"Without restricting the permissible limits of the applicable zoning district, the height and scale of each building shall be compatible with its site and existing (or anticipated) adjoining buildings."

2. Relationship of Buildings and Site to Adjoining Area

a. Adjacent buildings of different architectural styles shall be made compatible by such means as screens, sight breaks, and materials.

b. Attractive landscape transition to adjoining properties shall be provided.

c. Harmony in texture, lines, and masses is required. Monotony shall be avoided.

3. Landscape and Site Treatment

Landscape elements included in these criteria consist of all forms of planting and vegetation, ground forms, rock groupings, water patterns, and all visible construction except buildings and utilitarian structures.

a. Where natural or existing topographic patterns contribute to beauty and utility of a development, they shall be preserved and developed. Modification to topography will be permitted where it contributes to good appearance. . . .

b. Grades of walks, parking spaces, terraces, and other paved areas shall provide an inviting and stable appearance for walking and, if seating is provided, for sitting.

c. Landscape treatment shall be provided to enhance architectural features, strengthen vistas and important axes, and provide shade. Spectator effects shall be reserved for special locations only.

d. Utility of design shall be achieved by repetition of certain plant varieties and other materials and by correlation with adjacent developments.

e. Plant material shall be selected for interest in its structure, texture, and color, and for its ultimate growth. Plants that are indigenous to the area and others that will be hardy, harmonious to the design, and of good appearance shall be used.

f. In locations where plants will be susceptible to injury by pedestrian or motor traffic, they shall be protected by appropriate curbs, tree guards, or other devices.

g. Parking areas and traffic ways shall be enhanced with landscaped spaces containing trees or tree groupings.

h. Where building sites limit planting, the placement of trees in parkways or paved areas is encouraged. . . .

i. Screening of service yards and other places that tend to be unsightly shall be accomplished by use of walls, fencing, planting, or combinations of these. . . . Screening shall be equally effective in winter and summer.

j. In areas where general planting will not prosper, other materials such as fences, walls, and pavings of wood, brick, stone, gravel, and cobbles shall be used. Carefully selected plants shall be combined with such materials where possible.

k. Exterior lighting, when used, shall enhance the building design and the adjoining landscape. Lighting standards and building fixtures shall be of a design and size compatible with the building and adjacent areas . . . . Lighting shall be restrained in design and excessive brightness avoided.

4. Building Design

a. Architectural style is not restricted. Evaluation of the appearance of a project shall be based on the quality of its design and relationship to surroundings.

b. Buildings shall have good scale and be in harmonious conformance with permanent neighboring development.

c. (i) Materials shall have good architectural character and shall be selected for harmony of the building with adjoining buildings.

(ii) Materials shall be selected for suitability to the type of buildings and the design in which they are used. Buildings shall have the same materials, or those that are architecturally harmonious, used for all building walls and other exterior building components wholly or partly visible from public ways.

(iii) Materials shall be of durable quality.

(iv) In any design in which the structural frame is exposed to view, the structural materials shall be compatible within themselves and harmonious with their surroundings.

d. Building components, such as windows, doors, eaves, and parapets, shall have good proportions and relationships to one another.

e. Colors shall be harmonious and shall use only compatible accents.

f. Mechanical equipment or other utility hardware on roof, ground, or buildings shall be screened from public view with materials harmonious with the buildings, or they shall be so located as not to be visible from any public ways.

g. Exterior lighting shall be part of the architectural

concept. Fixtures, standards, and all exposed accessories shall be harmonious with building design.

h. Refuse and waste removal areas, service yards, storage yards, and exterior work areas shall be screened from view from public ways, using materials as stated in criteria for equipment screening.

i. Monotony of design in single or multiple building projects shall be avoided. Variation of detail, form, and siting shall be used to provide visual interest. In multiple building projects, variable siting or individual buildings may be used to prevent a monotonous appearance.

5. Signs

a. Every sign shall have good scale and proportion in its design and in its visual relationship to buildings and surroundings.

b. Every sign shall be designed as an integral architectural element of the building and site to which it principally relates.

c. The colors, materials, and lighting of every sign shall be restrained and harmonious with the building and site to which it principally relates.

d. The number of graphic elements on a sign shall be held to the minimum needed to convey the sign's major message and shall be composed in proportion to the area of the sign face.

e. Each sign shall be compatible with the signs on adjoining premises and shall not compete for attention.

f. Identification signs of a prototype design and corporation logos shall conform to the criteria for all other signs.

6. Miscellaneous Structures and Street Hardware

a. Miscellaneous structures and street hardware shall be designed to be part of the architectural concept of design and landscape. Materials shall be compatible with buildings, scale shall be good, colors shall be in harmony with buildings and surroundings, and proportions shall be attractive.

b. Lighting in connection with miscellaneous structures and street hardware shall meet the criteria applicable to site, landscape, buildings and signs.

7. Maintenance—Planning and Design Factors

a. Continued good appearance depends upon the extent and quality of maintenance. The choice of materials and their use, together with the types of finishes and other protective measures, must be conducive to easy maintenance and upkeep.

b. Materials and finishes shall be selected for their durability and wear as well as for their beauty. Proper measures and devices shall be incorporated for protection against the elements, neglect, damage, and abuse.

c. Provision for washing and cleaning of buildings and structures, and control of dirt and refuse, shall be included in the design. Configurations that tend to catch and accumulate debris, leaves, trash, dirt, and rubbish shall be avoided.

8. Factors for Evaluation

The following factors and characteristics, which affect the appearance of a development, will govern the Appearance Review Commission's evaluation of a design submission:

a. Conformance to ordinances and the Appearance Code

b. Logic of design

c. Exterior space utilization

d. Architectural character

e. Attractiveness

f. Material selection

g. Harmony and compatibility

h. Circulation—vehicular and pedestrian

i. Maintenance aspects

Appendix 7.C

Submittal Requirements

Libertyville, Illinois

All exhibits required for the permanent file (noted in the following paragraphs) must be able to be reduced to "legal size" (8½" × 14") by folding, photo reduction, etc. However, larger mounting boards, material samples, or other exhibits not meeting this criteria may be used for Commission presentation.

Three (3) black- or blue-line prints (one of which shall be colored) of the following required drawings shall be submitted to the building commissioner for presentation to the Commission.

An adequate number of color photographs (Polaroid-type) are required to illustrate the size, including buildings and other existing features. Photos may also be used to illustrate installation on other sites that are similar to the applicant's proposal.

BUILDING CONSTRUCTION, EXTERIOR REMODELING, AND ADDITIONS (INCLUDING PARKING LOTS AND LANDSCAPING) SUBMITTAL REQUIREMENTS

A. Site Plan. A site plan is required containing the following information:
• Scale and north arrow,
• Address of site,
• All property and street pavement lines,
• Existing and proposed contours,
• Gross area of tract stated in square feet,
• If parking is involved, show calculations for determining the required number of off-street parking spaces as required by the village's zoning ordinance. Give the number of spaces actually proposed. Give the maximum number of employees, customers, and office vehicles that would be at the facility at any one time,
• Proposed ingress and egress to the site, including on-site parking areas(s), parking stalls, and adjacent streets. Delineate traffic flow with directional arrows and indi-

cate the location of direction signs or other motorist's aids (if any),
• Calculations for determining the required number of trees to be placed within the proposed parking area must be shown, as well as the designation of required buffer screens (if any) between the parking area and adjacent property,
• Location of all isolated trees having a diameter of six (6) inches or more (tree masses may be shown with a diagrammatic outline and a written inventory of individual trees included),
• Existing landscaping that will be retained and proposed landscaping shall be differentiated and shown on the plan. The type, size, number, and spacing of all plantings must be illustrated,
• Location of all existing (to remain) and proposed buildings on the site and all buildings within fifty (50) feet of the site's boundaries,
• Location of all existing (to remain) and proposed lighting standards, complete with routing of electrical supply and isofootcandle diagram.

B. Elevations. Complete elevations of all proposed construction and related elevations of existing structures (if any) are required containing the following information:
• Scale,
• All signs to be mounted on the elevations,
• Designation of the kind, color, and texture of all primary materials to be used.

C. Section Profiles. Two (2) section profiles through the site are required containing the following information:
• Scale,
• Building(s),
• Lighting fixtures and standards,
• Signs.

D. Material Samples. Material samples are required for all major materials.

"Materials shall have good architectural character and shall be selected for harmony of the building with adjoining buildings."

Library and Addition

FREE-STANDING GROUND SIGNS SUBMITTAL REQUIREMENTS

A. Site Plan. A site plan is required containing the following information:
- Scale and north arrow,
- Address of site,
- All property and street pavement lines,
- Proposed ingress and egress to the site, including on-site parking area(s), parking stalls, and adjacent streets. Delineate the traffic flow with directional arrows and indicate the location of direction signs and other motorist's aids (if any),
- Location of existing and proposed landscaping,
- Location and height of all buildings on the site and all buildings within fifty (50) feet of the site's boundaries,
- Location and height of all existing (to remain) and proposed signs on the site, complete with route of electrical supply signs. Show required setbacks for sign from property lines,
- Location of all existing (to remain) routing of electrical supply.

B. Elevation. An elevation is required of each face of the proposed sign showing the following information:
- All specifications including size of letters and graphics,

- Description of sign and frame materials and colors including supports,
- Planter box details (if provided); i.e., construction of box, materials, plant types, sizes, number, and spacing.

C. Section Profile. A section profile through the site is required containing the following information:
- Scale,
- Buildings,
- Lighting standards,
- Landscaping.

D. Detailed Drawings. Detailed drawings showing the following information will be required to be submitted to the building department for technical review:
- Footings,
- Electrical wiring diagram,
- Wind stress calculations.

WALL SIGN SUBMITTAL REQUIREMENTS

A. Sign Drawing. A scaled drawing of each face of the proposed wall sign is required showing the following information:
- All size specifications, including the size of letters and graphics,

• Description of sign and frame materials and colors,
• Wall anchorage details (note: anchorage must be interior to the sign or camouflaged).

B. Elevation. An elevation drawn to scale of the entire wall of the building to which the sign is to be fixed, correctly locating the sign.

C. Detailed Drawings. Detailed drawings showing the following information will be required to be submitted to the building department for technical review:
• Electrical wiring diagram,
• Wind stress calculations.

LIGHTING SUBMITTAL REQUIREMENTS

A. Site Plan. A site plan is required containing the following information:
• Scale and north arrow,
• Address of site,

• Proposed ingress and egress to the site, including on-site parking area(s), parking stalls, and adjacent streets,
• Existing landscaping that will be retained and proposed landscaping,
• Location and height of all existing (to remain) and proposed buildings on the site and all buildings within fifty (50) feet of the site's boundaries,
• Location of all existing (to remain) and proposed lighting standards, complete with routing of electrical supply and circumference area that will be lighted by each standard.

B. Lighting Standard Drawing. A scaled drawing of the proposed lighting standard(s) is required and should contain the following information:
• All size specifications,
• Information on lighting intensity (number of watts, isofootcandle diagram, etc.),
• Materials, colors,
• Ground or wall anchorage details.

Appendix 7.D

Design Review Commission Project Evaluation Checklist

Walnut Creek, California

Site Planning

A. General

	Not Applicable	Excellent	Fair	Poor	Remarks
1. Minimize the disruption of existing natural features such as trees and other vegetation, natural ground forms, rocks, water, and view.					
2. Illustrate design compatibility with the desired developing character of the surrounding area.					
3. Create a development which is pleasant in character, human in scale, and facilitates easy circulation.					
4. Recognize views, climate, and the nature of outside activities in the design of exterior spaces.					
5. Insure in each step of a phased project that the design is complete in its functional, traffic, visual, drainage, and landscaping aspects wherever possible.					
6. Insure that all exterior lighting is functional, subtle, and architecturally integrated with the building style, material, and colors.					

B. Buffering

	Not Applicable	Excellent	Fair	Poor	Remarks
1. Screen exterior trash and storage areas, service yards, loading docks and ramps, and electrical utility boxes, etc., from view of all nearby streets and adjacent structures in a manner that is compatible with building site design.					

	Not Applicable	Excellent	Fair	Poor	Remarks
2. Minimize the visual impact and presence of vehicles by generally siting parking areas to the rear or side of the property rather than along street frontages, utilizing underground parking and screening parking areas from view both interior and exterior to the site.					
3. Minimize noise created by the proposed project (traffic, air conditioning, use, etc.) that may negatively impact the surrounding area.					
4. Minimize noise from the surrounding area that may negatively impact the proposed project.					

C. Grading

	Not Applicable	Excellent	Fair	Poor	Remarks
1. Blend any proposed grading with the contours of adjacent properties.					
2. Contour round all proposed cut and fill slopes both horizontally and vertically.					
3. Insure that all on-site drainage patterns will occur on or through areas designed to serve this function.					

D. Circulation

	Not Applicable	Excellent	Fair	Poor	Remarks
1. Create traffic patterns which minimize impact on surrounding streets and property and accommodate emergency vehicles.					
2. Create circulation systems which avoid conflicts between vehicular, bicycle, and pedestrian traffic.					

	Not Applicable	Excellent	Fair	Poor	Remarks
3. Insure that the propsed project accommodates individuals with physical disabilities via the provision of handicapped parking stalls, ramps and the like.					

Building Design

A. General

	Not Applicable	Excellent	Fair	Poor	Remarks
1. Create a design compatible with the developing character of the neighboring area. Design compatability includes harmonious building style, form, size, color, and material.					
2. Coordinate exterior building design on all elevations with regard to color, materials, architectural form, and detailing to achieve design harmony and continuity.					
3. Limit the number of materials on the exterior face of the building.					

B. Building-Site-Plan Relationships

	Not Applicable	Excellent	Fair	Poor	Remarks
1. Site buildings so as to avoid crowding and to allow for a functional use of the space between buildings.					
2. Site buildings so as to consider shadows, changing climatic conditions, noise impacts, safety, and privacy on adjacent outdoor spaces.					

C. Roof Design

	Not Applicable	Excellent	Fair	Poor	Remarks
1. Coordinate roof shape, color, and texture with the treatment of the perimeter walls.					

	Not Applicable	Excellent	Fair	Poor	Remarks
2. Minimize roof penetration by grouping all plumbing vents and ducts together.					
3. Design and/or screen all rooftop mechanical and electrical equipment as an integral part of the building design.					

Landscaping

A. General

1. Design landscaping to create a pleasing appearance from both within and off the site.					
2. Size all landscaping so that a mature appearance will be attained within three years of planting.					
3. Tree and shrub planting should be grouped together unless circumstances dictate otherwise in order to create strong accent points.					
4. Insure that landscaping permits adequate sight distance for motorists and pedestrians entering and exiting the site and does not interfere with circulation effectiveness.					
5. Provide landscaping adjacent to and within parking areas in order to screen vehicles from view and minimize the expansive appearance of parking areas. This landscaping should include fast growing deciduous or evergreen trees in parking lots to create maximum summer shade.					

	Not Applicable	Excellent	Fair	Poor	Remarks
6. Retain and integrate native and significant trees such as Oaks, Buckeyes, and Black Walnut.					

B. Architectural Relationship

1. Utilize landscaping to complement building elevations.					
2. Provide dense landscaping to screen unattractive views and features such as storage areas, trash enclosures, freeway structures, transformers, generators, and other elements which do not contribute to the enhancement of the surroundings.					

C. Climatic Relationships

1. Provide landscaping which will grow well in Walnut Creek's climate without requiring extensive irrigation.					
2. Provide deciduous trees along southern building exposures, coniferous and broad-leaf evergreen trees along east and west building exposures, and evergreens along the north exposures to conserve energy usage within structures.					

Residential Subdivisions

1. In general no more than two detached two-story dwelling units should be placed adjacent to one another.					

	Not Applicable	Excellent	Fair	Poor	Remarks
2. Site only one-story detached dwelling units adjacent to major collector or arterial streets or on corner lots.					
3. Vary front yard setbacks a minimum of 3 feet on straight line portions of streets.					
4. Insure that houses with identical or similar building elevations are not on adjacent lots or directly across the street from one another.					
5. Insure a compatibility (not duplication) of color schemes on homes on adjacent lots.					
6. Continue the design motif on each individual house completely around the structure.					
7. Trim out all doors and windows whenever such treatment would be compatible with the architectural style of the building.					

Comments: _____

_____

_____

_____

_____

_____

_____

8

Writing Better Zoning Reports

Duncan Erley

One of the most important functions of any local planning staff is providing technical advice on zoning decisions to the planning commission and zoning board. Good zoning decisions depend not only on the quality of staff analysis and recommendations, but also on the staff's ability to communicate those recommendations clearly and effectively. Most staffs use written reports to relay their findings and recommendations. These reports allow commissioners to study each case before attending a meeting. In addition, the staff presents oral findings and recommendations at meetings.

This chapter is intended as a guide to improving staff reporting to planning commissioners. Its primary focus is on written staff reports—their content, organization, format, and depth of analysis, as well as practical considerations of good report writing. Oral presentations are briefly discussed.

Many agencies are under time constraints and must meet ordinance requirements or guidelines in analyzing zoning cases and in writing their reports. This chapter is not meant to prescribe an ideal method, style, or format for zoning staff reports; rather, it should serve to identify particular elements of good report design that are adaptable for use in light of individual agency constraints and needs.

THE READERS: PLANNING COMMISSIONERS

Before getting into the details of report writing, carefully consider the readers. Much of the staff's effectiveness in communicating depends on how well the needs of the readers are understood. How knowledgeable about planning and zoning matters are the commissioners? And what are their time constraints?

Planning expertise. Planning commissioners usually are not professional planners. Commissions are composed of lay people, only some of whom may come from fields related to land development. Even the commissioner who has been a real estate agent or developer for many years may not be familiar with all the current theory and jargon of professional planning. Staff report writers should keep this in mind when choosing the content, level of technical detail, and diction. Writers should also be aware of opportunities to teach commissioners new planning concepts and terms. An awareness of these considerations does not suggest condescension in writing staff reports but rather common sense and empathy.

Time constraints. The job of the planning commissioner is usually a voluntary, time-consuming task involving heavy meeting agendas and a good deal of preparation. There are often more than ten cases to prepare for, and many report packets are sent to commissioners only a few days before the meeting. In addition, the commissioners have other, full-time professional and social commitments. Thus, staff reports should be written so that they can be read easily and quickly, without sacrificing thoroughness. A format that is consistent and that makes the information readily accessible is best. Avoid wordiness while ensuring that all of the information is contained in the report.

BASIC PROBLEMS

Report writers fall prey to several types of writing problems. They include the following.

Poor Organization and Format. One of the most common weaknesses of zoning staff reports is poor organization and format. Bits of information often are scattered throughout the reports, and types of information appear in different places from report to report. Various data are not listed by category, forcing the reader to search for specifics. Poor layout is another common problem. Report writers often fail to label information or use subheads that identify the various sections of the report.

In the following example it is hard to distin-guish categories of information. The text runs on without any subheads or labels:

> The owners seek a special use permit for institutional hall uses in an R-3 zone. The site is approximately one acre in area with access and frontage on Green Street. The applicant intends to build a lodge meeting hall which will comply with the standards of the R-3 zone. The site is presently vacant and is surrounded by single-family residential development. The Official Plan designates this site for low-density residential development. The plan states that consideration will be given to institutional uses by zoning amendment in this district. Traffic flow on Green Street has increased considerably in the past year due to the completion of Crossroads Mall, one mile to the south.

Mixing Facts with Subjective Information. It is relatively common practice in zoning staff reports to mix factual information, such as the location and the adjacent land uses, with subjective information, such as staff opinion on specific impacts or recommendations for approval. This practice is especially confusing when it is done indiscriminately or unpredictably throughout a report. Facts should be kept separate from analysis and recommendations. The case analysis and recommendations should refer back to a list of easily accessible facts.

Here is an example of the confusion caused by running together the case facts and the conditions of approval:

> Adjacent Land Use. To the north is agricultural land. To the south, east, and west are single-family homes. There are a barn and three smaller outbuildings on the agricultural land to the north. *The applicant should be required to remove all four structures upon completion of the new facility.*

Obviously, the recommendation (in italics) should be separate from the section on adjacent land use.

Pomposity. Report writers in all professions fall into the habit of using pompous, high-toned language when plain English will do. For some reason, they feel compelled to use the long, complex, inflated word or sentence instead of the simple word or phrase. They are addicted to words with Latin roots, when good old Anglo-Saxon terms are readily available.

The following is an example of the use of pompous language in report writing.

> The area designated for the surface parking of vehicles and the ingress and egress thereto has not been considered as usable open space other than for automobiles. Signing on the subject parcel will not impede safety to vehicular access.

Excessive or Incomplete Information. Commissioners often complain that zoning staff reports are simply too long to be read and digested within the time allotted. Other staff reports suffer from incompleteness. Both problems stem from carelessness in deciding which information to include and which to omit. Unnecessary information often keeps the reader from getting to the facts. Missing information leaves commissioners uninformed and ill-prepared to make decisions.

Excessive detail only wastes the reader's time and obscures the message, as in the following example:

> Soils. According to a report from the Soil Conservation Service, two soil types were discovered on the site, both using subtypes of the Hayesville Loam group. These soils consist of typically poorly to moderately sorted soils. In those areas where material was reworked, they may be well sorted.
>
> The depth of the A horizon ranges from six to eight inches across the parcel, depending upon topography. The soil study was made to check the suitability of the site with regard to soil stability for the proposed use as long as design recommendations are followed.

The only information the planning commissioners need is that the soil was found suitable for the proposed use. Everything else is extraneous.

Redundacy. Zoning staff reports often contain two kinds of redundancies: stating the same fact twice (not for the purpose of emphasis) and making the same point over and over again. Redundancy makes the report unnecessarily long and undermines a reader's confidence in the report and its writer.

The following example illustrates redundancy in staff reports:

> *Case No.:* 66987
> *Applicant:* George Warner
> *Request:* Rezoning from Commercial 1 to Commercial 2 to construct a dry cleaning store
> *Purpose:* Dry Cleaning Store
> *Location:* 457 Montrose
> *Size:* 0.6 acres
> *Existing Zoning:* Commercial

The information about existing zoning (commercial) and the purpose of the request (to permit a dry cleaning store) is unnecessarily repeated.

REPORT CONTENT: BASIC REQUIREMENTS

All zoning staff reports should include certain basic information about the applicant's proposal. Regardless of the type of request, information such as the applicant's name, the zoning status of the land involved, or the purpose for the request should be included in every case.

Much of this information is included in the application and can simply be transferred to the report. If application forms are coordinated with the staff report, the writer can merely fill in the blanks on the report form. Taken one step further, if the information on the application does not need correction or clarification, it can be used as part of the staff report itself. In either case, the staff saves time by having the applicant do some of the work. Any information that is not available to the applicant himself may be available to the staff and can be added to the report later.

The following example identifies the main information categories commonly found in zoning staff reports:

Information Categories	Examples
Applicant Information	Dorothy Morris Owner 4567 Trumbull Street
Requested Action	Rezone to Special Use, Medical Complex District
Existing Zoning	Residential-3
Purpose	Dental/Medical Building
Location	9700 Block of South Wave St. (see map)
Size	3.5 acres
Existing Land Use	Vacant open space
Surrounding Land Uses	East—Single-family residential (see map) West—Single-family residential South—Townhouse residential North—Vacant open space
Master Plan Specifications	Medium-density residential
Zoning History	No previous zoning actions have been requested for the site
Applicable Land Use Regulations	Regulations for Special Use District: Minimum Lot Area: 3 acres Maximum Height: 6 stories Maximum Lot Coverage: 60%

Special Information Needs: Tailoring the Report to Suit the Case

In addition to the above information which automatically should be included in every staff report, more specific information is often required to address the specific needs of each case.

For example, a report on a variance to erect a sign in a shopping area should be different from a report on a rezoning to construct an apartment building in a single-family zone. In the first instance, nothing more than the basic information about the applicant, the location, the request, and so forth is necessary. But in the second case, information on public utilities, parking, and landscaping also might be required. The amount of detail required also depends on the type and scale of each case. Complex cases often require not only more kinds of information, but also greater depth of information.

Special Information Categories

The following list presents a range of specific information categories often needed in zoning staff reports.

• *Public Utilities.* Information on the public water supply and central sewerage, including availability of service to the site, capacity of existing service, current demand on existing service, summary of planned improvements or additions to water and sewerage systems and facilities.

• *Public Services.* Information on fire and police protection, refuse collection (including availability of these services to the site), capacity of and current demand on fire, police, and sanitation departments, special equipment necessitated by the proposal.

• *Public Schools.* Information on existing educational facilities, including their current student loads and excess capacity, improvements to existing schools, or new facilities planned.

• *Transportation.* Information on streets (including size and capacity), state of repair, planned improvements or additions, and traffic (including data on volume and direction of flow).

• *Physical Site Characteristics.* Information on natural conditions of the site, including data on soil type, topography, existing vegetation, groundwater, drainage, and flooding.

• *Environmental Quality.* Information on environmental conditions, including data on air quality, water quality, wildlife, and habitat.

• *Aesthetics/Landscaping.* Information on visual quality and landscaping needs.

• *Recreation.* Information on recreational facilities and opportunities, including location of existing or proposed facilities, capacity, and demand on those facilities.

• *Energy Consumption.* Information on energy efficiency ramifications of the proposal.

Special and additional information is often needed for PUDs, including the following information categories.

• *Density.* Information on density, including proposed dwelling units per acre, floor-to-area ratio, and other density-related data.

• *Dwelling Units.* Information on the type and mix of dwelling units, including number and size of units and number of bedrooms and bathrooms.

• *Amenities.* Information on proposed recreational facilities or common buildings.

• *Ownership of Common Facilities.* Information on ownership and maintenance of common facilities, homeowners association, public dedication, responsibility for upkeep.

Tailoring reports to fit specific cases requires deciding which of the above categories are relevant and how much detail is needed. Only the information necessary to make a sound decision on the application needs to be included. The extent of detail should be based on the staff's knowledge of the commission. Technical information must be interpreted and translated into clear, simple forms of expression. Unnecessarily detailed and esoteric information should be eliminated.

STRENGTHENING REPORTS

With audience needs defined, basic writing problems identified, and basic content requirements met, the report writer can move forward by realizing that two reports, even if they contain exactly the same information, can differ greatly in their success in communicating that information to the planning commissioners. Four practices that can help the report writer avoid the pitfalls of inconsistent format, redundancy, mixing fact with opinion, and illogical ordering information follow.

1. Separate Facts from Analysis. It is helpful to separate the presentation of the factual information in the report from the staff analysis of the case. Certainly, facts will be referred to in the analysis, but, if fact and analysis are mixed together in one narrative body, a potentially simple report may become too involved and confusing. Separating facts from opinion and analysis makes the planning commissioners' job that much easier.

2. Separate Information Categories. An easily read and referenced report is the result of separating information categories to the greatest extent possible. Where the information is labeled and set apart visually, the commissioners can scan the whole report readily for a quick overview or concentrate on the parts that need more attention. Using headings indexes the information, making it easy to find.

3. Use a Standard Format. Although report content varies greatly, most zoning staff reports can be organized into a standard format usable in every case simply by adding or omitting relevant or irrelevant components of the form. Not only does this simplify report writing, it also means that commissioners come to expect the same style of report and need not waste time reorienting themselves to every new report or searching for a certain category of information. If they want to find out the current zoning or the response from the school board, they should know where to look.

4. Present Facts with a Minimum of Narrative. Simple, factual information of the kind included in zoning staff reports doesn't need to be surrounded by prose. Instead of saying, "The current zoning of the parcel is R-1, residential," the writer might say, "Current zoning: R-1, residential."

The use of narrative should be restricted to sections such as the analysis and recommendations. Dropping the narrative whenever possible reduces the number of words substantially and makes the facts stand out.

Exhibit 8.1 is an example of a well-organized zoning staff report. Information is clearly labeled, narrative is kept to a minimum, and staff analysis and recommendations are separated from the factual portion of the report. While any number of variations are possible, this example serves to illustrate the major elements of good format.

Exhibit 8.1
STAFF REPORT

To: County Planning Commission	**Prepared By:** BF

Case No.: 349-15	**Date:** September 15, 1987

General Information

Applicant	Mt. Carmel Baptist Church 458 North Avenue
Status of Applicant	Owner
Requested Action	Special Permit
Purpose	To construct an 80-seat church and a 30-space parking lot.
Existing Zoning	Residential-1
Location	South side of Oak St. approximately 40 feet west of 34th St.
Size	3.2 acres
Existing Land Use	Vacant
Surrounding Land Use and Zoning	North—Single-family and R-1 (see map) South—School and R-1 East—Vacant and R-1 West—Vacant and R-1
Master Plan	Area is designated for low-density residential use.
Zoning History	June 1987—Rezoning application to R-2 for townhouse construction was denied.
Applicable Regulations	Churches are permitted uses in the R-1 district.

Special Information

Public Utilities	Adequate central water and sewage service are available.
Public Services	Sanitation service is available. Police department has responded that it has adequate staff to handle potential traffic problems on Sundays. Fire department has responded that it has adequate equipment to handle potential fires.
Transportation	Additional traffic flow of 20 to 30 automobiles will be generated on Sunday mornings. Oak Street is a principal arterial street. Current loads are below capacity.

Physical Characteristics	Soil is well drained and stable for building foundations. Topography is approximately 5 percent, very gentle. Vegetation consists of grass and weeds.

Analysis

The staff recommends approval of this special permit.

Churches are a permitted use in the Residential-1 District and the facility proposed by Mt. Carmel Baptist complies completely with the requirements for the permit.

Proposed parking facilities are more than adequate to meet the demand generated by churchgoers. In addition, landscaping plans for the proposed parking lots surpass minimum requirements.

The proposed church will not place an unreasonable or unacceptable demand on existing public utilities and services. Central water and sewerage systems can easily accommodate the increased demand created by the church. The same is true for sanitation, fire, and police services.

The response from residents of the neighborhood has been positive. Many of the adjacent residents will attend the church after it is constructed.

Recommendations

The following recommendations must be met as conditions for approval of this special permit:

1. Access to the church parking lot will be from Elm Street.
2. The church will be constructed according to the submitted site plan.
3. The grounds will be maintained in a neat condition.
4. One additional street light will be provided at the southwest corner of the parking lot.

Attachments

1. Site plan
2. Zoning and location map
3. Memo dated 5/6/87 from Police Department.
4. Memo dated 5/15/87 from Public Works Department.

TONE AND STYLE

Most zoning staff reports include a separate section with an analysis of the case. This is where facts and educated opinion from among themselves and from other sources are used to make a case for or against a proposal. The analysis should develop the case of the staff position through a logical argument.

Logical Persuasion

The analysis section of the staff report should appeal to the planning commissioners' senses of reason rather than to their emotions. This is the difference between argument and persuasion. In all forms of technical writing, the author should appeal to reason. Argumentation involves a logical ordering of minor ideas of propositions to support a major proposition.

For any zoning case there are three possible recommendations: approval, approval with conditions, or denial. The analysis section should begin by stating the staff position; for example, "The staff recommends denial of the application."

The staff's position must be supported through a series of major propositions. Minor propositions are the case issues or findings of fact. If groundwater impact or noncompliance with the master plan are the major issues of the case, they are the ideas most important to use in supporting the staff position. For example, in support of the recommendation for denial, an analysis might make the following points:

1. The proposal is not in accordance with community master plan goals.
2. The proposal will create traffic demands that would cause a safety hazard.
3. Approval of the application would constitute a spot zoning.

Factual information on the case already presented is restated or referred to in support of the minor propositions. For example, the analysis may say, "Topography is unsuitable for the proposed use." The analysis can go on to state, "Slope is nearly 35 percent," or might simply refer to the information section of the report, "See Topography Section." Referring to the information rather than repeating it has the advantage of shortening the report; on the other hand the argument may be strengthened by repeating the information in the analysis.

Examples of Zoning Case Analysis

The following examples represent three types of staff report analyses. Like factual information in zoning staff reports, analyses may be as detailed as necessary for the individual case. Controversial cases may require fairly extensive analysis sections. The examples here are relatively brief but can be used as guidelines for more complex and detailed analyses.

Example 1: Findings of Fact Analysis
In order to approve this permit, the Board is first required to find that:

　1. The use is in accordance with objectives of the ordinance.

　2. The use will not be detrimental to public health and safety or be injurious to properties in the vicinity.

　3. The use will comply with applicable provisions of the ordinance.

　The staff recommends approval. With regard to these required findings, the staff comments that:

　1. The proposal is a permitted conditional use in a General Agricultural (AG) Zone.

　2. The use will promote an appropriately located agricultural pursuit—an objective of the ordinance.

　3. The conditions of approval of the conditional use permit and the requirements of the Pleasantville Health Department will insure that public health and safety are maintained and that the use will comply with applicable provisions of the ordinance.

Example 2: Special Use Permit Analysis
The staff recommends approval of this special use permit because appliance repair is an appropriate use in

this type of light manufacturing and warehouse district. The Pleasantville zoning ordinance specifically lists appliance repair as a conditionally permitted use in the Light Industrial Zone. Repair activities permitted are limited to those that are free from nuisance factors such as dust, odor, and noise. Based on the staff's past experience with appliance repair, the proposed use is appropriate and would not generate excessive parking, noise, and other nuisance factors.

Example 3: Rezoning Analysis
The staff recommends denial of the rezoning. Several issues are involved in this request, including master plan goals, impact on public schools, site topography, and impact on runoff and erosion.

　The applicant's proposal to develop a large tract of multifamily residential use is not in accordance with community master plan goals and specifications. As stated earlier, the master plan specifies the area of the proposed development for low-density, single-family development. The higher density, multifamily use is encouraged in various other areas of the city, and such development in this area, if allowed, could establish a precedent for other low-density, single-family areas.

　The proposed density of the development (see previous section) would generate a greater number of school children than the existing school (McArthur Grade School) can accommodate. The school is presently serving a near maximum number of students. Certainly, permitted low-density development of this tract will increase pupil loads, but the higher density development would mean a faster rate of increase and less time for the school board to make plans for additional facilities.

　Much of the site is of significantly severe topography and is unsuitable for multifamily construction. Slope stability characteristics are such that the load created by a multiple-unit dwelling could create a safety hazard. The master plan specifies low-density, single-family development partially for this reason. The lower density requirements facilitate greater open space and less impervious coverage in an area where runoff and erosion potential are great.

　Finally, the proposed development would require extension of central sewerage to service it. Surrounding single-family development is adequately served by individual septic systems, but the higher density use, especially in light of the topographic conditions, would require central sewerage for adequate sanitation.

Style Tips

Technical reports should be simple. They should also be distinguished by the information they convey, not by their showy style. Experts agree that the best way to keep technical writing simple is to use short words and sentences. In writing staff reports, planners should use short, brisk sentences, and short words.

The following sentence is windy and overblown:

> Due to the extensive sedimentation on the subject parcel and the increased potential for further erosion, the agency staff has reached the conclusion that this site is not highly appropriate for the intended use and that the requested conditional use permit be denied.

The sentence could read:

> The staff recommends that the use permit be denied because the proposed use might increase the already severe erosion and sedimentation.

Also avoid pomposity and overblown language whenever possible. Instead of saying "the subject parcel," say "the site." It means the same thing.

CONDITIONAL RECOMMENDATIONS AND ATTACHMENTS TO STAFF REPORTS

Planners' report writing is not confined to reports to commissioners. Conditional recommendations and attachments to staff reports also require attention.

Conditions for Approval

A zoning case report that recommends approval of an application often includes a list of recommended conditions or requirements to be met by the applicant. Because these con-

ditions serve as an agreement between the applicant and the local government, it is important that they be as clear and concise as possible. They should be listed item by item and without unnecessary discussion and wordiness. If the recommendations are ambiguous, problems will arise when the time comes to interpret them.

The conditions in Exhibit 8.2, for example, leave little room for speculation about what is required of the applicant.

Exhibit 8.2
APPLICATION APPROVAL WITH CONDITIONS

Recommendations
The staff recommends that the application be approved subject to the following conditions:

1. That all proposals of the applicant be conditions of approval unless stated here.

2. That the site be developed according to all General Agriculture Zone District regulations.

3. That development be in accordance with the approved site plan.

4. That all necessary building permits be secured from the County Planning Agency.

5. That a minimum of one parking space for every two beds be provided and that these parking spaces be covered with a durable, dustless surface.

6. That the structure be set back 80 feet from the centerline of Eucalyptus Road.

7. That any necessary approval or permits be secured from the County Health Department.

Report Attachments

Maps, memos, petitions, correspondence, or other documents pertinent to the case often are added to the staff report. Most commonly, a zoning map covering the site and a site plan of the proposed project are attached. Other attachments, such as specialized information in the report itself, are required in some cases but not others. Such attachments include correspondence with public agencies, private utilities, and other interested parties, or special detailed reports on, for example, soil drainage or traffic safety.

The most common problem with report attachments is improper labeling. Many staff reports have a sheaf of letters and memos stapled to them that are identified only by a signature of the writer or by the content of the document itself. Attachments should be clearly labeled in the same place (for instance the upper right corner), so that particular attachments can be found quickly. In addition, if certain attachments are routinely included in staff reports, use a standard order for those attachments. For example, routinely place the zoning map first, the site plan second, the public works report third, and so forth. The commissioners will become familiar with the system and know where to look for particular items.

ORAL PRESENTATIONS

No matter how well written, staff reports cannot always convey to the commissioners all of the information about a case. Some information may come in too late to be included in the report or some maps and plans may be too large to fit. Certain issues may be too complex to treat adequately. Some commissioners simply may not not have read the report. The planning staff's oral presentation to the planning commission provides an opportunity to supplement the written report and compensate for any limitations.

Many planners involved in writing and presenting staff reports feel that the oral presentation is as important as the written report in communicating with commissioners; many place more emphasis on it than on the written report. The oral presentation can provide the facts of the case to outsiders and can refresh the memories of the commissioners. It can stimulate discussion about the case and it can flesh out the details and rationale of the case.

We do not go into detail about oral presentation techniques and procedures here, but several points can be made briefly. Many of the tenets of written reports apply to oral presentations. Indeed, a well-written report can be valuable as a guideline for the oral presentation.

The oral presentation should be short and simple. Time constraints at commission meetings are even greater than constraints on commissioners' preparation time, and they involve more people. The staff report should not be read verbatim; rather, the main points should be summarized in the order that they appear in the report. Using the written report format for the oral presentation simplifies the procedure for commissioners and also can help the secretary in recording and preparing minutes. If an applicant's presentation includes a good deal of overlapping information, the staff should make every effort to avoid repetition. Because planners' verbal skills vary as much as those of any other group, those planners who are particularly adept at speaking should be given priority as representatives at commission meetings. Any planner giving an oral presentation should remember that as in written reports, jargon, flowery speech, and elaborate explanations will diminish the effectiveness of the presentation.

The sections of the oral presentation should be distinct and appropriately identified. For example, an oral presentation might be divided into four sections: (1) applicant's presentation, (2) staff report summary, (3) display of maps and illustrations, and (4) discussion of the case. The important issue here is not the order of events, but rather the separation of the sections. Furthermore, if the order of presentation is consistent, the efficiency of individual presentations and the meeting in general will be improved.

Zoning cases often involve maps, site plans, architectural sketches, photographs, and other graphic materials. Much of this material is too large or too expensive to include in the written report and must be displayed at the commission meeting. Audiovisual aids are helpful, especially in large meeting rooms or when documents are not quite large enough to be legible. An overhead or opaque projector or a slide project or will make the material more accessible to audience and commissioners alike. Easels, flip charts, or bulletin boards also can be used.

The Public Economics of Development Impacts

Albert Solnit

One of the most common goals of community leaders---is that of fiscal profitability. The criterion they use is the change (increase) in the tax revenue and the public costs associated with the act---- Fiscal profitability is too crude a criterion. There are interdependencies that are ignored and it is silent on the problem of evaluation of public services.
JULIUS MARGOLIS

When developers present their cases for project approval, they invariably claim that building their development will enrich the tax base, increase local trade, create new jobs and investment opportunities, and generally stimulate the local economy. What they never reveal are the spillover or hidden costs of the development. These costs have both economic and noneconomic impacts.

What the planner working for the public interest must reveal to decision makers is what the development will do to the community's present and planned public facilities, public services, and the general livability of the surrounding area.

This chapter discusses how to determine whether a new development will be a long-term asset or a long-term liability.

THE INITIAL EVALUATION

The first thing the planner should check is whether the proposed project conforms to the general neighborhood and capital improvement plans. This assumes that these plans are up to date, realistic in terms of economic and environmental considerations, and that there is a consensus on policy matters related to the project.

The staff report on a significant project should describe the projected conformance or nonconformance in terms of the plan's logic and applicable data. The planner then needs to compare the future as proposed with the project to the future as proposed by the plan. For example, the plan may call for a compact downtown serving as the community center for shopping, government installations, education, and so forth, while the project presents a future with dispersed shopping and a greatly diminished downtown center. The staff report should highlight the policy alternatives before getting into the specifics of cost·benefit considerations.

When the plans are obsolete or deficient, the planner should develop an analysis using the following basic questions:

1. *Is this an appropriate place for this project compared with alternative locations?* Even the most attractive and well-designed project will not work if it is in the wrong place. Far too often, public hearings degenerate into debate about site-specific issues in an attempt to "fix up the project," rather than facing the problem that it simply is in the wrong place.

2. *Is this the right time for this project or is it premature?* Often a developer will point to the general plan's colored map which projects land use 20 years into the future and say, "Our project conforms to the plan because it is a multiple use that will be located in the brown multiple-use area." Unfortunately, many plans simply project a result without any staging or information on how to get from here to there.

3. *Is the land use compatible with the surrounding area?* Theoretically, the selection of alternatives that best tie into a communitywide framework should have been done during plan preparation. When a small or medium project is submitted there should be no great question

about whether the use will be appropriate; the issue of which alternatives are best for each location should have been settled when the plan was adopted. Having to handle issues such as growth policy, public services overloads at a city or regional level, and major cost revenue changes detracts from the time available for staff analysis and the design of positive changes of the project itself.

QUANTIFICATION

Too often, time is wasted trying to develop precise data about every aspect of a project's economic impact. Except for very large projects, the fiscal impact of a project will not make enought difference in the big economic picture to make the complex and time-consuming work required to secure cost revenue data and make it understandable to a lay city council worthwhile.

It simply is not relevant to ask whether each project pays its own way. Take, for example, the question of schools. Low-cost housing with a large school-age population will not generate enough property tax to pay for the education costs it incurs. But the basic education of American children is considered a right independent of the local tax base; the California Supreme Court ruled that the equal protection clause of the Constitution applied to children's education and that support of education should not be a function of the wealth of a district (*Serrano* v. *Priest*). To a lesser extent, most people-oriented services involve a redistribution of wealth. Very poor or slum neighborhoods usually use far more police, fire, health department, and social services than rich ones.

Classic economic theory claims that the real cost of an impact depends on the willingness of a particular public to pay for offsetting it. However, this approach has serious drawbacks in that the willingness to pay is often a function of the income available and the distribution of the effect. The impact of overcrowded schools theoretically can be measured by the willingness of taxpayers to pay a higher property tax to create more classrooms. However, the disadvantage of overcrowded schools is felt most keenly by the parents of school-aged children—parents who may represent only a fraction of the public that is asked to pay for more schools.[1] Moreover, the social value of education may be interpreted differently by different cultural and income groups. Assume that the parent is interested in his or her child's future income-earning ability and integration into society. Even so, our society does not trust the parent with full control over the education of the child because society does not accept that what the parent would budget would be a proper measure of what the child would be willing to pay, assuming the child could make an informed choice. If we reject parental judgments about willingness to pay with regard to a child's education, should this rejection extend to other public services such as public safety?

Consider also that money values cannot measure environmental and social values with the same degree of specificity as they can things like tax rates and bond costs.

Then there is the shadow price method of unpriced goods. It, for example, might establish the price of good air quality by a polluter's willingness to pay for licenses and fines until he stops polluting. This, however, does not get at the value to be set on the loss of health, death of plant life, and chipping of paint for those individuals and properties impacted by the polluter (consider acid rain). Some economists claim that the value to the sufferers could be estimated as the cost of having the polluter move to an alternate location versus the social costs of continuing to breathe foul air. The problem with this approach is that many physical impacts are permanent and irreversible, and costs of substitution do not generally apply. Even when they might, people really cannot choose all the alternatives in order to find the cheapest. Again, the choice would have an income bias. This was pointed up at an international environmental conference where developing nations opposed developed nations on the issue of strict environmental controls because they wanted to have the chance to develop before any restrictions were placed on growth.

In essence, almost all attempts to translate social and environmental effects into economic terms wind up with explanations of whose pocketbook the money comes from (rich or poor) and discussion of the extension of price theory whereby scarce resources are allocated among competing ends. In private economics, the profit-maximizing ends of the firm dominate the decision. In public economics, decisions on whether to produce a public good usually are economically evaluated only in terms of whether they pay off their costs with revenues from and savings to the users. Unfortunately, this process has ignored the existence of spillovers and external costs (e.g., the new sewer plant makes it possible to develop residential densities, but those densities may seriously strain other functional service agencies such as schools and fire).

More importantly, public goods are rarely produced on a single-product basis. Producing one product invariably leads to the need for others and the impacts then are cumulative, stemming from the relationships between the public goods.

CUMULATIVE EFFECTS

Many communities are currently embracing the belief that no growth is the best policy for maintaining a sound municipal economy. In the Palo Alto Foothills Environmental Design Study (Livingstone and Blayney, Consultants), 22 alternative development patterns were studied as possibilities for several thousand acres of vacant land above the city. In every case, the cost of local public services and facilities exceeded revenues from property, sales, and other tax sources. It then was found that the cost of buying and keeping the land for open space would cost the taxpayers less than the long-term costs of development.

After this, other communities wanted to assume development strategies that minimized residential growth and school enrollment (cash flow to the school district was consistently negative and school costs made the difference between net plus revenues and negative net costs to the community in about one-third of the Palo Alto alternatives tested). Even the consultants who carried out the project cautioned other places about blindly accepting the Palo Alto findings as universally applicable. First, Palo Alto is a wealthy municipality, in which two-thirds of each property tax dollar is paid by nonresidential development and where only a third of the people employed in this nonresidential development can afford a new home in the city. Second, the area surveyed has special environmental characteristics (among them high fire hazard and some unstable slopes). Third, there is an assumption that federal subsidy funds for low- and moderate-income housing will continue to be scarce well into the future, thus practically limiting the foothills area to luxury housing and in return making the open space recommended of least benefit to low- and moderate-income families consigned to live farthest from it.

Nevertheless, the notion of rationing residential development has caught on without being properly examined. In San Rafael, California, voters approved a tax increase for open space bonds by a majority of 75 percent, even though many other bond issues had been rejected in recent years. That city, like Palo Alto, has a tax base that is mostly nonresidential; by buying the open lands, whose development potential is almost entirely residential, the residents preserve the favorable property tax ratio in a city that has the greatest scarcity of low- and moderate-income family housing in rich Marin County. Other California communities, most notably Sacramento, Pleasanton-Livermore, and Petaluma, where runaway growth has swamped public facilities and degraded the environment, have gone in for various formulas for restricting growth to areas peripheral to existing development.

Obviously, as each community gets "smart" about limiting development to that which produces the most favorable cash flow into the municipal coffers, then the "unfavorable" development has to find a place where the drawbridge has not been raised. This serves to compound the social inequities—of housing, schools, and other public services—that no single unit of local government can do much about righting.

What seems to be happening is that mutually exclusive systems of environmental protection, cost·benefit analysis, and social planning often are canceling each other out in the name of improving on the present results of urban expansion, commonly known as "the mess we're in." A way of considering these systems in a more integrated manner is clearly needed.

What communities that ration residential growth fail to realize is that immigration and employment—not housing—is the engine that generates growth. Thus every community that raises its drawbridge with zoning or pricing mechanisms causes spillover effects that are passed onto the cities up the road, and also cause other costs such as doubling up, illegal residential units, and a one-class (usually childless) community.

Most communities do not fall into the high-investment/high-tax-revenue class and the political approach to fiscal impacts is more a function of the degree of perceived economic stress than the real impacts of a project. One of the most revealing studies of this problem of urban fiscal stress was conducted by Touche Ross & Co. and the First National Bank of Boston[2].

The study covered 66 cities with populations of more than 50,000 and analyzed them in terms of 13 financial and 11 nonfinancial variables. The study quantified what most planners already knew: Older cities in decline have higher operating costs because as private investment and employment leave, costs of services increase. For example, the tax rates as a percentage of personal income of older Rust Belt cities like Trenton and Buffalo were 8.5 percent, compared to 3.8 percent for younger cities like Jacksonville and Indianapolis. The findings were that declining cities needed to forego lower priority services in order to balance revenues and costs. The paradox is that as older cities are less able to maintain capital investment there are corresponding declines in private investment. They thus are forced to choose between immediate services and long-term opportunities for tax base and employment.

One does not need a doctorate in economics to know that the fiscal impacts of a project that promised jobs and a rise in assessed values would be read differently in Buffalo than in Palo Alto, especially if one city has unused fiscal and facility capacities and the other is an old industrial city with a 500-year street maintenance schedule and a large dependent and unemployed population.

FACTORS OF PUBLIC SERVICE DEMAND

The levels of public service that actually are delivered by a local government only rarely are in direct response to a measurable public demand such as that encountered in the private sector, where market mechanisms such as pricing, propensity to consume, and advertising combine to establish the required quantity of goods and services.

In the public sector, public services are allocated by a political process that may hear individual preferences but has no mechanism for aggregating the preferences as is done in the private marketplace. Thus, service levels are determined by the goals and standards of the community leaders and quite often the goal of fiscal profitability may be paramount. In terms of timing, however, the government arrives first on the scene[3]. It plans, zones, and provides the services and facilities that allows land to urbanize at certain densities. The offsetting revenues to these new fixed costs may or may not arrive in time to prevent the burdens of these costs from shifting to the residents already taxed for their own shares of governmental costs. Very few costs-benefit analyses take a hard look at the cash-flow risks of new projects. Moreover, several studies of urban growth have indicated that fiscal profitability is more a function of a jurisdiction's fiscal condition, rather than the nature of a specific movement of growth.

A second important factor of service demand is the assessment of need. Most often this is done by those who deliver the service, rather than by the recipients. The assessment of need usually is based on the standards of professional associations that not only seek to expand their services on a basis of zero pricing, but also seek uniformity of service levels so that administrators can control the rationing of services in response to what is always "excess demand" in comparison with public funds available. Many times these standards are imposed from above by subsidizing agencies at the state and federal levels, with resulting diseconomies[4].

A SIMPLE GUIDE TO FISCAL IMPACT ANALYSIS

Fiscal impact analysis is defined as "a projection of the direct current public costs and revenues associated with residential or nonresidential growth to the local jurisdiction(s) in which this growth is taking place."[5] Before using the methodology, the user should first be aware of the risks involved. They are:

1. *Making inappropriate assumptions about the ratios of residential to nonresidential land uses.* Home owners in communities with much business and industry generally pay lower property taxes than home owners in largely residential communities. In the first instance, nonresidential land uses produce tax revenue without making major demands on schools and other public services. Thus, the mix between residential and nonresidential land uses that is assumed as a context for analyzing any given development project is critical to the analysis of fiscal feasibility. The analyst needs accurate answers to these questions: What are the overall development trends within the community? Will the present ratios of residential to nonresidential land uses persist? Will preproject and postproject land use ratios be the same?

The intent here is not that every project produce a surplus of revenue but that land uses remain balanced. Nonresidential uses that have "carried" residential land uses in the past should continue to carry them in the future. In sum, the analyst needs an understanding of the entire range of projects taking place within the community so that the surpluses of some can offset the deficits of others.

2. *Overestimating or underestimating intergovernmental transfers.* In the 1976 fiscal year, fully 40 percent of all general revenues received by local governments took the form of intergovernmental transfers. Chief among the sources was state and federal aid to public schools. However, the stagnant or declining enrollments that now characterize many school districts should cause concern about the impact of new development on intergovernmental transfers. In many states, a development that causes an increase in school enrollment will result in a net reduction of school aid to the community.

3. *Perpetuating the mystique of computerized models.* Too often, elected officials, planners, administrators, and citizen commissioners regard computer analyses as more precise and credible than analyses performed by hand. This assignment of magical powers is unfortunate, since all fiscal impact analyses require the same computations. Computers simply perform them faster.

Further, the use of computerized models tends to hide the high degree of uncertainty involved in all fiscal impact analysis. Fiscal impact methods are all ad hoc in nature, with very little in the way of statistical precision.

If the problems to be analyzed are massive and detailed, a computer can make sense. But for small-scale, relatively straightforward fiscal impact analyses—the great majority—such models are often difficult to understand.

Computer analysis does have a particular virtue, however. That is its potential for sensitivity analysis. Sensitivity analysis makes it possible to explore different land use mixtures and to assess various revenue sources and the costs associated with different public service systems.

4. *Neglecting to weigh fiscal impacts against other impacts.* A common pitfall involves placing too much weight on fiscal factors and ignoring factors that are less easily quantified. Other kinds of impacts include those typically considered in environmental impact statements: environmental impacts on air, water, flora, and fauna; traffic impacts; social consequences for neighborhoods, housing markets, racial balance; economic impacts; and land use and transportation impacts.

One way to gain a better perspective on the relative importance of fiscal consequences is to relate all the impacts in a broader cost-effectiveness or cost-benefit framework. Monetary impacts—those involving public costs and revenues—then become only one of several important consequences that must be assessed, compared, and traded off.

5. *Not knowing when to use average costing approaches.* Average costing is by far the most commonly used approach in fiscal impact analysis. This approach assumes that the average costs of municipal services will remain stable in the future, with some adjustment for inflation. That assumption is fair in relatively slow-growing communities where the supply of public services matches demand and financing systems are stable. The most popular analysis method, the per capita multiplier technique, is based on this assumption.

However, in communities with population decline or rapid growth, a different situation exists. Public service capacity is then likely to be either underutilized or deficient. In these situations, marginal costing makes the most sense. Here the costs associated with public services needed for new developments should reflect the amount of excess capacity available (in which case marginal costs will be relatively low) or the degree of overcrowding (in which case there will be higher marginal costs). Basic to the use of marginal costing is an understanding of the existing supply of and demand for local public services. Highly misleading results may emerge if the inappropriate fiscal impact technique is used.

6. *Using fiscal impact analysis to support exclusionary zoning.* Fiscal impact analysis can be used to exclude certain land uses, such as low- and moderate-income housing. This application in invalid and has been banned in court in certain areas. New Jersey, which has paid more attention to fiscal zoning than any other state, is an example.

As a type of land use regulation, fiscal impact analysis can be a valid exercise of the police power, but, like other forms of land use management, it must be used in support of a comprehensive plan. In general, the courts have held that fiscal impact analyses that favor certain land uses—while explicitly excluding others—are invalid. The courts have concluded that zoning based on fiscal well-being may be considered locally but that it may be neither the sole basis for zoning nor a means to exclude certain groups.

7. *Risking the increasing skepticism of public officials by not using standardized methods.* Many communities that have included requirements for fiscal impact analysis in their zoning codes or subdivision regulations have beome disenchanted with the effectiveness of such requirements. The reason is that virtually every analysis has turned up a positive fiscal impact regardless of the type of development, density, or land use mix. In other words, analysts have tinkered with the various techniques until they have found one that presents the development in a favorable fiscal light.

Public officials become skeptical when confronted with lack of standardization among the various fiscal impact methods. Depending on local growth and development conditions, as well as fiscal relationships and data, different methods can produce dramatically different   cost·revenue ratios. It then appears that the methods have been manipulated to produce desired results. The recent Fiscal Impact Handbook, developed with HUD funding, represents a major step forward in the standardization of methods, but more needs to be done.

8. *Neglecting to devote enough time to the presentation of conclusions.* Most planners prefer the simplest methods of fiscal impact analysis. The per capita multiplier method, which is the easiest to understand and most logical, seems to be the most credible. But it is also the most simplistic, making many shaky assumtions about average costing, land use mixes, and so on.

Because they are harder to understand, more sophisticated techniques require more effective communication of methods and results. It is particularly important to match the results of fiscal impact analysis with other pertinent impact analyses. Too often, local officials cannot determine how the results of fiscal impact analysis should be weighed.[6]

Projecting Costs

For rough approximations of project costs, the following methodology generally is sufficient.[7]

A. *Education.* This is generally the largest single item in the tax bill. The planner will have to determine the answers to the following questions.

• How many new students will the project bring into the local school system?

• Is there enough space, teachers, etc., to ab-

sorb this additional enrollment?
• If not, what will be the cost of more teachers, buildings, playgrounds, etc.?
• Where will the funds to cover these increased costs come from?

The quickest way to approximate increased costs is to derive a per pupil cost by taking the present school budget and dividing it by the total enrollment. Then multiply the costs per pupil by the pupils per household for the particular types of housing proposed for the project.

> **Example:** Project proposes 100 two-bedroom condos and 200 single-family homes. Current per pupil costs for local area is $2,000 per annum. Average pupil per household figures are: 0.20 for two-bedroom condos and 0.80 for single family homes.
>
> $100 \times 0.2 + 500 \times 0.8 = 420$ pupils.
>
> $420 \times \$2,000 = \$840,000$.
>
> The proposed project would cause an $840,000 per annum increase in school costs. (Note: this many pupils may require a new school.)

B. *Municipal Costs.* (Fire, police, general government). Again taking a per capita cost figure derived from current budgets, the project's costs are the average population per household multiplied by the per capita cost figure. In the case of the above project with its 100 two-bedroom condos and 200 single-family homes:

> Two-bedroom condos have 1.2 persons per unit and single-family homes have 2.5 persons per unit. The current per person municipal cost is $300 per annum.
>
> Total increase in costs $= (1.2 \times 100 + 2.5 \times 500) \times \$300 = \$411,000$.

Some of the specific municipal service cost questions that may arise include the following.

Police. How many more police personnel and equipment will be required to maintain the same quality of protection? Will a new police station be required? Will new jail space be needed?

Fire Protection. Will the community have to change from a volunteer department to a paid staff? Will new fire stations have to be built? Is the present water system adequate to provide proper fire protection?

Public Utilities. At what stage of the project will a new sewage treatment plant be required or the existing one's capacity expanded? How will the local water supply by affected? Will wells from the project seriously lower the water table? Can the present water supply be increased and at what cost? Will additional land fill space be required to handle solid wastes from this project?

Roads. What new roads will have to be built and what old roads will have to be improved to accomodate the increased traffic flow from the project? How much of this will the project pay for? What will the added cost of street maintenance be? Will the level of service on the adjacent road system be lowered by congestion from the project?

Projecting Revenues

The property tax is usually the most significant source of revenue. To project the revenues from a new development, the planner projects the expected assessed value against the tax rate for each jurisdiction analyzed. If the project has not been assessed, the market value or the assessed selling price of each residential unit may be used. In commercial or industrial projects, the planner can accept the developer's building cost estimate and add the average value of land in that type of land use if the new assessment has not yet been made. In general terms, nonresidential developments pay higher prices for their sites with costs ranging from 15 to 35 percent of building values.

The sales tax is one that is not necessarily entirely captured from the residents of a city, nor limited to those same residents. Therefore, it is very hard for an analyst to be precise about where new residents will shop or from how far away new commercial development will draw customers. The following sample calculation can help to project this income, however.

Sales Tax Revenues from a Residential Project

Local annual per capita taxable purchases	= $1,000.
Regional per capita taxable purchases	= $2,000.
Local capture ratio	= 50%.
Projected project population	= 4,000.
Projected increase in taxable sales in city = $4,000 × $1,000	= $4,000,000.
Sales tax remitted to city	= 1% × 4,000,000.
Total projected annual increase in sales tax revenues	= $40,000.

Sales Tax Revenue from a Shopping Center

Shopping center retail floor space	= 100,000 square feet.
Annual tenant sales per square foot	= $75.
Annual retail sales	= $7,500,000.
Taxable retail sales	= $5,000,000
Sales tax remitted to city = 1% × $5,000,000	= $50,000 per year.

CASE STUDY: LAKEWOOD HILLS AND WINDSOR, CALIFORNIA

Some years ago, this author headed a demonstration project aimed at developing a simple methodology for comparing a major development's revenue impacts in a rural (leapfrog) location to those in a compact growth urban location. While the dollar amounts do not represent current prices, the results and comparisons are enlightening.

Project Description

The sponsor of the Lakewood Hills development drew up plans for a planned residential unit of 1,488 dwelling units, consisting of 440 apartments, 534 townhouses or cluster homes, 408 single-family detached homes, and 116 hillside estate houses. The development plan also promised a 181-acre 18-hole golf course, a swim and tennis center, a 16-acre shopping center, and 139 acres of open space, mainly in the steep hillsides to the rear of the estate area. In addition, a 9-acre school site would be reserved for future purchase by the school district. The proposed development was to be near Winsor, California.

The developer's plans were based on building and selling off the entire Lakewood Hills complex in less than 12 years. (For market absorption analysis, 10 years was used as the sales period after discounting the lead time for governmental approvals and construction.)

The cluster homes (townhouses) would cost about $25,000 and sell to people making at least $11,000 per year. The single-family detached homes would be marketed at an average price of $32,500, so that their owners would have to have incomes of around $14,000 per year. The hillside estate housing was to be priced at $40,000 and up; the income floor for that part of the development started at $17,000 per year. The apartments were slated to rent for $200 or more per month and the income needed by their occupants would be $10,000 or more per annum. As a so-called selling point to the wider community, the developer's prospectus made the point that the development was not meant for "young families with high child dependency ratios—this group has yet to accumulate the financial means to afford a unit within this project." In projecting the elementary pupil population for the development, the project planners foresaw 0.46 pupils per household.

A crude test of the developer's prognostications was the market absorption rate verification. The Santa Rosa Planning Department had estimated that the annual market demand for new housing in the coming decade would be about 13,000 units (including multiple units) for the Santa Rosa and environs area. Assuming that the market demand would be roughly proportional to the current income structure of the area (median income for Santa Rosa area was $10,763), then Lakewood Hills had to capture the following percentages of total demand over the next 10 years:

• **Cluster Houses** ($11,000 to $14,000 incomes)—Total demand was figured by calculating the percentage of area residents in that income range and multiplying by 13,000 to obtain the 2,390 figure (17.8% × 13,000). The project would offer 534 cluster homes—enough housing to meet 23.4 percent of demand in this income range.

• **Single-Family Homes** (incomes of $14,000 to $17,000)—Total demand was for 1,339 houses (10.3% × 13,000); the project would offer 408 single-family detached houses, or enough housing to meet 30.2 percent of total single-family housing market demand.

• **Estate Homes** (incomes of more than $17,000)—Total demand was for 2,210 estate homes (17.0% × 13,000); the project would offer 116 estate houses, or enough to meet 5.2 percent of total estate house demand.

Conclusion

Except for the custom houses for families with incomes of $17,000 and over, the project was attempting to capture a very ambitious share of estimated housing demand for each of the housing types it planned to market. Since a recent survey by the Sonoma County Planning Department had indicated that the overwhelming majority of county residents preferred single-family detached homes, it was figured that perhaps not more than one out of two families in this income range would choose to move way out of town to live in townhouses. This meant that the cluster houses might have to get about one out of two buyers in the market area within the next 10 years. Since a number of other townhouse developments closer to Santa Rosa had been approved in the past few years, the belief was that the project would be competing with a formidable inventory of cluster housing already on the market. Given the front costs and the costs of site preparation, utilities, as well as special facilities such as a golf course, tennis and swim center, hiking and riding trails, off-site road improvements, and the establishment of an on-site water system, it was hard to imagine how cash flow problems would be met if sales targets were not met. Other concerns included the possibility that the final value of the homes sold would be less than anticipated, and that other developments with high-cost private recreational facilities had been forced to either support the facilities publicly or close them, once the facilities no longer were useful as sales gimmicks or when the developer no longer could swallow their cost.

THE LARGER ISSUES

The most important question about a development like Lakewood Hills concerns public questions of timing and equity. Is it fair to give so much of foreseeable market demand to a single developer, especially when the development does not provide any housing opportunities for the majority of the county's families who have lower incomes and children? If a local government gives an approval to a development that will more than take care of any foreseeable need for certain residential market sectors, how is land similarly situated and next in line with a development proposal to be treated? Is this next development premature? Does the public have an interest in what the impacts of an oversupply of vacant urbanized land may mean? These are questions that the usual project-by-project analysis procedures overlook. Lakewood Hills was a case in point, and the discussion of these issues follows in the context of the evaluation of the Windsor-area location for the Lakewood Hills development.

Lakewood Hills and Windsor, California

IN THE FIRST PLACE–THE VILLAGE OF WINDSOR

Citizens of this sleepy half-urban, half-rural hamlet which is laced with trailer parks and low-income housing developments, are in a snit. . . . Some Windsorites suspect the county has a clandestine policy of turning their town into a slum. Two low-income developments housing 500 people have been built here in the past few years, and construction has begun on 100 additional units.

Even county planners are worried that Windsor may become a dumping ground for the area's poor.

Already Windsor elementary schools are in double session. Community leaders feel the volunteer fire department and police protection provided by a roving sheriff's deputy are inadequate.

The unanimous sentiment among community representatives who have testified before county planning agencies is that Lakewood Hills, by dramatically hiking the tax base, "could make Windsor."

Townspeople assert that the 573-acre Lakewood Hills development with its hillside homes, shopping center, and golf course could turn things around. . . . Ideally, county planners would like to see development take place within the Windsor Water District, where nearly 70 percent of the land is vacant.

The problem there. . . is, "How do you get developers to build high-quality housing in the midst of trailer courts, run-down commercial areas, and low-income housing projects?"

The proposed Lakewood Hills development lies just outside the water district in a relatively unscathed farming area.

County officials are also concerned about underlying social issues. Will low-income housing starts cease if Lakewood Hills is approved? Will Windsor be split into a new and old town, the existing areas becoming a slum disconnected in all but a geographical sense from the posh new development?

"We're tired of outside influence," said Jerry Fletcher, school board chairman and chamber of commerce member. "The county says we're going to be part of an urban corridor between Healdsburg and Santa Rosa–the hell we are."

Source: San Francisco *Examiner*, June 25, 1971.

The main job for the study was to see what difference Lakewood Hills would make in solving Windsor's fiscal problems, under varying assumptions of growth, assessed value, and levels of service. Fire and police services were considered to be the essential services to examine for fiscal impacts because these services cost the most in proportion to others and are perceived as essential by citizens; the others, while important, are often viewed in terms of citizen preferences.

School services include elementary, junior high, senior high, and community college functions. Analysis in this case study was confined to the elementary school district, because as the smallest education jurisdiction, it presented the most sensitive unit for recording possible changes in quality and costs.

Finally, there were the utility services of sewer and water districts. These services were financed by both user charges and property tax levies. With such a mixed system, it is often difficult, as in the case of Windsor, to determine if the pricing system charges new development the full price of growth in the form of hook-up and other fees, or whether there are hidden costs passed on to the district at large. For this reason, it was considered unfeasible to try and pin down whether new development was fully paying its way for additional land and operating costs, and so consideration of the impact on these services was not made in the first round of impact evaluations.

Windsor was an unincorporated place without urban police and fire services, and had no parks, library, or medical clinic. Government was represented by the post office and fire house in the village center. There was no plan for the community and the development pattern was a hodgepodge of agricultural and rural residential mixed up with spots of urban residential, homegrown roadside businesses, trailer parks, trailers outside of parks, and an astonishing collection of sheds, shacks, and do-it-yourself structures.

Although Windsor's history as a village went back further than its larger neighbor, Santa Rosa, it hadn't taken on its present aspect until recently. Three governmental actions were probably responsible for the most of the community's current predicament. First, the village had been bisected into east and west sections by the State Highway Engineers when they ruled, rather than designed, U.S. 101 through the heart of the crossroads that gave the village its geographical reason for existence.

Second, the Farmer's Home Administration, whose low-income housing loan program was limited to rural areas at least 10 miles from cities over 10,000, selected Windsor as the place to push its program.

Third, to make a cheap land area like Windsor feasible, (land costs could not exceed 20 percent of total housing cost), sewers had to be available and the rural zoning had to be changed to permit 6,000-square-foot lots (seven units to the net acre). The federal government gave the Windsor Sewer District grants and low-interest loans to extend sewer service well beyond the original village confines and the county passed out the necessary zone changes, so that in a very few years more than 250 low-income homes had been approved and, as a result, the local school had gone on double sessions.

Against this background of concern about the social and economic consequences of a concentration of low-cost housing, citizens in the community petitioned to form a county service district with the Lakewood Hills development. A county service area is a special district that can be formed in unincorporated areas to raise special revenues, mainly from the property tax, to purchase an urban level of municipal services (such as police and fire protection) that the county does not provide through its own general fund. The question then became, what effect would approval of the Lakewood Hills development have on the chances of Windsor improving its civic lot?

Calculations

The differential tax rates for fire, police, and elementary school services were calculated for the following sets of assumptions in this preliminary round:

Police
Minimum level = 0.5 police per 1,000 population, at $25,000 per officer/year.

Intermediate = 1.0 police per 1,000 population, at $18,000 per officer/year.

Full service = 1.5 police per 1,000 population, at $18,000 per officer/year.

The minimum level cost was based on the cost of a full-time resident sheriff, while the other levels represented the costs of additional officers. In addition, residents would continue to pay the $0.36/$100 assessed valuation to the county that they currently paid.

Fire service costs were based on the replacement of the volunteer department with professional fire fighters at the cost of $32,000 per year without Lakewood Hills and $62,000 per year if it were developed.

School assumptions were based on Lakewood Hills at full development adding either 530, 595, or 660 elementary pupils to the then average daily attendance of 629.

Evaluation of First Approximation Fiscal Impacts

Several things stood out from the results of the first approximation analysis. The first was that Windsor alone (the Water District) probably had too weak a tax base to afford to step-up its municipal services to the quality normally provided in incorporated areas.

A county service district with boundaries embracing the much vaster school district would quadruple the tax base, while actually adding less than 1,000 people to the population. While such figures may look good on paper, it was not feasible to assume that the owners of all the agricultural and vacant rural land beyond the water district would hold still for a significant jump in their taxes to provide urban services to benefit only the people in town. This was because the availability of sewer service extensions was quite limited for lands well beyond the district boundaries unless heavy costs for treatment plant and sewer line expansion were incurred. This situation made development at residential densities unlikely for the foreseeable future, and thus the benefits to farmers and ranchers from joining a service area would be difficult to sell.

On the other hand, much of the agriculture around Windsor was struggling to survive rising costs, lower rates of return, crop losses and so forth. The effect of a significant jump in taxes could very well push marginal agricultural enterprises out of business. For example, assume that a 100-acre farm is valued at $5,000 per acre. The assessed value would be $125,000 and the farm's smallest probable tax increase brought on by a service area that included Lakewood Hills and the school district with intermediate police service, and the lowest (530) pupil increase would be $0.47 per $100 assessed valuation. This would cost the farmer $587 more per year. It might push him into cutting down his orchard, pulling up his grape vines, or selling off his milk cows to reduce his tax assessment and to allow him to hang on to the land while he took a job in town, dreamed of a developer coming to his door with the "big offer," and speculate about selling off an acre here and there for lot split housing. (Lot splits are subdivisions of property into four or less parcels. This kind of subdividing escapes many of the improvement requirements of the subdivision ordinance). The homeowner, however, with a $25,000 house and lot, who receives much more benefit from higher quality municipal services, would pay only $35.25 per year in additional taxes.

Further analysis of the first approximation was not warranted because there were no significant variations in the tax rates among other possible Lakewood Hills locations. Perhaps more importantly, these alternatives were really comparing apples to oranges by lumping the present assessed value for the Windsor water and school districts with the possible assessed valuation of a development that would not be completed for at least 10 years.

Fiscal Analysis: Round Two

A second round of analysis that carried the growth of both Windsor and Lakewood Hills forward on a yearly basis for 10 years was then done to learn what the road from here to there might look like. The analysis included the possibility that the developer might sell his houses only half as fast as he said he would, due to the high market absorption rate the development would have to meet to sell out in 10 years. In the second analysis, it also was necessary to look more thoroughly at Windsor. First, it was one of the poorest communities in Sonoma County. Almost half (48 percent) of the families there earned less than $8,000. The median family income of the Windsor area was 16 percent below the countywide median of $9,673. At the same time, the sizable (18 percent) Hispanic population had incomes that were 38 percent below the countywide median.

As would be expected, the 69 percent of the housing stock there that was owner-occupied had a median value that was 32 percent less than the countywide figure. What this meant in terms of fiscal weakness was that a penny of tax increase in the Windsor Elementary School District would raise only $862; in the nearby similarly sized cities of Sebastopol and Healdsburg, a penny increase would raise $987 and $1,005 respectively. A penny increase in the Windsor water district would bring in only $270. In addition, Sebastopol and Healdsburg had sizable commercial centers whose sales tax revenues were the property tax equivalent of $1.50 and $1.83 respectively. The sales tax raised in Windsor went into the general county fund, but was not considered to amount to much even if it could be kept at home because of Windsor's comparatively tiny commercial center. The almost total dependence on the regressive property tax is an institutional liability that severely penalizes county service areas when compared with municipalities.

The trend of growth in Windsor was not very encouraging either. Most of the growth had been residential, and in the previous seven and a half years, 8.3 percent of the new homes built

there were valued (not including land) at less than $20,000 by the county building department. In the previous two and a half years, since the Farmer's Home Administration had become active in the area, the percentage of new single-family home construction less than $20,000 in value had risen to 9.2 percent while the volume had more than tripled in recent years. Furthermore, the occupants of these low-income housing projects had many school-age children (about 0.9 elementary school children per household).

Therefore, in carrying forward the analysis, it appeared reasonable to try to discern how a higher income development like Lakewood Hills would offset a likely continuation of this trend.

A secondary issue was how much subsidy does or should an area like the Windsor water district receive when it has only $6,860 of assessed value per person in a county with $23,500 of assessed value per person. Given the California Supreme Court decision that the quality of education should not be entirely dependent on the size of the local tax base, it could also be strongly argued under the equal protection clause of the Constitution that public safety (police and fire services) as well should be freed from the limitations of how much assessed value an area has to use for paying the costs.

In this second analysis, for the sake of internal consistency and comparability, it was assumed that in each instance the community would choose the recommended standard of 1.5 police per 1,000 residents, that it would opt for an increasingly higher quality of fire protection, and that it would add schools to the system at the recommended rate of one new school for each increment of 500 additional pupils. It must be remembered, however, that these assumptions meant that Windsor was envisioned as already accepting the same levels of service without Lakewood Hills as it would want with it. In this analysis, the capital costs of a new firehouse to serve Lakewood Hills and East Windsor, plus equipment, new police cars and equipment, and the costs of new schools in terms of payments on principal and interest were added to the estimated operating costs to obtain the total tax levy for each service.

Other assumptions were that the water district's tax base would increase 5 percent per year over the 1971·72 base, with a pupil-residence ratio of 0.6, while Lakewood Hills was calculated as contributing only 0.4 pupils per dwelling unit. This was done so as to come up with the most conservative school cost increases. The low-income housing then being built in Windsor was contributing students to the elementary schools at 0.9 pupils per residence. Windsor's water district was assumed to contain all of the community's 1971·72 population, rather than dividing it with the school district.

In the case of fire protection, Windsor had a Class X rating, on a scale of I to X with X being the lowest. A fire district moves up this rating scale, which was devised by fire insurance underwriters, by meeting certain standards in seven categories; the categories including water supply, adequacy of the fire department, alarm system, and structural conditions are given the most weight. By adding equipment, having trained personnel, and improving its hydrant and water system a district can improve its ratings. However, it becomes increasingly more expensive for a district to advance in the scale, especially beyond Class VII.

In Windsor's case an advance to a Class IX zone rating would have saved the owner of a $20,000 home $9 a year on structural insurance and $4 on dwelling-contents insurance. Certain parts of the central area of the community might reach an VIII rating, in which case the structural rate would drop by $32 and the con-

tents rate by $16.

Additionally, the community of Windsor then paid $0.12 per $100 for fire protection provided by the state division of forestry. Formation of its own fire district was expected to excuse Windsor from this charge, which would further offset the cost of having improved service.

Analysis of the aggregate tax costs revealed that, as expected, the addition of Lakewood Hills to the Windsor community would offset the costs of improved services five and ten years out. Furthermore, since Windsor had been launched on the road to urbanization by actions taken before Lakewood Hills came on the scene, it had probably passed the point of no return between remaining rural and developing into a full-fledged urban area. Lowering the cost of services, however, still does not reveal whether people can afford them. To begin with, homeowners in the Windsor area already paid high taxes. Forming a new county service area simply meant new taxes on top of the old ones. For example, homeowners with a tax bill that added up to a rate of $14.34 per $100 of assessed value could expect to pay as much as $5.50 more per $100 assessed valuation in ten years as a result of buying improved urban services and paying for growth in the school district.

For the owner of a federally assisted home valued at $20,000, the payments and insurance would come to $1,560 a year. Taxes then were about $13 per $100 assessed valuation or $650 per year for the owner of a house in the Windsor water district. That meant that the typical family that made $8,000 a year had to spend about 28 percent of its income on housing due to the tax loads. The generally accepted rule of thumb is that a family should not have to spend more than 25 percent of its income on housing or else it may forego other necessities like food, clothing, transportation, and medical care.

Every $1.60 rise in the property tax at this rate would raise the cost of housing for such a family by another 1 percent of annual income. On the other hand, the typical $14,000-per-year family envisioned for some of Lakewood Hills could pay a tax bill of $2.80, which is 75 percent higher, before it meant another 1 percent of their income being taken by taxes on shelter ($140 versus $80). This is where the seeming objectivity of cost·revenue analysis breaks down, for there is no objective way to really pin down the impacts on people with widely varying abilities to pay, when these abilities are largely unknown. Which is of greater benefit: Raising taxes to improve public services or keeping taxes at a level that allows lower income families to keep their homes? One answer is that it is wrong to have to make such a choice. Some say that revenue sharing and revenue pooling should be employed to protect people and their property and to educate their children to decent standards without dependence on their ability to pay.

Other Impacts of Lakewood Hills in Windsor

Water Supply. The developer planned to build a storage reservoir and drill two or three wells in the on-site aquifier. This would probably provide an adequate supply for the foreseeable future. The developer would then turn these facilities over to the Windsor water district. The costs of maintaining and operating the system would be neutral, probably changing to slightly positive as the development built up to provide enough additional customers to allow economies of scale to be passed on to the district customers in the form of reduced charges. Because of a large aquifer underneath the Windsor area, the district could continue to depend on wells that would provide a water

supply on a minisystem basis as each subarea of the district developed. However, in seven years the district might find it advisable to link up with the county aqueduct system and use the wells as a back-up system. This was a situation that required a level of countywide planning—planning that was not yet available. The increased revenue and size that Lakewood Hills would bring to the district would make capital improvements by revenue bonding such as an aqueduct hook up somewhat more feasible.

Roads. As Windsor became more urbanized, its people would no longer live on the land but on the highway. It was virtually without public transit, and it was doubtful that the Golden Gate Bridge District's service would be extended there soon unless the county was willing to subsidize the growth. The residents thus had to look forward to continued dependence on automobiles. The county road system and state highway interchange in the vicinity of Lakewood Hills were inadequate; an engineering analysis of the situation by the county public works department concluded that:

> Freeway access at the junction with Old Redwood Road is difficult and without considerable expenditure by the State in construction of a "clover leaf" will turn from difficult to impossible with the phased construction of this (Lakewood Hills) development.

Because most of the development's traffic would probably be traveling toward employment centers in Santa Rosa and beyond, it was probable that the freeway interchange snarl would divert southbound traffic onto local streets, to other interchanges, or even on to county roads leading to the city.

In order to develop a minimum of proper access for Lakewood Hills, a considerable amount of off-site road improvements would have to be completed. The construction costs for improving roadways external to the site had been estimated to be $321,000. (It is assumed that all rights-of-way are dedicated at no cost. This may be a dubious assumption if the contributing lands are restricted for future use as agriculture or open space purposes.) To the degree the developer did not pick up this cost—there was also $982,000 of on-site roadway costs—then the taxpayers of the county would either pay for it, leaving other projects undone, or the Windsor area would simply live with the traffic being generated from the development onto a very inadequate circulation pattern.

Since there was no plan for the Windsor area, there was no way to be certain that the roads built to serve Windsor would tie in with adjoining development or fit in any way with an overall circulation system serving the whole community. Assuming this were the case, the county road fund would have to maintain about seven and a half miles of county roads largely for the benefit of the traffic generated by Lakewood Hills. To a great extent the Lakewood Hills residents would be relocated county residents and thus there would be no new revenue from gas tax funds to offset this cost. The county then was spending $1,150 per mile per year on road maintenance. The approximate annual costs of maintaining the roads that would serve Lakewood Hills was $86,000. To be fair, new roads do not cost as much to maintain as old ones, but given the thousands of daily trips that the shopping center, golf course, and homes would generate, maintenance costs well above those of the average county road in a rural area soon would arise.

In summarizing the fiscal effects of Lakewood Hills on the Windsor community, it seemed fair to say that while Lakewood Hills with its proportionally higher valuation would offset the burden of improved public service to some degree, it was also probable that Windsor alone would be more likely to settle for a lower cost service package than it would when spurred on by the hope of fiscal rescue by the "rich folks" who would live out by the golf course. The slower they were in moving in, the more the front end costs of this package would fall onto those who could least afford it. The development was being looked to "to turn things around," and it also would have to perform prodigious feats for the next decade to capture its predicted share of an uncertain and highly competitive market. The situation called for more rather than less caution, and that was the strongest recommendation the study made about any of the county service area proposals for Windsor.

SUMMING UP

In places like Windsor, a development like Lakewood Hills is evaluated on whether it can change things from the way they are instead of on how well it will fit in.

This asks a development to do much more than just be a good neighbor and contribute to the commonwealth in proportion to what it is getting. Some voices in Windsor expected the newcomers to subsidize their civic aspirations as well as confer new status on the community. It was beyond the methodology of the project to search out how these kinds of impacts can come to pass. However, it is entirely relevant to point out that new status and subsidies have been the goals of urban renewal projects for several years now, with the usual result being that "areas" have been upgraded by having the people in them removed. In Windsor, too, civic striving had to be weighed against what it would do to the housing costs and opportunities of the low- and moderate-income people who made up the majority of the population living there.

The impact that a development like Lakewood Hills makes on the community around it is largely conditioned by the makeup of the place at the time that the impact is being assessed. Thus, in the case, Windsor, one encountered a place undergoing rapid residential growth with a fragmented and impoverished local government structure supported by a population characterized by low incomes, large families, and most of the disadvantages that accrue to those who inhabit the lower end of the income scale.

Windsor's federal sewer grants and loans, plus the subsidized housing of the Farm Home Administration, resulted in a prime example of the disorder that the national government bestowed on local governments by distributing the benefits of its programs in an uncoordinated way. The federally assisted sewers and housing introduced there really are examples of income transfers from richer to poorer people. The notion that Lakewood Hills would subsidize the resulting need for improved urban services is really the same thing, for the people who would live there, not the developer, were being counted on to contribute taxes for the benefit of their poorer neighbors. This is bad welfare economics, for the subsidy to be taken out of the pockets of a relatively small group of the more well-to-do residents would have been substantial and they would not directly benefit.

The social benefits obtained from giving lower income people an opportunity for decent housing had already been partially recognized as being in the national interest. The provision of adequate funds for a decent education has been ruled by the courts as being a right independent of the size of the local tax base. Many think it is not stretching this point to include adequate protection of life and property as a right that ought to be equally independent of the size of a local tax base. Thus the creation of an urbanized place with no attention to whether the area has the means to support or attract the support for adequate public services and facilities means that continued subvention by some larger unit of government will be the only answer. If there is no government treasury that will pick up the tab for making places like Windsor livable, then urbanizing is a major mistake and it should be left a semirural community, with service demands that can be met more fully by county and local resources.

Given these conditions, plus the other uncertainties and risks involved in proceeding to develop without a plan, Lakewood Hills could not be viewed very favorably at the time. The only certainty was that there would be either a substantial rise in an already burdensome property tax rate or a deferred improvement in services until the hoped-for offsets from Lakewood Hills might arrive some years later. Good business practice discounts future returns against current outlays. Since Lakewood Hills would have to perform incredible feats of market capture in the next decade for the upper-income housing market to come to full development, a discount rate of 10 percent per year seemed reasonable. That meant at least $1.60 of future offset five years out was needed to equal $1.00 of additional current cost (10 percent compounded). As Willis H. Shapley of the United States Bureau of the Budget said:

> The primary concern is the effect of the various choices that are before us on the total rate of expenditures, i.e., the total outlays required each year for the foreseeable future. When we are looking six or seven years into the future, there is little to go on and everything gets quite hazy. The effects of the total ultimate cost of a particular program on overall future budgets are generally overshadowed by the inherent uncertainties and effect of other decisions to be made between now and then.

Further work is needed to deal with the following.

1. Does the question of marginal public costs and revenues resulting from new development hinge largely on the existing capacity levels of public services and facilities? If this is the case, then when the excess capacities are large, additional development may help spread fixed costs and thus confer a net plus. These effects need to be studied with respect to the so-called advantages of compact development. Urban form considerations based on aesthetic judgments have been implied as having economic grounds as well. We suspect that there are probably many instances where further contiguous development may be less beneficial and more costly than moving out to a self-contained location, especially if the new development is sizable, diversified, and reasonably well-to-do, as many planned unit developments are.

2. When properly served, the poor and disadvantaged require more from government than the affluent. When rich and poor are mixed, the more well-to-do subsidize their poorer neighbors. Most conscious attempts to bring the poor to live near the affluent have been bitterly resisted. Further work, however, is needed to probe for the limits at which this kind of local subsidy to the low-income people becomes socially and economically inappropriate and disadvantageous to both groups.

THE ANALYTIC PROCESS OF THE SAMPLE STUDY

The analytic process demonstrated in the case study is principally concerned with the comparative evaluation of alternative locations for an activity. There are five major evaluation categories used in this process:[8]

1. *Fiscal impacts*—The costs and revenues to all relevant public jurisdictions.

2. *Nonfiscal impacts*—These include externalities or uncompensated costs and benefits. Examples include significant changes in the environment, neighborhood character, traffic flows, and social conditions arising from an activity being introduced into an area.

3. *Distribution of impacts*—Impacts are distributed among jurisdictions, various income levels, various land uses, and so forth.

4. *Comparative effects between alternative locations*—This focuses on the differentials between impacts which arise from the nature of the place rather than the nature of the development. Thus a development that reduces property taxes by spreading fixed costs onto a larger tax base in one location may increase taxes in another by incurring congestion or expansion costs for which it does not fully compensate those bearing these costs. This is easily evident in such public facilities as schools, roads, sewers, and others of fixed capacities.

5. *Relation of net impacts to public objectives and plans*—In the Windsor case study, the initial public objective related to the analysis was whether the development to be added to the community gave Windsor a fiscal assist in meeting its needs for higher levels of public services. However, as this analysis proceeded, other public objectives were called into question, which might offset the purely fiscal favorable findings (e.g., impacts on low-income home owners, agriculture, environmental changes, etc.) In the second analysis, the focus was on objectives of compatability with existing neighborhood character and trade-offs between the new development and the facilities in place. It was hoped that the comparison between the two locations would focus on the relative costs and benefits of compact versus noncompact growth. However, the findings in this instance were unclear, due at least partially to the fact that in the case of Windsor there was no plan for the area to clearly designate Lakewood Hills as either a next-in-line location or a leapfrog development with respect to the orderly growth plans of Windsor. However, it did illuminate the side effects likely to occur in two different economic and institutional settings, thus raising a number of important issues for future planning and policymaking to resolve. This is seen as a decided advantage of this analytical process because while the traditional process *starts* with goals, analysis is directed at defining the questions toward which a search for goals or a reexamination of existing ones must be directed. This is done by evaluating the impacts stemming from achieving a certain goal compared to its alternatives.

The first analysis helped to avoid the data trap of most research programs that become mired down in collecting and sifting through mountains of information in order to find a few nuggets of relevancy. The first approximation technique made it possible to quickly assemble estimates of the significance of impacts by preparing a precise approach for interviewing knowledgeable people about what would happen if, for example, 1,488 dwelling units were placed in a certain location. The people interviewed were briefed on specifically what they were supposed to respond to (e.g., when would the sewer plant need expanded capacity if there is a 5 percent growth level in the community each year?). This kind of analysis is quite different from conventional planning choices that usually ask how much growth shall there be. Instead, the analysis appraises what is involved in accommodating a given amount of growth under the variations that are inherent in different locations, thus giving policymakers information on choices, rather than a grand design. The first approximation technique is simply the formation of an unmeasured, judgmental consensus on problem parameters (costs, realistic rates of market absorption, etc.) by use of generally accepted estimates obtained from discussion with knowledgeable people and analysis of available data.

Often it also will be necessary to develop logical approximations of land use configurations as part of this process in order to properly determine the setting for impacts. This is known as creating a sketch plan. Then when first approximations are developed, the first step preceding analysis is to separate the factors that would be neutral or insignificant in cost and benefit from those that appear to be critical. This is a procedure designated as *sensitivity analysis*. The study found that the significance of the same factor would change markedly in alternate locations.

Finally, there is the analysis of fiscal and nonfiscal impacts and their distribution. The study considered the stream of costs and benefits over time. In the case of Lakewood Hills, the full benefits of its increased assessed valuation would not arrive for ten or more years when full development was supposed to take place. Without even discounting future returns, one finds that it is the baseline growth rate of 5 percent per year (in mainly low-cost housing) that is the critical timing element in pushing up demand for services faster than revenues can be obtained without ruinous taxes.

NOTES

1. In Portland, Oregon, the school district has been paying for television commercials to favorably impress the 83 percent of households that do not have children in the public school system. In other cities, voters have refused to approve the tax levies necessary to keep the schools open a full year; some schools have had to close their doors early.

2. The hidden agenda in this study is that even the most expensive residences will appear to have negative cost-revenue net return because they are heavily subsidized by the nonresidential tax.

3. Charles F. Stam, "Urban Fiscal Stress: Is It Inevitable?" in *Tempo,* Vol. 25, No. 1, 1979, pp. 13-18.

4. In "Taxes and the Death of Cities" (*Architectural Forum,* June 1966, p. 87), Perry Prentice wrote, "Actually, the value of unimproved suburban land and underimproved urban land derives 100 percent and perhaps more than 100 percent from money the community has had to invest in roads, streets, sewers, schools, water supplies, fire protection, police protection, and other community facilities without which that land would be neither accessible nor liveable."

5. A case in point was the pressure felt by small rural communities to accept federal grants for sewer systems. Led by pressure from local health departments, which declared local residential septic tanks to be "failing" (although in most cases they could be repaired), the 90 percent federal capital grant for sewers committed the community to unplanned growth and urbanization. For example, one community in California was offered a sewage system whose cost was equal to 81 percent of the community's assessed value. The project report dismissed this cost-revenue disaster by implying that new growth following the sewers would take care of the problem.

6. Richard B. Stern and Darwin G. Stuart, "Beware the Pitfalls in Fiscal Impact Analysis," in *Planning,* April 1980, pp. 15-17.

7. Where more richness of detail or specific impacts over time for each category of service is desired, several more complex methodologies are explained in *Practitioner's Guide to Fiscal Impact Analysis,* by Robert W. Burchell and David Listokin (Piscataway, NJ.: Rutgers University Center for Urban Research).

8. Nathaniel Litchfield, who has pioneered in this kind of economic analysis, states: "When a public agency provides services to be paid through taxes, its benefits are the taxes. But those paying taxes may not be the ones who receive the benefits, and where necessary a distinction is made. Analysis attempts to forecast, prior to the time of decision, the difference in all costs and benefits accruing to each producer or consumer if the project were implemented. This being the case, we compare costs and benefits which would arise 'with' the project's implementation *against those arising without undertaking the project at all.*"

CHAPTER

10

Ethics and
the Planner

Albert Solnit

There is such a thing as the public interest, higher than any and all private interests, and it is something of which a politician must at least be dimly conscious. HENDRICK HERTZBERG, "The Education of Mr. Smith," in *Esquire*, February 1986, p. 37

To plan is to make waves. This happens because real planning has to steer a course between community values, political dealing, private interest pressures, and professional views of the public interest. A few years ago, many planners could escape the development controversies of the time by dwelling at the drafting board on the plan for 20 years into the future. There, what happened at the next council meeting wasn't too relevant to the "big picture." Today, it is still okay to look into the future, but it is not okay to get caught staring at it. The planner who comes out in public these days has to speak to the action needed for here and now. The days of fat federal grants to make lengthy studies and long-range

colored map plans for every section of the city or county are over.[1]

THE GRAY AREAS

This chapter deals with how a planner can deal with the problems of loyalty to the jurisdiction and agency, of dissent and compromise, of building effectiveness as an advisor to politicians, citizens, and other agencies, and of working as a regulator of business interests. These are gray areas, and are not as easy to address as queries such as, "Shall I take bribes?" The assumption here is that the reader has an operational conscience and can distinguish between right and wrong at the felony level.

Hendrick Hertzberg advises:

First, everyone should start out with a clear idea of "This is as far as I go and I don't care if it gets me fired." This is to know what freedom really is.[2]

But as Hertzberg pointed out: "There are few opportunities to step so boldly into the moral

173

sunshine." He notes that the planner learns that the real choices leave him in the grey area. "From the best of motives he begins to make compromises. He wishes to build his effectiveness. He seeks to accumulate credits that will be used at some future date in some unspecified way on some issue he doesn't know about yet. And then he begins to put his soul in danger. He begins to imagine that his...advancement is so important to the cause of good and right that the cause of good and right is served by his advancement in and of itself."[3]

THE HOWE-KAUFMAN STUDY

Many planners will never perceive situations where there is an ethical conflict. A few years ago a large randomly selected group of American planners were given scenarios in which a theoretical planner acts in a certain way.[4] For example, a planner gives a land developer draft recommendations from a development plan for a largely vacant part of the city upon the developer's request. No agency policy on releasing such information exists. The theory behind Elizabeth Howe and Jerome Kaufman's study was that:

1. For planners, ethics set the boundaries of acceptable behavior.

2. A set of commonly held behavioral norms make up the body of professional ethics.

3. Some, but by no means all, of these norms have been codified in the American Institute of Planners' Code (see Exhibit 10.1).

Exhibit 10.1
CODE OF ETHICS AND PROFESSIONAL CONDUCT, AMERICAN INSTITUTE OF CERTIFIED PLANNERS

The Planner's Responsibility to the Public
A. A planner's primary obligation is to serve the public interest. While the definition of the public interest is formulated through continuous debate, a planner owes allegiance to a conscientiously attained concept of the public interest, which requires these special obligations:

1. A planner must have special concern for the long-range consequences of present actions.

2. A planner must pay special attention to the interrelatedness of decisions.

3. A planner must strive to provide full, clear, and accurate information on planning issues to citizens and governmental decision makers.

4. A planner must strive to give citizens the opportunity to have a meaningful impact on the development of plans and programs. Participation should be broad enough to include people who lack formal organization or influence.

5. A planner must strive to expand choice and opportunity for all persons, recognizing a special responsibility to plan for the needs of disadvantaged groups and persons, and must urge the alteration of policies, institutions, and decisions which oppose such needs.

6. A planner must strive to protect the integrity of the natural environment.

7. A planner must strive for excellence of environmental design and endeavor to conserve the heritage of the built environment.

The Planner's Responsibility to Clients and Employers
B. A planner owes diligent, creative, independent and competent performance of work in pursuit of the client's or employer's interest. Such performance should be consistent with the planner's faithful service to the public interest.

1. A planner must exercise independent professional judgment on behalf of clients and employers.

2. A planner must accept the decisions of a client or employer concerning the objectives and nature of the professional services to be performed unless the course of action to be pursued involves conduct which is illegal or inconsistent with the planner's primary obligation to the public interest.

3. A planner must not, without the consent of the client or employer, and only after full disclosure, accept or continue to perform work if there is an actual, apparent, or reasonably foreseeable conflict between the interests of the client or employer and the personal or financial interest of the planner or of another past or present client or employer of the planner.

4. A planner must not solicit prospective clients or employment through use of false or misleading claims, harassment or duress.

5. A planner must not sell or offer to sell services by stating or implying an ability to influence decisions by improper means.

6. A planner must not use the power of any office to seek or obtain a special advantage that is not in the public interest nor any special advantage that is not a matter of public knowledge.

7. A planner must not accept or continue to perform work beyond the planner's professional competence or accept work which cannot be performed with the promptness required by the prospective client or employer, or which is required by the circumstances of the assignment.

8. A planner must not reveal information gained in a professional relationship which the client or employer has requested be held inviolate. Exceptions to this requirement of non-disclosure may be made only when (a) required by process of law, or (b) required to prevent a clear violation of law, or (c) required to prevent a substantial injury to the public. Disclosure pursuant to (b) and (c) must not be made until after the planner has verified the facts and issues involved and, when practicable, has exhausted efforts to obtain reconsideration of the matter and has sought separate opinions on the issue from other qualified professionals employed by the client or employer.

The Planner's Responsibility to the Profession and to Colleagues

C. A planner should contribute to the develoment of the profession by improving knowledge and techniques, making work relevant to solutions of community problems, and increasing public understanding of planning activities. A planner should treat fairly the professional views of qualified colleagues and members of other professions.

1. A planner must protect and enhance the integrity of the profession and must be responsible in criticism of the profession.

2. A planner must accurately represent the qualifications, views and findings of colleagues.

3. A planner, who has responsibility for reviewing the work of other professionals, must fulfill his responsibility in a fair, considerate, professional and equitable manner.

4. A planner must share the results of experience and research which contribute to the body of planning knowledge.

5. A planner must examine the applicability of planning theories, methods and standards to the facts and analysis of each particular situation and must not accept the applicability of a customary solution without first establishing its appropriateness to the situation.

6. A planner must contribute time and information to the professional development of students, interns, beginning professionals and other colleagues.

7. A planner must strive to increase the opportunities for women and members of recognized minorities to become professional planners.

The Planner's Self-Responsibility

D. A planner should strive for high standards of professional integrity, proficiency and knowledge.

1. A planner must not commit a deliberately wrongful act which reflects adversely on the planner's professional fitness.

2. A planner must respect the rights of others and, in particular, must not improperly discriminate against persons.

3. A planner must strive to continue professional education.

4. A planner must accurately represent professional qualifications, education and affiliations.

5. A planner must systematically and critically analyze ethical issues in the practice of planning.

6. A planner must strive to contribute time and effort to groups lacking in adequate planning resources and to voluntary professional activities.

What the study found was that:

1. The most acceptable tactics involved the planner playing an activist role, such as acting to dramatize a problem in the face of existing apathy and using expendables as trade-offs, (e.g., strong recommendations to really be used as bargaining chips, and a planner working with a group trying to overturn an official action on his own time). See Table 10.1.

2. Least acceptable tactics were the use of threats, distortion, and leaking of information.

3. There was widespread disagreement about leaking inside information to outside groups or interests (see Table 10.2).

4. The greatest uncertainty occurred when the planner bowing to pressure from a superior changed his technical judgment.

5. The benefiting issue of a tactic had some efffect on how the planners viewed the ethics of a tactic, probably due to the value system

TABLE 10.1
RANK ORDER OF TACTICS BY ETHICAL ACCEPTABILITY

Rank	Tactic	Total Response Ethical	Total Response Unethical	Total Response Not sure
1.	Dramatize problem to overcome apathy	82%	13%	5%
2.	Use expendables as trade-off	68	21	11
3.	Assist group overturn official action	67	24	9
4.	Release draft information on request to environmental group	64	27	8
5.	Release draft information on request to white homeowners group	54	34	11
6.	Organize coalition of support to induce pressure	53	35	11
7.	Release draft information on request to developer	47	43	9
8.	Change technical judgment due to pressure	42	39	18
9.	Leak information to low-income group	33	55	12
10.	Leak information to environmental group	31	59	10
11.	Distort information	22	70	9
12.	Distort information	17	74	9
13.	Leak information to Chamber of Commerce	16	75	8
14.	Distort information	13	81	8
15.	Threaten	11	84	5

Note: Totals for some scenarios are less than 100 percent due to rounding.

Source: Elizabeth Home and Jerome Kaufman, "Ethics of Contemporary American Planners," in *Journal of the American Planning Association*, July 1979, p. 247.

planners espouse. Thus, tactics benefiting issues like environment and low-income housing were considered more ethical than the same tactics benefiting business or developer groups.

6. There was a strong relation between ethical attitudes and potential behavior (from 75 to more than 80 percent in every scenario).

7. The most acceptable tactics were the least risky.

8. The central variable in the differences among planners was probably role. Politically oriented planners found the tactics in the scenarios more acceptable than technically oriented planners did.

9. Planners who wanted to combine both the technical and political roles outnumbered the number at both extremes.

10. The majority of planners were "quite loyal or committed to their agencies" where the scenario involved dissent with agency policy.

TABLE 10.2
EFFECT OF VALUES ON
RELEASING DRAFT RECOMMENDATION

Releasing draft recommendations	Total Responses Ethical	Total Responses Unethical
1. To a representative of an environmental group	64%	27%
2. To a representative of a white homeowners group	54	34
3. To a land developer	47	43

Source: Elizabeth Howe and Jerome Kaufman, "Ethics of Contemporary American Planners," in *Journal of the American Planning Association*, July 1979, p. 252.

11. However, the majority of planners think it is acceptable to be open about their values and express them in their work.

12. Technicians hold to the traditional value-free image of a planner whose effectiveness is based on purely objective in-depth analysis. These technicians were more loyal to agency policy. Politicians are much more interested in influencing policy and are much more willing to use political tactics to do so. They are usually more committed to issues or client groups than to their agencies. Obviously, they are much more value oriented than technicians.

Howe and Kaufman found that the majority of planners are hybrids.

Hybrids are close to technicians in their attitudes about analysis, and to politicans in their attitudes about political tactics. Overall, they seem to be more like politicians than technicians in being value committed and not totally committed to agency policy. The only place they hold views stronger than other role groups is in the belief planning should be long range, which may indicate a more ambitious view of what planning should be than is held by either other group.[5]

Study Conclusion

Ethical standards in planning are relative. But the traditional approach of the American Institute of Planners (dissolved in 1978) was to set up a code of conduct treating the planner as a pure number-crunching technician. (The newer Code of Ethics and Professional Conduct of the American Institute of Certified Planners does recognize that "planners' primary obligation is to serve the public interest.") The fact still remains that practicing planners face ethical dilemmas.

ETHICAL DILEMMAS

Sit any group of seasoned public agency planners together and out of their career war stories will inevitably come many versions of common ethical dilemmas. Client allegiance versus planner autonomy is one of the most common. If one assumes that the professional-client relationship is with the person or agency that pays the planner's salary, then, in Peter Marcuse's words, the following obligations fall on the professional:

a. Confidentiality within the client-professional relationship;
b. Avoidance of representation of conflicting interests;
c. Uniform espousal of the client's interests in dealing with others.

But as a professional, according to Howe and Kaufman, the planner also is supposed to:

a. Give the client sound and independent advice whether or not the client will be offended...
b. Take responsibility for formulation of the problem as well as of the answer and must be willing to challenge the client's preconceptions and refuse too limited instructions in order to do so.[6]

All this usually raises more questions: Who is the client? Isn't the "public interest" sometimes a superior client to the paying client? Even if the elected representatives are considered the client, how about the city manager or county administrator who usually considers himself the executive arm of these people *and* the boss of the planning director, with a budget knife to punish dissenters?

Is bringing bad news to the king an ethical issue? Especially when the manager says do not make waves, the votes are already in place? What can determine when serving the public interest shall override keeping peace in the family?

Consider the following occurrence: The county supervisors shared Community Development Block Grant funds with several cities. At the ritualistic public meeting where the funds—supposedly aimed at improving the housing opportunities of the poorer residents—were to be distributed, the use to which each jurisdiction was going to put the funds and how that use met the federal "helping the poor" criteria were read into the record. One of the most affluent cities announced that it was going to buy a millionaire's mansion and hadn't connected this expenditure to any qualifying language yet, but would submit something later. Many of the planners wanted to confront this arrogant contempt for the legal intent of the grant program; however, they were ordered not to make any futile protests at the meeting. So they offered the press the qualifying language the city had omitted: "The purchase of the D-Mansion offered the low-income residents of the city an outstanding opportunity to understand what kind of housing they'd live in if they got rich." They learned that off-the-record ridicule can often illuminate an issue more effectively than confrontational rhetoric.

Discussions of these gray zones usually conclude that there are no stock, all-purpose answers to cover every ethical question.

FINDING THE RIGHT NICHE

The most important decision a planner may make is to follow Polonius's advice: "To thine own self be true." This means the planner should choose the role in planning that best suits his or her internal makeup. If analytical work and rigorous statistical work is a planner's forte, it is probably unwise to take a job that emphasizes public relations and debating against attorneys. By the same token, a planner with a strong inclination to work for social justice for the poor will not be too well fitted in a computerized traffic modeling project.

After mapping the internal terrain—the role, the risks, and the values that the planner wants to assume in his or her career—it then becomes important to be selective about the agency and clients for whom the planner will work. If Norman Krumholz is right, then enlisting in the right cause will be difficult. He dismissed the majority of the planning profession with the following put-down:

> Most planners, I began to think, were ordinary bureaucrats seeking a secure career, some status, and regular increases in salary. They rarely took unpopular public positions since these might prejudice these modest objectives.[8]

To an extent he is right: Working under a planning director whose major priority in life is to collect full measure from the retirement fund usually means that in that department issues of social equity, saving the environment, or simply resisting bad development will not often be raised. The facts also are that political power is in the hands of the politicians and the rich business and residential interests. But planners have one power not given to the politically strong—the power of information.

When a dispute arises over some aspect of zoning or development, it is the planning department that should be giving out the truth in plain language to the people in the community.

A good planning department does not hide behind a staff report delivered at a public hearing. It should have a strong liaison with community groups to explain what is at issue, what the rules and options of the game are, how this piece of growth fits into long-range plans, and how it will impact on the environment, the local economy, the traffic system, and everything else that people might bring up. Obviously, a well-organized development corporation will have a sales team of slick attorneys and high-status experts at work long before a hearing. If the planner's version is not out and comprehended well before a hearing, then the planners usually lose. This is because of the very nature of public hearings, where the pro and con sides can engage in tactics suitable to an adversary courtroom fight, but the planner is staff. Rebuttals, cross-examinations to disclose false statements or reveal concealed facts, and springing surprise witnesses, exhibits, and experts are tactics usually prohibited to the planner but generously allowed the interested parties who play to win. Moreover, in some instances, the hearing chairperson will muzzle the planners with statements such as, "We've already read the staff reports and minutes of the planning commission; there's no need to take up time with a repetition by the planning staff."

Under circumstances like these many planners would be tempted to issue/use leaks to the media, coach the opposition to the council action, and use other questionable tactics. This is the place where a planner needs to turn his analytical skills inward. For example, Sissela Bok's "practical moral reasoning in three steps" could be applied.

1. Consider alternative ways of achieving the purpose underlying the intention to lie or to use some other questionable tactic.
2. Weigh the moral reason for and against the contemplated actions.
3. Consider the test of publicity—how a jury of peers would judge the contemplated action.[8]

Albert Einstein put the ethical imperative succinctly when he stated:

The right to search for truth,
implies also a duty.
One must not conceal
any part
of what one has recognized
to be true.[9]

Finally, ethics require wisdom. As Rod McLiesh noted on National Public Radio, NASA had great technological skills in putting together a space shuttle that could go into space, but lacked wisdom about when *not* to launch. Wisdom for planners is the same. Great technical skill in assembling and analyzing information also requires the wisdom to ethically decide how and where to use the technical product.

NOTES

1. Earl Finkler, "Viewpoint," in *Planning,* June 1984, p. 42

2. Hendrick Hertzberg, "The Education of Mr. Smith," in *Esquire,* February 1968, pp. 37-38.

3. Hertzberg, p. 38

4. Elizabeth Howe and Jerome Kaufman, "The Ethics of Contemporary American Planners," in *Journal of the American Planning Association,* July 1979, pp. 243-55.

5. Howe and Kaufman, p. 252.

6. Howe and Kaufman, p. 254.

7. Norman Krumholz, "A Retrospective View of Equity Planning," in *Journal of the American Planning Association,* Spring 1982, pp. 164-165.

8. Sissela Bok, *Lying: Moral Choice in Public and Private Life,* quoted in *Ethical Awareness in Planning,* October 1983, p. 65.

9. Inscribed on Albert Einstein memorial, Washington, D.C.

Glossary

Many of these terms and their definitions are adapted from Miriam Laukers, compiler, *The Language of Planning, An Explanation of Selected Land Use Planning and Zoning Words and Phrases* (Olympia, Washington: Washington State Planning and Community Affairs Agency, 1980).

Aesthetic zoning Aesthetic zoning is designed to create, preserve, and promote beauty, or a particular architectural theme. Like all zoning, whether aesthetic or otherwise, it promotes community interest and is based on the principle that the public welfare outweighs the interests of the individual property owner. Justification for aesthetic zoning is to be found within the broad confines of general welfare. In the past, the courts were reluctant to recognize aesthetics as a main reason without joining it with other reasons such as property values. In the last decade, though, aesthetics has gained increasing acceptance in the courts as a legitimate reason to exercise police power in a more advanced and mature society.

Agricultural zoning Agricultural zones are primarily intended to retain productive agricultural lands for agricultural purposes, but they may also be used as means of preserving open space and preventing loss of important aesthetic qualities, especially in close proximity to metropolitan areas. Agricultural zoning may be effectively employed to prevent increases in property taxes that would otherwise result from assessment based on maximum development potential on lands near densely populated areas. Under agricultural zoning, suitable large parcels of land are identified and designated as agricultural zones, but the actual uses may include not only the growing of crops and raising of farm animals, but also some food processing and selling of farm-grown products. Other compatible uses may be permitted as conditional uses, such as recreation and very low density residential. The regulations also typically provide for minimum building sites of 20 to 40 acres. Agricultural zoning is just one of the techniques available to prevent the loss of open space and farm lands and to manage growth by directing the spread of development into areas where growth can be accommodated.

Buffer areas (zones) A parcel of land established to seprate incompatible adjacent land uses, such as a commercial use and a residential use. The area may be only 10 to 25 feet wide and include walls, fences, screen plantings, or earthen mounds (berms) to insulate the adjoining properties from noise, traffic, or visual intrusions. Some ordinances require commercial and industrial districts to install a buffer area wherever the property line abuts a residential district. The term may also be used more broadly to describe any zone that separates two unlike zones, such as a transitional multiple-family or professional-business zone between the central business district and a single-family zone.

Bulk regulations The combination of requirements that establishes the maximum size and shape of a building and its location on the lot. Their purpose is, first, to assure sufficient light, air, and open space on the ground and at all levels of a building and, second, to maintain a compatible and pleasing appearance.

Components of bulk regulations include: size and height of building; location of exterior walls at all levels with respect to lot lines, streets, or other buildings; building coverage; gross floor area of buildings in relation to lot area (floor area ratio); open space (yard) requirements; and amount of lot area provided per dwelling unit.

Capital improvement program (CIP) A community's plan that matches the costs of future projects such as water, sewers, roads, and schools to anticipated revenues. It is a governmental timetable for constructing the permanent improvements and includes timing of the projects, their costs, and the methods for financing. CIPs are usually prepared for five or six years, updated annually, and should be coordinated with the comprehensive planning process.

Carrying capacity The level of use that can be accomodated and continued without irreversible damage to natural or human resources, the ecosystem, and the quality of air, land, and water.

Central business district (CBD) That part of a city or town, usually centrally located, where most of its commercial activities are concentrated, such as financial, service, retail, government, entertainment, and office. It is distinguished from shopping centers by the wider range of business activities, multiple ownership of property, more intense development, and the traditional street pattern.

Cluster zoning Cluster zoning generally refers to a development pattern for residential, commercial, industrial, institutional, or combination uses in which buildings are grouped or "clustered," rather than evenly spread throughout a parcel as in a conventional lot-by-lot development. A zoning ordinance may authorize such development by permitting smaller lot sizes and higher density if a specified portion of the land is kept in permanent open space, usually through public dedication or designation on a site plan or plat. Cluster zoning is encouraged by many communities and developers since it allows them to keep in open space land they may have found unbuildable anyway, such as steep slopes, ravines or wetlands, to create innovative designs, and save money by building shorter streets and utility lines.

Comprehensive plan A document or series of documents for guiding the future development of a county or city, or a part of one, and is based upon the stated long-term goals and objectives of a community. Such a plan is the result of public input, study, and analysis of existing physical, economic, environmental, and social conditions and is a projection of what future conditions are likely to be. Certain elements of a comprehensive plan, such as land use and circulation elements, are required by the enabling legislation. Other elements, such as those dealing with housing, recreation, open space, or conservation, are optional elements under the enabling laws, but some are required by other state statutes or federal programs.

Once adopted, the plan serves as a guide for making land use changes, preparation of implementing ordinances (zoning, platting), preparation of capital improvement programs, and the rate, timing, and location of future growth.

Comprehensive planning programs (process) The whole of the continuing planning process, including gathering and analysis of data, consideration of alternatives, formulation of the comprehensive development plan, and measures for implementing the plan, including regulatory, administrative, education, and updating measures related to the plan.

Condemnation and eminent domain *Condemnation* is the taking of private property by a government unit for public use when the owner will not relinquish it through sale or other means. The power to take the property is based on the concept of *eminent domain*, which is the legal right of a government to acquire private property for public use of public purpose upon paying just compensation to the owner.

Condemnation is commonly used to acquire property for highways, street widening, parks and utility construction. Property has also been condemned under eminent domain powers for private use in the public interest, such as urban renewal where the public purpose is the removal of dilapidated structures.

The terms *eminent domain* and *condemnation* are often used interchangeably, although condemnation may also mean the demolition by public authority of an unsafe structure where no compensation is paid to the owner and the condemned property does not become public land.

Conditional use and permit Because of their size, special requirements, or possible safety hazards, certain uses are expected to have detrimental effects on surrounding properties but may be compatible with the other uses if they are properly designed. Such uses are classified in zoning ordinances as conditional uses if they are properly designed. Such uses are classified in zoning ordinances as conditional uses requiring conditional use permits.

A conditional use permit is granted after a careful review by either the board of adjustment, hearing officer, or zoning adjustor. The zoning ordinance prescribes the necessary standards (conditions) that will make the use acceptable in the district. Most zoning ordinances specify permitted, accessory, conditional, and limited use activities within each zone designation and establish criteria for determining the conditions to be imposed.

Public utilities, schools, churches, and community centers are often considered as conditional uses in a single-family residential zone.

Conflict of interest It is a common law principle that public officers have the duty of serving the public with undivided loyalty uninfluenced in their official actions by any private bias or interest, including financial and property interests, business associations with interested parties, prejudgement, and family relationships with interested parties.

The specific interest or bias which would disqualify a public officer from voting on a particular matter should be a personal or private one and not the common interests that the officer shares with other citizens and property owners. Whether the particular interest is sufficient to disqualify an officer from participating depends upon the circumstances of the particular case. What is required is that actions of a public body be fair in fact. An action that is not fair is invalid. This concept is expanded in the appearance-of-fairness doctrine.

Covenant A covenant is an agreement written into deeds and other instruments promising performance or nonperformance of certain acts or stipulating certain uses or nonuses of property. There may be certain legal requirements for formal establishment of a covenant such as a written document, a mutual interest in the property, a concern with the use of land rather than with individual characteristics of ownership. Covenants are commonly used in the establishment of a subdivision to restrict the use of lots in the development to a certain type of use such as single-family dwellings. They are also used in rezoning situations, in conjunction with a contract or conditional rezoning to bind the landowner to use property in a specific manner to achieve a desired goal.

Cumulative (pyramidal) zoning A zoning scheme that begins with the most-protected land use, usually the single-family home, and permits in each "lower" district all of the uses in the "higher" districts plus new ones. Thus, the least-protected zone, such as a heavy industrial district, would permit all uses allowed in all other districts and in effect is not zoned. Most modern zoning ordinances have dropped the cumulative feature in favor of exclusive use zoning.

Dedication The assignment of private property to a specific public use and its acceptance for such use by the appropriate governmental agency. Dedication for roads, parks, open space, school sites, and other public uses are increasingly required as a condition for approval of a development. Where costs are high or a fee simple transfer is unnecesary, the owner may, where authorized, dedicate a portion of the rights through an easement or other form of less-than-fee transfer. Such easements may include dedications for scenic, nonaccess, pedestrian, utility, drainage, floodway, air space, and other purposes.

Where land dedication is not appropriate, a cash payment (fee in lieu of) may be authorized. Both methods assess the developer with more of the costs of the new development to the community.

Dedication, fee in lieu of This technique involves cash payments as a substitute for dedications authorized under subdivision regulations when requirements for mandatory dedication of land are inappropriate. The conditions under which such payments will be allowed must be spelled out in the regulations. Payment in lieu of provisions have a relatively unknown legal status in some states.

Density The number of families, persons, or housing units per unit of land usually expressed as "per acre." Density is controlled through zoning, based upon the density indicated in the comprehensive plan.

Density zoning Density zoning, which often resembles cluster zoning and/or performance standards, offers both the community and the developer substantial flexibility in site design as long as overall density restrictions and other requirements are met. Under this approach any type of dwelling is permitted, from detached homes to apartments, so long as total density does not exceed the maximum permitted. It is a somewhat further extension of cluster development provisions common in planned unit development ordinances, and is usually subject to a site plan review process.

Development-impact fees A fee or tax imposed on developers to help pay for the community's costs of providing services to a new development. Such charges are an extension of efforts to make new developments help pay for their impact on the community. Impact fees may also involve some effort to predict the total cost to the community for servicing the new development and to relate it to the tax revenues that will be produced by the development once it is completed.

Development ordinance The combining of zoning, subdivision, and other regulations into a single, integrated code to cover all the provisions appropriate to the conversion and development of land. While considered a radical departure 10 or 15 years ago and never enacted except as part of planned unit development provisions, the development ordinance is a basic feature of the American Law Institute's *A Model Land Development Code* and is likely to be more widely used in the future.

Development rights When a piece of property is purchased, the purchaser also acquires a number of rights toward the use of that property, such as the right to build a home, a right to develop commercially, a right to remove gravel or other minerals, a right to use water, a right to raise crops. Which rights are purchased with each property depends on the zoning, other applicable regulations, and the terms of the purchase.

Acquisition of development rights is a method for controlling urban growth and conserving natural resources. Essentially, the concept involves buying the future development potential for land and permits the owners to continue the existing use, usually agriculture, in urbanizing areas. Hence, a county could acquire a fee or any lesser interest necessary (development rights) to conserve selected open space, timber, or agricultural lands. A county could also acquire fee title to such property and convey or lease the property back to its original owner using covenants or contractual agreements to limit the future use of the property.

Downzoning A change in the zoning classification of land to classification requiring less intensive development, such as change from multifamily to single family or from commercial to residential. A change in the opposite direction would be upzoning.

Due process A general requirement that proceedings be carried out in accordance with established rules and principles. Commonly, it takes two forms: procedural and substantive. *Procedural* due process means an assurance that all parties to a proceeding are treated fairly and equally, that citizens have a right to have their view heard, that necessary information is available for informed opinions to be developed, that conflicts of interest are avoided, and that the appearance of, as well as the fact of, corruption does not exist. Procedural due process requirements are increasingly being expanded by the legislature and the courts in proceedings involving zoning changes.

The meaning of *substantive* due process is less precise, but it usually refers to the payment by government of "just compensation" to property owners when their property is condemned by government or is severly diminished in value because of government action.

Easement An easement is a right granted by the owner of land to another party for specific limited use of that land. For example, a property owner may give or sell an easement on property to allow light to reach a neighbor's window or to allow access to other property. In recent years, there has been increasing use of open space easement under which property owners sell their development rights to the government and thereby keep the land open for agricultural conservation, recreation, or scenic purposes.

Environmental impact statement (EIS) A fact finding report required by either a State Environmental Policy Act (SEPA) or the National Environmental Policy Act (NEPA) before a government may authorize a proposed project, program, law, or any other major activity requiring a governmental authorization. The EIS (also known as EIR, Environmental Impact Report, in California), usually contains a description of the proposal and its location, its environmental effects, plus available alternatives to the proposal and possible ways to mitigate the expected negative effects.

The purpose of the EIS is to make known to the decision makers what is likely to happen if the proposed project or program goes ahead and thus help them arrive at an informed decision.

Euclidean zoning Derived from the *Euclid (Ohio)* v. *Ambler Realty Company* 1926 U.S. Supreme Court decision affirming the validity of comprehensive zoning (considered the first major court decision). Refers as a convenient nickname, to traditional zoning in which district regulations are explicit, uses are segregated, districts are cumulative, and bulk and height controls are imposed.

Exclusionary zoning Zoning practice that has the effect of keeping out racial minorities, poor people, or additional population of any kind from entering a community is known as exclusionary zoning and may be subject to court action. The techniques include large-lot zoning, high minimum residential floor area requirements that increase housing costs, and discretionary decision making processes that may permit a community to deny certain applications and conceal the real reasons. Exclusionary zoning, in all its subtle variations, is considered by many to be one of the most effective and pervasive tools used by suburbs to maintain their homogenous character. A growing number of state court decisions are invalidating exlusionary practices, whether intentional or unintentional, and in some cases are requiring affirmative inclusionary practices. However, the U.S. Supreme Court has refused to invalidate exclusionary zoning and has maintained that such zoning is not unconstitutional, unless it can be proven that the discrimination was intentional. If discrimination has occurred as a side effect of the zoning regulation, it is not a sufficient reason to consider the ordinance unconstitutional.

Ex parte contact Some form of contact between a party to a proceeding and a public official responsible for making the decision, occurring outside the formal decision-making process.

Extraterritorial zoning The authority granted to a local municipality to exercise zoning powers for a specified distance outside of its corporate boundaries. It is intended to protect activities on the edge of communities from being adversely affected by incompatible activities outside city limits.

Fill The placement of sand, sediment, or other material, usually in submerged lands or wetlands, to create new uplands or raise the elevation of land.

Fiscal zoning Fiscal zoning means designing zoning regulations for the purpose of attracting uses that will bring in more local tax revenue than they will cost in public services. Since the greatest single cost to local government is education, sophisticated fiscal zoning would tend to limit single-family housing in favor of small apartments generating few school children and business and industry generating higher taxes. Because of such policies, competition for high tax generators may be heightened. Fiscal zoning is utilized primarily for economic motives.

In many instances, fiscal zoning has been based only on the tax-revenue side of the ledger with no regard to service costs.

Flexible zoning Under the traditional zoning system, a city or county is divided into various land use districts and only conforming or homogenious uses are permitted within each district. In recent years, a growing number of states facing increasingly complex development problems have sought to bring a greater flexibility to the system of land use controls without sacrificing the traditional zoning objectives for health, safety, and welfare of residents. Numerous techniques have been developed to achieve the desired flexibil-

ity. Among these are conditional rezoning, bonus and incentive zoning, floating zones, overlay zones, performance standards, planned unit development districts, and others.

The intent of flexible zoning techniques is to widen the range of options available to developers and thereby lead to more desirable and better designs. Rather than prescribing specified uses and standards for each and every parcel of land, only policies and criteria for decision making are established. Under most flexible techniques, public officials have discretion in their decision-making process and frequently negotiate with developers before final approval is given. Thus, while development options are broad, development permission, once granted, may be quite specific and require compliance with a site plan.

Floating zones A floating zone is a zoning district that is described in the text of a zoning ordinance but may not be associated with a specific location on a zoning map. When a project of sufficient size anywhere within restricted areas can meet certain requirements, the floating zone can be anchored and the area designated on the zoning map.

This technique has commonly been used for large-scale developments such as shopping centers, planned unit developments, and industrial parks. Frequently, the text describing a floating zone will require unified development of the parcel and give approximate standards for building height, lot coverage, setbacks, and frontages, and will generally prescribe parking areas and other site facilities.

Flood, a regional (100-year) A standard statistical calculation used by engineers to determine the probability of severe flooding. It represents the largest flood which has a 1 percent chance of occurring in any one year in an area as a result of periods of higher than normal rainfall or streamflows, extremely high tides, high winds, rapid snowmelt, natural stream blockages, tsunamis, or combinations thereof.

Floodplain zoning Floodplains are the plains next to a river which are subjected to flooding when a river overflows its normal channel. Floodplains have been used successfully for farming, and they also provide important wildlife habitats, recreation areas, and other uses compatible with periodic inundation. Because floodplains are flat, often scenic, and are easily built upon, they attract housing, roads, and other developments. The wildlife and farms disappear but the flooding inevitably reoccurs, which may result in extreme damage and need for costly disaster relief programs and expensive structures to control the flow potential.

Floodplain zoning has three objectives: (1) to prevent obstruction of the natural flow and capacity that may cause additional damage; (2) to protect individuals from poor choices of land use that may be detrimental to the safety, health, and property; and (3) to prevent burdening taxpayers with unnecessary expenditures for public works and disaster relief. Regulations generally limit floodplain uses to those not susceptible to flood damage such as farming and some forms of recreation. If other uses must occur, the structures are required to be flood proofed or constructed above the flood elevation.

Floodplain zoning, like any other type of zoning, is based on the police power. The validity of state and local floodplain zoning ordinances is generally upheld by the courts where there is a proper exercise of the police power, where the statutory objectives are related to the public health, safety, and welfare.

Floodway The normal stream channel and that adjoining area of the natural floodplain needed to convey the waters of a regional flood while causing less than one foot increase in upstream flood evaluations.

Functional plans A plan to deal with a particular activity or governmental service such as transportation, traffic control operations, community renewal, water and sewer systems, or other specific projects. Such functional plans represent detailing of the elements of a comprehensive plan and should follow the goals developed in the comprehensive planning process.

Goal A broad statement of what should exist in a community or what the community wants to achieve in the future, usually determined through citizen involvement.

Growth management A wide range of techniques in combination to determine the amount, type, and rate of growth and to direct it to designated areas. Comprehensive plans often form the backbone of the system. Techniques used to execute growth management policy may include zoning, emphasizing flexibility, capital improvements, public facilities ordinances, urban growth foundaries, population ceilings, and others. Some sophisticated systems have departed dramatically from the traditional land use controls by using a variety of innovative devices to achieve particular policies. Growth management differs conceptually from conventional approaches because it does not accept the likely population growth rate as inevitable, but as something open to question and subject to determination by public policy and action.

Hearing officer (also zoning and subdivision officer) An appointed official with authority to conduct hearings and make decisions on applications for zone changes, county subdivisions, variances, conditional uses, or other land use matters. The range of responsibilities varies with each jurisdiction, and the decision may have the effect of a recommendation to the legislative body or that of an administrative decision appealable within specified time to the legislative body.

The hearing officer system is a growing trend in local administration nationwide, because it relieves planning commissions from administrative decisions so that they may concentrate on their primary responsibilites, considering policy issues of comprehensive planning and rewriting zoning ordinances.

Highest and best use A real estate term describing the use of land in such a way that its development will bring maximum profit to the owner. The theory allows the economics of the real estate market to establish a maximum value for each parcel of land at any given time. This concept is not based upon public regulations, which may limit land use to some activity that will provide the owners with less than maximum profits. For example, a tavern on a particular site might give its owner the greatest return; however, if the site is zoned residential, the owner is prevented from utilizing the highest and best use potential.

Holding zones A holding zone is a zone established in the zoning ordinance on a temporary basis awaiting applications for rezoning to desired uses. Holding zones are usually very low density zones with the purpose either made explicit in the ordinance's statement of intent or left implicit. Typically, a holding zone is applied to an area which is undergoing transition, particularly where the ultimate use may be under consideration or involved in a comprehensive plan revision.

Illegal use A use, building, or activity is illegal if it is prohibited by the zoning ordinance and was established *after* the zoning ordinance became effective, as compared to a nonconforming use which is a prohibited use that was established *before* the zoning ordinance became effective.

Impact analysis The process of evaluating a proposal's expected impact on its surroundings in a community. The environmental effects are evaluated according to a State Environmental Policy Act (SEPA) or the National Environmental Policy Act (NEPA), and the information may be presented as an Environmental Impact Statement (EIS).

Closely related are economic, social, and fiscal analysis techniques that are being applied to projects at all levels of government. Impact analysis is a more sophisticated and systematic version of the reviews planning agencies have given public and private proposals for many years.

Impact zoning This relatively new, still-developing technique usually applies to an ordinance that identifies fiscal and environmental standards to be met by new development. The process involves a detailed analysis of existing conditions in the area to be developed and estimates what impacts the development will have on community facilities and environment. The goal is for the developer to show that the proposed development will not cost the community more than it will produce in taxes and incomes.

"In accordance with the comprehensive plan" Commonly found in state enabling laws, this phrase requires that zoning ordinances be applied uniformly, include all private property within the jurisdiction, be internally consistent with public policies arrived at through detailed study and analysis—that is, through a comprehensive plan.

Incentive (bonus) zoning Incentive or bonus zoning is another tool that permits greater flexibility in the zoning process. It is a negotiation process whereby a developer is awarded bonuses in exchange for adding amenities the community feels it needs. While a typical zoning ordinance is usually restrictive, incentive zoning permits the restrictions to be exceeded (for example, higher densities, greater floor area ratios, or reduced parking requirements). In return, the developer agrees to build pedestrian plazas or low- and moderate-income housing, to protect a fragile natural area, or to support some other critical need of the community.

Inclusionary zoning Inclusionary zoning is a positive and active program in a community to attract racial minorities or low- and moderate-income residents. Such policies, analogous to affirmative action in job recruitment, not only avoid techniques that discourage certain classes of people from moving into an area, but also actively seek to invite such groups. Inclusionary zoning devices usually include offering incentives or bonuses to developers for building low- or moderate-cost housing or exceptions to traditional controls. Such practices are still rare, but they are being experimented with in a number of communities. Inclusionary policies are developed in response to the challenges being levied at exclusionary zoning practices.

Intensity The degree to which land is used. Somewhat broader, though less clear in meaning than density, it usually refers to the levels of concentration or activities in use.

Interim zoning Interim zoning is a device to temporarily freeze or severely restrict development for an area while a comprehensive plan and a new set of zoning regulations are prepared. Interim zoning has three main purposes: (1) it permits planning and ordinance writing to proceed relatively free of development pressures; (2) it prevents uses that may not conform to the adopted ordinances; and (3) it encourage public debate on the issues. Occasionally, where the controls have been found to be a disguise for a more or less permanent effort to halt growth, courts have disallowed them.

Inverse condemnation Governmental action or the use of police power to regulate the use of land, reducing the value of a property to a level where it approaches a taking of private property for public benefit, but without the just compensaton. There is an extensive debate about how far government can go in using police power regulations that diminish property values before compensation must be paid (the "taking issue").

Judicial (or quasi-judicial) hearing A judicial hearing takes place when a planning commission or hearing examiner holds a hearing to ascertain the facts and then apply the law to the facts. Examples would be hearings on a variance, use permit, or rezoning. In such hearings the courts take a strict view of whether or not the legal safeguards of due process and proper procedure were followed (for example, notice, records, and findings).

Key facilities Basic facilities that are primarily planned for by local government but that also may be provided by private enterprise and are essential to the support of more intensive development, including public schools, transportation, water supply, sewage and solid-waste disposal.

Land use A term used to indicate the utilization of any piece of land. The way in which land is being used is the land use. A study of the existing use of land usually provides the basis for the formulation of a land use plan in a community and the establishment of district boundaries in a zoning ordinance.

Land use plan The proposed or projected utilization of land. It is usually presented in a map form, indicating areas best suited for residential, commerical, industrial, agricultural, and other types of use. The map is supported by a written text explaining the underlying policy and the principles upon which it is based. It is one of the major components of a community's comprehensive plan.

Leapfrog development Development that occurs well beyond the existing limits of urban development and thus leaves intervening vacant land behind.

Legislative hearing A legislative hearing takes place when a planning commission is seeking advice from the public on the type of law to pass. Examples would be hearings held on whether to adopt a master plan or whether to adopt a road setback line. The courts permit commissions considerable leeway in terms of evidence admissible and whether the evidence is presented in person or by petition or other indirect fashion.

Lot of record A lot that is part of a subdivision officially recorded or a lot or parcel described by metes and bounds, the description of which has been so recorded.

Metes and bounds A system of describing and identifying a tract of land by distance (metes) and directions (bounds) from an identifiable point of reference such as the monument of quarter section of land.

"Mistake or change" rule A rule that a zoning ordinance, once enacted, cannot be amended unless it can be demonstrated by the applicant that there has been a mistake in the original zoning designation or a change in conditions.

Mixed-use zoning Mixed-use zoning permits a combination of several uses within a single development. While traditional zoning often separated land uses, improved performance controls and some rethinking of old values on the part of planners and their clients has led to a loosening of the narrowly defined districts to permit appropriate mixtures. This can result in more interesting, livelier, and convenient neighborhoods.

Many planned unit development ordinances specify permitted combinations such as various residential types and local businesses. Recently, the term has been applied in a more limited way to major inner-city developments with high-rise buildings, which may contain offices, shops, hotels, apartments, and other related uses.

Moratorium In planning, a moratorium means a temporary freeze on all new development pending the completion and adoption of a comprehensive plan or other guiding document. In recent years, building moratoriums have also been instituted by water and sewer agencies when sewage treatment facilities are inadequate or when water shortages are threatened. They have also been voted into being by residents of communities whose schools and other public facilities have been overwhelmed by rapid growth. Moratoriums are increasingly common and are generally considered legal when not abused.

National Environmental Policy Act (NEPA) The National Environmental Policy Act of 1969 (NEPA) requires that prior to an authorization by the federal government of a project or other major action, environmental effects be considered and made available to the decision makers and public. Usually, an environmental impact statement must be prepared. In passing the act, Congress recognized that each person should enjoy a healthful environment.

Nonconforming uses, lots, structures Lots, structures, uses of land and structures, and characteristics of uses that are prohibited under the terms of a zoning ordinance but that were lawful at the date of the ordinance's enactment. They may be permitted to continue, or they are given time to become conforming. The continuation of such nonconformities is based on the principle that laws cannot be applied retroactively unless there is a compelling reason, such as imminent danger to health or safety. While many ordinances permit legal nonconformities to continue and to rebuild immediately after a fire, they usually prohibit the extension and enlargement of the degree of such nonconformities. Some ordinances provide for the abatement (amortization) of all or some nonconformities at the end of a prescribed period. Increasingly, ordinances are distinguishing among classes of nonconformities and are providing for their individual treatment. Such classes include: nonconforming lots, nonconforming buildings or structures, nonconforming uses of land with minor structures only, nonconforming uses of major buildings and premises, and nonconforming characteristics of use.

Nuisance Anything that interferes with the use or enjoyment of property, endangers personal health or safety, or is offensive to the senses may be considered a nuisance. There are many types of nuisances, and the law can be invoked to determine when, in fact, a nuisance exists and should be abated. Nuisance law forms part of the basis for zoning. The separation of uses through zoning (for example, separating industrial from residential areas to keep them free of pollution, noise, congestion, and the other characteristics of industrial areas) had its origins in nuisance law.

Official map A legal document, adopted by the legislative body of a community, that pinpoints the location of future streets and sites for other anticipated public facilities. It allows land to be reserved for a limited time and to be protected from unauthorized encroachment, giving the community a chance to acquire the land before it becomes developed. Official mapping provisions are also another type of land use control implementing the comprehensive plan.

Originally intended to serve the future street-widening process by establishing building setback lines, official mapping has also been used to locate land for future public uses such as parks, playgrounds, reservoirs, fire houses, and other public facilities or easements. Once a site is officially reserved, it may not be used for other purposes without the consent of the local administering agency.

Open space Land with nondevelopment or minimum development types of uses (examples: golf courses, agricultural uses, parks, very low density residential development) or land left undeveloped for aesthetic reasons (examples: greenbelts, floodways, steep unstable slopes, or wetlands).

Open space can also be classified based on ownership: (1) privately owned open space—the yards or acreage associated with private homes or farms; (2) common-use open space—land designated at the time of recording a plat or site plan as open space for the common access and use of the residents of the development; or (3) public open space—publicly owned land for the active or passive recreational use of the public.

Ordinance A legislative enactment of a county or city. It is a governmental statute or regulation and its adoption requires a public hearing and publication of the complete text of the ordinance in a local newspaper.

Overlay zones A set of zoning requirements that are described in the ordinance text, mapped, and subsequently imposed in addition to those of the underlying district. Development within the overlay zone must conform to the requirements of both zones. They are usually employed to deal with special physical characteristics such as floodplains, historic preservation, steep slopes, shorelines or other environmentally sensitive areas, but have other applications as well.

Overzoning Zoning more land than can reasonably be expected to be developed for a particular use or zoning for an excessive population. Recognition of overzoning has led in recent years to a movement for downzoning.

Performance standards Rather than listing permitted uses within a certain zoning district, performance standards deal with the effects the uses may have on the surrounding area. Measurable minimum standards are established for such effects as smoke, noise, toxic emission, water pollutants, glare, vibration, shade, radioactivity, electrical disturbances, heat, odors, and traffic generation for each zoning district. Theoretically, any use may locate in any zone, because as long as the standards for the particular zone are met, the effects on the surrounding area will be acceptable. Performance standards are always measurable unlike *subjective standards*, which only state a desired policy but cannot be enforced without making discretionary judgment. Terms like "limited," "objectional," and "substantial" characterize subjective standards.

Another type of regulation that tends to be confused with performance standards is *specification standards*. For example, building heights, setback requirements, density limits, and road widths can all be measured but are not performance standards because they deal with the uses and structures themselves rather than the effects that the uses will produce.

In a complete zoning ordinance, all three types of regulation—specification standards, subjective standards, and performance standards—may be employed, since each accomplishes a specific purpose.

Phased zoning Phased zoning is a term referring to programs or techniques to guide the timing and sequence of development. Under phased zoning, land designated for residential use but presently undeveloped would receive permission to subdivide only if the developer could show the availability of adequate public services such as sewers, drainage, park sites, and roads. The special-use permit or rezoning usually serves as the control vehicle. Through it, development in the designated areas would be phased as the community is willing and able to provide the public services. Phased zoning is one growth-management technique and may be included in the process of establishing urban growth boundaries.

Planned unit development (PUD) This is a development preplanned in its entirety with the subdivision and zoning controls applied to the project as a whole rather than to individual lots. Therefore, densities are calculated for the entire development, usually permitting a trade-off between clustering of housing and provision of common open space.

The PUD is usually characterized by a unified site design. While most commonly used for residential development, the technique is also frequently applied to other forms of development such as shopping centers and industrial parks. Occasionally, a PUD may have a mix of uses.

The PUD also refers to the process of site plan review, in which public officials have considerable involvement in determining the nature of the development. The technique includes aspects of both subdivision and zoning regulations but permits a variation in the rigid zoning and subdivision regulations. A PUD is usually administered through a special permit.

Planning The process of setting development goals and policy, gathering information, evaluating that information, and developing alternatives for future action based on previous analysis is commonly referred to as planning.

In a community, planning is a joint effort of the citizens, elected officials, planning commission, and planning staff. It consists of identifying the physical, social, and economic factors that affect and are part of the community; defining the community's goals and objectives; and after careful evaluation of the information and possible alternatives for the future, selecting a course of action most likely to bring the community closer to its desired goals.

The products of this process usually include a comprehensive plan (goals, policies, generalized land use, housing, transportation, and other elements), plus one or more regulatory ordinances to carry out the plan. A comprehensive plan may range from a single page with policy statements to a series of reports, plans, and programs. It may consist of a single plan for the entire jurisdiction or separate plans for geographic subareas of a city or county.

Planning is a continuous process, because community goals and attitudes change, new information and philosophies emerge, and new economic and social conditions develop. This process requires periodic reevaluation of the previously established values and programs.

Planning commission A group of citizens appointed by the mayor or chairperson of the board of county commissioners to research, survey, analyze, and make recommendations on current and long-range land development policies, resource management, ordinances and administrative decisions such as subdivision plats, shoreline permits, and rezone requests. The planning commission functions as a fact-finding and advisory board to the elected officials, but its main function is to recommend a comprehensive plan and implement measures to be adopted by the city council or board of county commissioners.

Plat A plat is a map representing a subdivision of a parcel of land into lots, blocks, and streets or other divisions and dedications. A *preliminary plat* is an approximate drawing of a proposed subdivision showing the general layout of streets and alleys, lots, blocks, and restrictive convenants to be applicable to the subdivision. A *final plat* is the final drawing of the subdivision prepared for filing for record with the county auditor and containing all requirements set forth in applicable state and local regulations.

Police power Police power is the right of government to regulate personal conduct and the use of land in order to protect the public health, safety, and welfare. The use of police power by a unit of government must follow "due process" and be "reasonable" but the government does not have to pay compensation for related losses. In this last respect, it differs from the government's use of the power of eminent domain, which involves taking of property where just compensation is mandatory. The degree to which such exercise of police power becomes, in effect, a taking of property is a question of long standing and has arisen again lately in connection with the restrictive growth management and environmental controls being imposed by many communities.

Policy A more specific statement than a goal; a policy describes a particular course of action to accomplish the purposes of the comprehensive plan. Policies represent the will of the people translated into decision-oriented statements that are continuously available to the legislative body while it evaluates a new project or a proposed change in ordinance.

Policy plans As the name implies, a policy plan is a plan that consists mainly of policies, deemphasizes rigid land use maps in favor of textual statements expressing general community goals and policies and desirable relationships among human activities. A policy plan may be a comprehensive plan, although more flexible and general than traditional comprehensive plans.

Preservation Preservation means to save from change or loss and reserve for a special purpose. It is the most restrictive among management principles and should not be confused with conservation.

Regulatory measures The legal tools available to the local political unit under police power to implement a local comprehensive plan or other documents expressing community goals. Regulatory measures include but are not limited to zoning, subdivision regulations and building permits, shoreline permits,

and occupancy permits.

Resolution In the proceedings of city council or a board of county commissioners, a resolution is something less formal and binding than an ordinance. Generally speaking, it is only a formal statement of opinoin or determination, adopted by the governmental body. Adoption of a resolution does not require a public hearing or publication of the complete text in the local newspaper as is the case with an ordinance.

Rezoning Rezoning is a change in the designation or boundaries of the zoning ordinance. Rezoning is a legislative act and can be legal only if enacted by the governing body. Rezoning can take two forms: (1) a comprehensive revision or modification of the zoning text and map; and (2) a change in the map, such as the zoning designation of a particular parcel or parcels. One form of text change, the importance of which may be overlooked, is a change in a definition. For example, changing the definition of mobile homes to include them under multifamily and single-family dwellings may significantly affect where and how they are permitted.

Rezoning with conditions One of the most important and controversial of the flexible zoning techniques is rezoning with conditions, which actually refers to two separate but similar techniques: conditional rezoning and contract zoning.

Conditional rezoning means that the property owner agrees to perform certain specific conditions limiting the use of the property as a prerequisite to rezoning, but the local government is not formally committed to the rezone that would permit the intended use. The purpose of the conditions is to ensure that the new use will be compatible with the surrounding neighborhood. Typical restrictions are: limiting property to a single use; conditions relating to building size; open space requirements; construction of buffers; dedication of other property for parks and streets; payment for new public facilities, such as streets, caused by the rezoning.

Conditional zoning is vulnerable to legal attacks that claim such agreements constitute illegal spot zoning and violate uniformity requirements.

Contract zoning means that a landowner enters into a reciprocal agreement (contract) with the local government agreeing to restrict the use of his property in return to the local government's agreement to approve a rezone. The purpose of the restrictions, as with the conditional zoning, is to assure that the new use and its impacts will be compatible with the surrounding neighborhood.

Contract zoning has been challenged in the courts because it has been interpreted as bargaining away of police power, and a local government is not authorized to give away powers that have been delegated to it by the constitution. However, the Washington State Supreme Court has ruled that contract zoning or a concomitant agreement with respect to a rezone are valid if they represent another way for the local legislative body to determine that a rezone and the subsequent development will serve public interest.

Right-of-way The right-of-way is the right to pass over the property of another. It usually refers to the land required for the traffic lanes plus shoulders on both sides of highways, railroads, bikeways, and hiking trails. In short, it is the land purchased by or dedicated to the public for traffic purposes. The pathways over which utilities and drainageways run are usually referred to as easements.

Significant habitat areas A land or water area where sustaining the natural resource characteristics is important or essential to the production and maintenance of aquatic life or wildlife populations.

Site plan A scale drawing showing proposed uses and structures for a parcel of land as required by the applicable regulations. It includes lot lines, lot area, streets, parking spaces, private roadways, walkways, topographic features, reserved open space, buildings and other structures, major landscape features, and the location of proposed utility easements. A site plan is a more detailed representation of a proposed development than is shown in a plat and may also include density and statistical data.

Site plan review The process whereby local officials, usually the planning commission and staff, review the site plan of a development to assure that it meets the stated purposes and standards of zoning and other regulations, provides for the necessary public facilities such as roads and schools, and protects and preserves desirable features and adjacent properties through the appropriate location of structures and the use of landscaping.

Site plan review is usually required in connection with many flexible land use regulation techniques. The process often allows considerable discretion to be exercised by local officials since it may deal with hard to define aesthetic and design considerations.

Social consequences The tangible and intangible effects upon people and their relationships with the community in which they live resulting from a particular action or decision.

Special districts A special district in a zoning ordinance is established for a special purpose or to accommodate a special set of uses. The term can signify any district beyond the conventional residential, commercial, industrial, and agricultural districts. Examples include open space districts, hotel/motel districts, planned development districts, transit-impact districts, historic preservation districts, research park districts, and highway/commercial districts. Not to be confused with "special districts" as units of local government (see next entry).

Special districts (local government) Special district is a term generally applied to any local government entity which is neither city, town, nor county. They are municipal corporations created by statute and endowed with a definite governmental organization and revenue-raising authority for the purpose of performing a single function or a few closely related functions. The function or functions, the way the district is established, and its method of financing are determined by the state law under which it is authorized.

There are sometimes more than 40 varieties of special districts of various size and complexity in some states. Examples: school districts, library districts, diking and drainage districts, port districts, public utility districts, health districts, mosquito-control districts.

Not to be confused with "special districts" as one of the land designation categories in a zoning ordinance (see preceding entry).

Special use and permit The special use permit, although no longer used extensively, accommodates essentially the same concerns that are addressed by the conditional use permit, whereby a use or activity, otherwise excluded, may be permitted to locate within a specific zone or district after sufficient review by the appropriate administrative official, planning commission, or elected officials and the granting of a special use permit. This permit differs from the conditional use permit in that there are no conditions or standards placed upon the activity once approved. For this reason the conditional use process has become more popular than the special use permit.

Spot zoning Spot zoning occurs when a parcel of land is rezoned to a classification that is inconsistent with the comprehensive plan and that would permit uses possibly detrimental or incompatible with existing surrounding uses, especially when the rezone favors a particular owner. Such zoning practices have been held to be illegal on the grounds that they are unreasonable and capricious. A general plan or special circumstance such as historical value, environmental importance, or scenic value may justify separate zoning for a small area.

Statement of intent (statement of purpose) A statement of policy or objectives, often incorporated in a zoning ordinance, which outlines the broad purpose of the ordinance and its relationship to the comprehensive plan; frequently, a statement preceding regulations for individual districts, which helps to characterize the districts and their legislative purpose. When the application of particular district requirements is challenged in court, the courts rely on the intent statement in deciding whether the application is reasonable and related to a defensible public purpose. As zoning ordinances become more complex, with numerous special districts and flexible applications, statements of intent, which guide users, administrative officials, and the courts, are making more frequent appearances.

Strip zoning A zone normally consisting of a ribbon of uses fronting both sides of an arterial roadway and extending inward for half a block. Strip zoning recognizes that since such development will not go away, its most irksome characteristics should be controlled.

Subdivision Subdivision is both the process and the result of laying out a parcel of undivided land into lots, blocks, streets, and public areas. Many state laws define "subdivision" as the division of land into five or more lots, tracts, parcels, or sites for the purpose of sale or lease and subject to applicable regulations. The division of land into four or less parcels is defined as "short subdivision" and subject to local short plat regulations.

Subdivision regulations Local ordinances that regulate the conversion of undivided land into building lots for residential or other purposes. The regulations establish requirements for streets, utilities, and site design; procedures for dedicating land for open space or other public purposes to the local government or for fees in lieu of dedication; and prescribe procedures for plan review and payment of fees. Subdivision regulations, which govern the land conversion process, and zoning ordinances, which establish permitted land uses, have been local government's primary development and land use tools.

Taking Taking of property is the appropriation by government of private land for which compensation must be paid. Under the U.S. Constitution, property cannot be condemned through eminent domain for public use or public purpose without just compensation. This is reasonbly clear when government buys land directly. But the "taking issue" is far less clear when the imposition of regulations through police power considerably diminishes the value of the property. Generally, the courts have ruled that if government regulations prevent any reasonable use of a property, then it can be regarded as inverse condemnation and requires compensation.

Transitional uses Uses or structures, permitted under the zoning ordinance, which act as a transition or buffer between incompatible uses. For example, where commercial uses are back to back against residences, some zoning ordinances recognize the conflicts across district boundaries by providing for transitional uses or structures such as more yard space, walls, fences, or screening or intermediate uses such as passenger-vehicle parking to create a spatial separation to minimize the conflict.

Urban growth boundary and spheres of influence *Urban growth boundary* is a line around an area identified through official public policy within which urban development will be allowed during a specified time period. Beyond this line development is prohibited or strongly discouraged through the use of growth management tools such as acreage zoning and limits on capital improvements. The establishment of such boundaries has become an important tool for implementing public decisions about where growth should occur, at what time, and what kinds of services a community can afford to supply. It is also intended to protect low-density areas from urban intrusion.

Spheres of influence is another term used to express a concept similar to the urban growth boundary, except that it refers more to the cooperation between jurisdictions in establishing service areas and extension and timing of utilities at jurisdictional boundaries.

Urbanizable land Urbanizable lands are those lands within the urban growth boundary that are identified and (a) determined to be necessary and suitable for future urban areas, (b) can be served by urban services and facilities, and (c) are needed for the expansion of an urban area.

Urban service area An area, identified through official public policy, within which urban development will be allowed during a specified time period.

Use variance A variance to permit a use in a district where it is prohibited. The process is generally regarded as illegal, because a use variance effectively rezones a property to a different classification , but the authority to rezone belongs to the city council or the board of county commissioners, not the boards of adjustment that generally administer variances.

Variance A variance is a relaxation of the terms of a zoning ordinance or another regulatory document in order to avoid unnecessary hardships to a landowner. A variance usually deals with some measurable physical requirements such as height, bulk, or setbacks and is based upon a finding that such relaxation will not be contrary to public interest. A typical use of the variance procedure would be to permit construction of a home on a lot too narrow to have the required side yards, because it was platted before the adoption of the current side yard regulations. The variance mechanisms is not to be used in hardship situations that are the result of an action by the landowner, but only when the particular physical surroundings, shape of the property, or topographic conditions render strict compliance with the zoning ordinance impractical. A mere inconvenience or desire to make more money are not regarded as sufficient reasons for a variance.

Authority to decide variances is vested in the board of adjustment or a hearing officer. The administrators have to be aware that the cumulative effect of repeated variances may significantly change the character of an area in violation of plans and policies. On the other hand, repeated requests for similar variances in the same vicinity indicate that a revision of existing regulations might be needed.

Wetlands Land areas where excess water is the dominant factor determining the nature of soil development and the types of plant and animal communities living at the soil surface. Wetland soils retain sufficient moisture to support aquatic or semiaquatic plant life. In marine and estuarine areas, wetlands are bounded at the lower extreme by extreme low water; in freshwater areas, by a depth of six feet. The area below wetlands is submerged land.

Windfalls and wipeouts The conferring of great financial benefits (windfalls) or losses (wipeouts) on a property owner as a result of a public action.

Zero lot line A development approach in which a building is sited on one or more lot lines with no yard. Conceivably, three of the four sides of the building could be on the lot lines. The intent is to allow more flexibility in site design and to increase the amount of usable open space on the lot between buildings, especially in urban areas with high density and small lots.

Virtually all zoning ordinances retain yard requirements; where zero lot line developments have been permitted, they have been handled through variances, planned unit development procedures, or other devices which allow for site plan review. The few ordinances that specifically authorized the zero lot line approach do so as an exception to prevailing regulations and under clearly defined circumstances.

Definitions of incompatibility often are difficult to make and public bodies or officials may be required to make individualized determinations of transitional needs and requirements in doubtful cases.

Zoning Zoning is the process by which a county or municipality legally controls the use of property and physical configuration of development upon tracts of land within its jurisdiciton. Zoning is an exercise of police power and as such must be enacted for the protection of public health, safety, and welfare. The power to regulate the use of land through zoning is delegated to local governments by state laws. Zoning must be based on comprehensive plans.

Zoning ordinance Zoning ordinance is the local law

adopted by the governing body to assure orderly development according to specific standards established for the general public welfare and to implement the comprehensive plan. A zoning ordinance may govern the types of permitted land uses, the maximum density or minimum lot size, building heights, setbacks, and so on.

Zoning ordinances usually consist of a text and a zoning district map. The map divides the jurisdiction in to districts (zones) for different types of development, while the text specifies what regulations apply to each district, including general provisions and administration. Generally, this conventional description of a zoning ordinance still applies, but many modern ordinances have advanced beyond the traditional format. They have a greater variety of districts and employ various techniques to provide flexibility, such as floating zones, conditional use permits, performance standards, and planned unit developments.

Bibliography

As the author prepared this book manuscript he was struck by the very small amount of published literature that is readily available on the nuts and bolts of development review. There are a number of excellent books cited here that discuss design and site planning; unfortunately these sources are more oriented toward the designer of a development project than the public agency reviewer. However, the reader should be alerted to the fact that a small amount of unpublished materials exists. Generally these materials are public planning agency documents and reports that are usually typed and photocopied for staff use, or may be distributed to developers and builders as an information guide to the development, zoning, subdivision, or design review process. The American Planning Association's Planning Advisory Service collects such unpublished materials and loans them to its subscribers. The reader is urged to periodically check with other planning agencies as to the development and availability of such materials.

American Institute of Architects Committee on Design. *Design Review Boards: A Handbook for Communities.* Washington, DC: AIA Press, 1974.

Babcock, Richard F. and Charles L. Siemon. *The Zoning Game—Revisited.* Cambridge, Mass.: Lincoln Institute of Land Policy, 1985.

Bair, Frederick H. *Planning Cities: Selected Writings on Principles and Practice.* Chicago: American Planning Association, 1970.

Barnett, Jonathan. *An Introduction to Urban Design.* New York: Harper & Row, 1982.

Burchell, Robert W. and David Listokin. *The Fiscal Impact Handbook.* Piscataway, New Jersey: Center for Urban Policy Research, 1978.

———. et al. *The New Practitioner's Guide to Fiscal Impact Analysis.* Piscataway, New Jersey: Center for Urban Policy Research, 1985.

DeChiara, Joseph. *Time-Saver Standards for Residential Development.* New York: McGraw-Hill, 1984.

——— and Lee Koppelman. *Time-Saver Standards for Site Planning.* New York: McGraw-Hill, 1984.

Duerksen, Christopher J. *Aesthetics and Land-Use Controls: Beyond Ecology and Economics.* Planning Advisory Service Report No. 399. Chicago: American Planning Association, 1987.

Hedman, Richard. *Fundamentals of Urban Design.* Chicago: American Planning Association, 1985.

Hendler, Bruce. *Caring for the Land: Environmental Principles for Site Design and Review.* Planning Advisory Service Report No. 328. Chicago: American Planning Association, 1977.

Jones, Warren W. and Albert Solnit. *What Do I Do Next: A Manual for People Just Entering Government Service.* Chicago: American Planning Association, 1980.

Lynch, Kevin and Gary Hack. *Site Planning.* 3rd ed. Cambridge, Mass.: MIT Press, 1984.

McHarg, Ian L. *Design With Nature.* Garden City, New York: Doubleday, 1969.

Meck, Stuart and Edith M. Netter, eds. *A Planner's Guide to Land Use Law.* Chicago: American Planning Association, 1983.

Meshenberg, Michael J. *The Administration of Flexible Zoning Techniques.* Planning Advisory Service Report No. 318. Chicago: American Planning Association, 1976.

———. *The Language of Zoning: A Glossary of Words and Phrases.* Planning Advisory Service Report No. 322. Chicago: American Planning Association, 1976.

Stryker, Perrin, ed. *How to Judge Environmental Planning for Subdivisions: A Citizen's Guide.* New York: Inform, Inc., 1981.

Thurow, Charles, William Toner, and Duncan Erley. *Performance Controls for Sensitive Lands: A Practical Guide for Local Administrators.* Planning Advisory Service Report Nos. 307/308. Chicago: American Planning Association, 1975.

Vranicar, John, et. at. *Streamlining Land Use Regulation: A Guidebook for Local Governments.* Reprint. Chicago: American Planning Association, 1982.

Index

Access easements, in preliminary plat, 61

Aesthetic controls, 3, 16, 115-16. *See also* Appearance code; Appearance review procedures
    appearance review procedures, 116-17
    cautions on using, 121-22
    criteria for appearance codes, 125-28
    design review commission project evaluation checklist, 132-37
    submittal requirements, 129-31
    survey on, 119-21
    terminology for, 124-25
    typical code for, 118-19

Aesthetics, definition of, 3

Ambler Realty v. *Village of Euclid*, 14

American Institute of Certified Planners, code of ethics of, 174-75

Appearance code. *See also* Aesthetic controls; Appearance review procedures
    adoption of, 121-22
    criteria
        building design, 126-27
        factors for evaluation, 127
        landscape and site treatment, 126
        miscellaneous structures and street hardware, 127
        planning and design factors, 127
        relationship of buildings and site to adjoining area, 126
        relationship of buildings to site, 125
        signs, 127
    terminology in, 124-25
    typical, 118-19

Appearance review procedures, 116-17
    design review commission project evaluation checklists, 132-37
    submittal requirements, 129-31

Architectural design covenants, 60

Architectural review, 3
    and appearance codes, 136
    required documentation for, 50-51

Architectural variety covenants, 60

Babcock, Richard, 16

Blackstone, 14

Block layout, in preliminary plat, 63

Boilerplate information, for site plans, 87

Bok, Sissela, 179

Boston
    combat zone effect in, 5
    regulation of building height in, 14

Branch, Melville, 40, 42

Buffering, in design review, 132-33

Building placement criteria, 102
    development pattern, 112-13
    drainage, 104
    movement pattern, 110-11
    soils, 104-5
    sound, 109
    sun, 102
    topography, 106-7
    vegetation, 105-6
    visual, 108-9
    wind, 103-4

Building requirements
    and appearance codes, 126-27, 134-35
    development of, 19*n*
    in site plans, 95

Buzz words, 28

Civil rights nondiscrimination clauses, 60

Claire, William, 45

Cluster zoned areas, in preliminary plat, 62

Collective property rights, and zoning, 15

Combat zone effect, 5

Commercial and office land uses, in site plans, 96-97

Communication, planner's need for skills in, 26-29

Communities facilities
    in preliminary plat, 62
    in site plans, 96

Comprehensive plan amendment, application for, 52-53

Comprehensive planning, 17

Conditional-use permits, required documentation for, 50-51

Conditions, 7

Contour line, definition of, 35

Contour lines, 75-77
    characteristics of, 77-78
    and variations in slope, 78-79

Covenants, protective, 60-61

Cribett, John E., 13

Curbs, in preliminary plats, 66-67